QUANTITATIVE METHODS
IN POLITICS

QUANTITATIVE METHODS

IN POLITICS

BY

STUART A. RICE, Ph.D.

*Professor of Sociology, Wharton School
of Finance and Commerce,
University of Pennsylvania*

NEW YORK / RUSSELL & RUSSELL

TO MY FRIEND
CHARLES J. STAKER

FIRST PUBLISHED IN 1928
REISSUED, 1969, BY RUSSELL & RUSSELL
A DIVISION OF ATHENEUM PUBLISHERS, INC.
BY ARRANGEMENT WITH APPLETON-CENTURY-CROFTS
DIVISION OF MEREDITH PUBLISHING CORP.
L. C. CATALOG CARD NO: 68-27082
PRINTED IN THE UNITED STATES OF AMERICA

PREFACE

Sociologists are often alleged to find their fields of special interest outside of their own domain. For this reason it will not seem strange to some readers that a sociologist should be writing upon politics. Congruity between the present subject and the writer's occupational classification, however, does not depend upon academic *wanderlust* or kleptomania. Nor is it dependent upon certain expansive views among political scientists themselves. The subject matter of politics has recently been so defined as to include much of what is often regarded as the special province of sociology. It might seem that a dweller in this *irredenta* could remain by the filial hearth and discuss old sociological thoughts under the guise of allegiance to the annexationist party in the sister subject.

Pleasantries aside, my justification for this book is of a different order. The phenomena of politics are functions of group life. The study of groups *per se* is a task of sociology. Yet an understanding of groups in general can only follow a study of some groups in particular. The field into which this volume essays to enter, as I view it, is a border realm upon which social psychology, political science and sociology all have some claim, but into which none of these has until recently penetrated. Its exploration should be of benefit to all of these subjects.

The data which are assembled here have accumulated for a number of years. The majority have already appeared in some published form. The present context surrounding them, however, is virtually new. I have endeavored to organize the book in such a way as to evidence the conceptual coherence which binds together the various topics.

In making the customary acknowledgments, an explanation of one in particular is required. Arrangements for the present publication were made in 1926. The arrangement of material was approved by the publishers in the early spring of 1927. A short time subsequently I was invited by the Committee on Scientific Method of the Social Science Research Council to make a "case study" of method in social science and through the courtesy of the University of Pennsylvania was given leave of absence during the academic year 1927–28 for that purpose. This study is in progress at the date of publication. In the final collation of material with its inevitable revisions it has been impossible to avoid some interchange of ideas between the separate projects. Not merely this, but I have also to acknowledge the stimulus, encouragement and suggestions gleaned at meetings of the Committee at which I have been a guest since the autumn of 1926. To the Council, to the Committee, to its individual members and to fellow guests at its conferences, therefore, I feel an indebtedness which is difficult to express and quite impossible to appraise.

To the American Council of Learned Societies I am indebted for a grant in aid of research which permitted access to printed materials by purchase and by the provision of traveling expenses. Editors of publications have been generous in granting permission to reprint. Individual acknowledgments have been made as called for. To associates who have allowed me to use work which was done in collaboration I am grateful. Especially to be mentioned among these are Professor Malcolm M. Willey and a number of former students. Professors Floyd H. Allport and D. A.

Hartman have permitted extensive quotation from a published article and the reproduction of a number of their charts in Chapter VI. Mrs. Mabel S. Brown has supplied that most invaluable of all assistance to a writer, competent secretarial service. Miss Dorothea Jung has given an expert touch to the preparation of some of the charts. Mr. Paul B. Thomas of Alfred A. Knopf, Inc., has been always generous and understanding in attending to numerous arrangements and details.

Only the most general acknowledgment can be given to the numerous individuals from whom I have received ideas that have become my own, or who have given encouragement or helpful suggestions. Of one only will I speak,— my teacher and friend, Professor Franklin H. Giddings of Columbia University, affectionately known to many as "The Chief."

CONTENTS

xi

65022

LIST OF TABLES

LIST OF FIGURES

PART ONE

INTRODUCTION

I. The Aim and Scope of this Volume

I

The Aim and Scope of this Volume

Fashion and vogue are prevalent in scientific thought as well as in more ordinary human activities. An appreciation of this seeming fact will suggest the need of caution whenever support is given to a new or divergent viewpoint which is rapidly gaining ground among scientists. This need of caution applies to the subject matter of this book. There is little doubt that insistence upon the value of quantitative methods has become fashionable among American social scientists. Talk about the matter has considerably outrun actual performance, yet the "volume" of quantitative research has greatly increased since the beginning of the present decade, if one may reach an opinion from the character of the articles and papers in the several publications within the field. The tendency, moreover, still seems to be gaining momentum.

As one who views this trend with favor, I wish to make a reservation with respect to any impetus which may be given it by this volume. The effort to obtain more exact numerical measurements of social phenomena, and to employ these in scientific reasoning, does not necessitate a depreciation of other, non-quantitative efforts to arrive at truth. Two antithetical but consistent considerations appeal to me in this connection. First, the quantitative expression of social fact is to be preferred for scientific purposes whenever it can be used. It reduces individual bias to a minimum,

3

permits verification by other investigators, reduces and at the same time makes evident the margin of error, and replaces the less exact meanings of descriptive words with the precision of mathematical notation. But this preference is limited by the second consideration; namely, that quantitative method is at present unavailable to the scientific investigator of many phenomena. This is true of inorganic and organic realms of inquiry, but it is particularly cogent in regard to human society. It would be foolhardy to contend concerning any particular situation or problem that a suitable method of measurement or quantitative analysis will not presently be found, but there may always be some subjects of inquiry which at a given time have resisted this type of approach. Investigation of these by other means should not for that reason be held lacking in scientific value. This statement would apply at the present time to much "descriptive" writing in political science. If exclusive stress be placed upon those aspects of "reality" which can be measured, other aspects will be neglected, with consequent loss to the sum total of knowledge.

An illustration may help to make my meaning clear. In Chapter XVI a method is presented for the mechanical, quantitative identification of "blocs" in small legislative bodies. Without any knowledge whatever of the individual members, the blocs may be discovered by means of analyzing the votes cast on roll call. But no one who was making an actual study of the work of a legislative body would proceed in this purely mechanical way. That is, the inquirer would allow his mind to be influenced by observation, by the opinions of others, in short by all the miscellaneous data entering into "common knowledge" or "inside information" concerning the blocs and the bloc-forming influences that were at work. On the basis of this information he would consciously or unconsciously set up certain hypotheses which he would then attempt to verify. The verification might be quantitative, but neither the preliminary processes leading thereto nor the interpretation placed upon the quantitative results obtained could be regarded as such.

To summarize: Quantitative method is one among various means of discovering truth. In political science it is a comparatively new and rare means. I necessarily hold a brief for it in presenting this volume, but I do not contend for its necessary or universal superiority as compared with traditional modes of inquiry. Each method, so far as it has validity as a means of discovery, should supplement and corroborate the others, when applied to the same subject matter. When corroboration fails, the science will gain by disclosure of the point of weakness. I am making, then, no effort to provide or suggest a complete methodology for the science of politics, nor am I attempting to apply quantitative method to the entire domain of that science. The aim, rather, is to demonstrate in some parts of the political field the possibilities of obtaining by quantitative procedure more exact statements of situation or relationship than have hitherto been secured. My point of view throughout is deterministic, inductive, and to a considerable extent experimental.

Before proceeding further it will be well to explain the sense in which the terms of the subject are to be employed. The word "method" is used very loosely in scientific literature. It frequently includes both the logical processes by which inference proceeds from evidences to conclusions, and the technical processes or devices which are auxiliary, either to procuring evidence or to the process of inference. The distinction between these two types of method has been stated succinctly by A. Wolf in a passage quoted here in a footnote.[1]   Unless otherwise indicated, "method" will be used in the lax sense which may include technical as well as logical procedure, but the distinction latent in the term will be useful for the reader to retain in mind.

As to a definition of "politics," I find myself in much sympathy with the following explanation by A. Gordon Dewey:[2] "From the point of view of the political scientist, this subject (political science) may perhaps be divided into four main fields — public law, political philosophy, politics and administration. As to the first two, they occupy a dual position, the former being also a branch of jurisprudence and the latter of philosophy. . . . Politics deals with the for-

---

[1] Wolf, A. — *Essentials of Scientific Method*, pp. 15–16. "On the one hand, there are the technical or technological methods of manipulating and measuring the phenomena under investigation, and the conditions under which they can be observed fruitfully . . . These technical methods are mostly different in the different sciences, and few men of science ever master the technical methods of more than one science or one group of connected sciences. On the other hand, there are the logical methods, that is to say, methods of reasoning according to the nature of the data obtained . . . The technical methods . . . are mainly auxiliary to the logical methods . . . They are aids either to observation or to inference. Sometimes they render possible the observation and measurement of certain phenomena which either could not be observed and measured at all otherwise, or could not be observed so well and measured so accurately. At other times the technical methods enable the investigator so to determine the conditions and circumstances of the occurrence of the phenomena which he is investigating that he can reason about them in a definite and reliable manner, instead of merely speculating about them vaguely . . . Whereas the technical methods are, for the most part, different from one science to another, the logical methods are more or less common to all the sciences. They are, moreover, the only scientific methods that can be studied with advantage by those who are not men of science, in the strict sense of the term, as well as by those who are."

[2] "On Methods in the Study of Politics," *Political Science Quarterly*, Vol. 38, pp. 636–637. This is a good illustration of the ambiguity of terms referred to on page 13, in that a "philosophy" is made a branch of a "science." Yet it seems to me to be in realistic accord with the present organization of the subjects involved. In an unpublished paper by Professor W. Y. Elliott which I have been privileged to read, "political science" and "political philosophy" are defined as branches of "politics," — a direct antithesis of Dewey's classification.

mulation of public policies and the machinery through which they are expressed; administration with the modes of making these policies effective." My inquiry is clearly within the field of "politics" as Mr. Dewey has delimited it from the broader field of political science. However, a precise definition is unnecessary for my purpose, and I prefer to avoid it. The political significance of matters discussed will be taken up in each case, or left to the reader.

In considering the term "quantitative," it will be useful at the same time to discuss the potential development of *political statistics* as a specialization, and the relationship thereto of the present volume. "Quantitative" has a broad and somewhat loose connotation. It includes simple arithmetical and algebraic processes which, because they do not relate to any definite units or to any well-defined technique can scarcely be called "statistical." Nevertheless, the distribution of the two terms covers much common ground. The former has been employed in the present work for two reasons: It makes unnecessary a determination whether some of the devices used in the studies on following pages are really statistical, and it avoids a pretense of schematized and comprehensive treatment which the latter term implies.

So far as it has been applied within the general field of social science, statistics has achieved its most noteworthy successes in the study of economics. One indication of this is found in the relatively large number of books dealing with the principles or technique of economic statistics in general or with statistical applications to limited aspects of the economic field, such as "business," or "insurance." There is no inherent reason why statistical method should not have similarly extensive application to politics. Both subjects hold a coördinate position as special social sciences, dealing with distinct but homologous modes of social relationship.[3] The priority in development of economic statistics must be attributed in part to the existence of standard units of exchange value, and in part to the utilitarian motive which has directed the attention of statisticians to the economic data. In part, also, it may be due to the superiority of the data themselves, as records or indicators of social relationship, and to some extent to the greater importance played by economic activity, as compared with political activity, in the lives of men. From whatever cause, there is no present book known to the writer dealing with *political statistics* as a separate group of applications of statistical principles.

When first planning the present volume, it was my ambition to write such a book. I am now persuaded that the time for it has not yet arrived. Statistical method has received its differentiation along the lines of the subject matter to which it has been applied. While to some degree it creates its own problems,[4] its systematization within any field must await the delineation of the problems of the field. That delineation in the science of politics has not yet been made with sufficient clarity to render attempts at statistical systematization profitable. To cite a single but important aspect of the situation, no critical estimate of the types of political data which can be used for statistical analysis is yet available. It is difficult to see in what way a text book

[3] I am adopting here the traditional view of the respective fields of the several social sciences. A different view has been presented by Professor George E. G. Catlin, in *The Science and Method of Politics*. Professor Catlin regards politics as the science of "the relationship of wills," a view which seems to give it a scope equivalent, or nearly so, to the field of general theoretical sociology.

[4] *Cf.* his presidential address before the American Economic Association by Wesley C. Mitchell, "Quantitative Analysis in Economic Theory," *American Economic Review*, 15 (1925), pp. 1-12.

on political statistics would differ essentially at the present time from a number of other familiar treatises which relate in a more general way to social science.

While an attempt to write an introduction to political statistics seems premature, there is in the present development of political science no lack of readiness for a book *preparatory to* such a development. The present work I regard in this light. For a number of years I have been making quantitative studies in a field that might be described as behavioristic political psychology. Several of these have employed elementary statistical procedure. If generalizations concerning the special applications of statistics to politics are subsequently to be made, they should come *out of* numerous individual studies such as these.

The present work, therefore, is primarily a case book on quantitative methods in the field indicated. The cases have all been selected from my own inquiries. The consistent motive and uniform point of view which this permits will perhaps be of advantage in a field which is still so largely in the pioneer stage of development. Secondarily, the book is a statement of this point of view — an exposition of theories which seem to me to be involved in the construction of a quantitative science of politics.

To fellow investigators whose interests are confined to the immediate methods and results of social or political research, it may seem like a case of strange bed-fellows to place these two sets of topics together in a single volume. This appears, however, to be one of the instances where closer juxtaposition between philosophical outlook and scientific method is desirable. I am sure that no one engages in scientific research unequipped with certain assumptions and presuppositions of a philosophical character. It is not so much a question, then, as to whether assumptions are present. The question is rather as to their nature, and whether the investigator is aware of them. As the detailed studies presented in this volume were made, they led to reflection upon various questions of more general character, and the constant readaptation of the investigator's philosophy to provide consistency between the work in hand and other elements in his thought. This in turn unavoidably influenced all further work done. A similar process no doubt goes on in the case of any other investigation or investigator.

From this standpoint, any scientific inquiry is *relative* to the philosophy of the person pursuing it. In presenting the views in Part II, I have little desire to uphold any particular position for its own sake, or merely as an intellectual exercise. On questions such as are there discussed, no two people will often agree. The aim is more especially to illuminate the specific inquiries in Parts III to VI by exhibiting some of the assumptions to which they are related. Professional philosophers will, no doubt, find the arguments in Part II faulty, for probably no writer is aware of all of the assumptions he is making, or, hence, of all of the inconsistencies in his own thinking. To discoverers of errors of this kind the reply is that the viewpoints presented have served a purpose in enabling me to feel consistency in my own work and thought; and, further, that the reader is entitled to this amount of aid in finding the deficiencies therein.

It is my hope that the present work will contribute to the eventual preparation of a more systematic and comprehensive treatment of the subject.

II

The Separation of Ends from Means [1]

The so-called social sciences hold an anomalous position in the scientific world. Whether or not the term "science" can be legitimately used at all in referring to them seems to be questioned even by "social scientists." In some cases the doubt is expressed openly, but more frequently it appears in tacit form. Thus the issue is sometimes evaded by reference to the "social disciplines," the "social subjects," or the "social studies." Sometimes the purpose to start afresh in a spirit more scientific than in the past is evidenced by a rearrangement of terminology, as when the "National Conference on the Science of Politics" was formed a few years ago from within the older "American Political Science Association." An assumption that the word "science" when prefixed by the word "social" does not carry its generalized meaning is also frequently encountered. For example, a college faculty was recently assembled for the purpose of considering changes in its curriculum which would place psychology in the social science division. "Why!" protested the chairman of the division, "I have always regarded psychology as a *science* and not as a *social science*." The absence of comment upon this statement seemed to be evidence of a general acceptance of the distinction implied.

To get at the roots of this hesitancy and vague confusion in terms, it is not enough to say that the social sciences in

---

[1] Portions of this chapter appear in an article, "A Viewpoint Concerning Scientific Social Science," *Social Science*, February 1928, Vol. 3, No. 2.

the past have been pervaded by speculation and philosophical assumptions, and that these must be eliminated before genuine sciences can emerge. Assumptions are necessary in any science, and speculation is essential for its continued active development. The diagnosis must be more specific. In my judgment there are two chief elements in the difficulty. The first of these concerns a confusion of ends, or values, with means. It is here that the social sciences have departed farthest from the scientific spirit. The second concerns a misconception of the nature of evidence in the natural sciences,[2] and a failure to recognize that at best it provides merely a high degree of probability, of a kind essentially similar to probability in the social sciences. The remedies seem to involve a certain *rapprochement* between the social and the natural sciences; from the side of the former in the case of the first element of difficulty and from the side of the latter in the case of the second. That is, the social sciences must assimilate the purpose of the natural sciences, at the same time that the latter are being found to possess much of the uncertainty and tentativeness of the former. The second element will be discussed at some length in Chapter III. The first forms the subject of the present chapter.

Whatever else it leads to in the way of analysis, science is first of all an attempt to *describe phenomena*, accurately and without personal bias. Thus the biologist may describe the life processes of an oyster. He has no interest in showing

---

[2] The use of "natural science" and "social science" as contrasted or mutually exclusive terms is wholly illogical. I am unable to conceive of a science which is not "natural," and I insist upon the naturalness of social phenomena. "Natural science" is used in the present discussion, however, as the commonly accepted and most available term for referring collectively to the sciences which have for subject matter phenomena of inorganic and organic character, excluding that which is social. I shall beg the question also in using the terms "social science" and "social scientist" without reference to their essential validity.

that the oyster *ought* to reproduce in one way rather than another, or that it has moral obligations of certain sorts to other oysters. To him it is merely a phenomenon. Is the scientist, then, debarred from efforts to produce bigger and better oysters? Not at all. As a business man or a philanthropist he may think it *valuable* to have better oysters, and as a scientist set about to discover the conditions under which they may be produced. But his judgment of the *value* of this achievement is wholly apart from his study of the methods of attaining it. He cannot reach a scientific determination of this value, except by referring it to other values, and these perhaps to still other values, and so on. For example, he may prove scientifically that the bigger oyster will reduce the cost of living; if he does so, he is merely substituting "low cost of living" as a more general value for that of "bigger oyster." He may then prove that "low cost of living" is conducive to "human welfare." He has here merely fallen back again on a still more general value. In the last analysis, the end which is sought must be posited or assumed. It cannot be arrived at by scientific procedure. When this point is reached, we have left the domain of science and have entered the domains of philosophy, of religion, of ethics, or of æsthetics. In other words, science can point the way to the attainment of ends, but it cannot determine these ends, except as they may be deduced from other ends.

Social scientists have frequently attempted the impossible task of eating their cake and keeping it too. They have sought to retain scientific status for themselves and their subjects at the same time that they have sought to become arbiters of social goals and values. They have pictured their task, in short, as the creation of a *science of moral ends.* That this task involves a contradiction in terms does not

seem to have occurred to them.   The late Albion W. Small
asserted: "Sociology, in its largest scope, and on its methodological side, is merely a moral philosophy conscious of its
task, and systematically pursuing knowledge of cause and
effect within this process of moral evolution." [3]   He criticized
economists for failing to follow Adam Smith in relating their
economic theory to a "more fundamental science" (p. 10)
of human ends.   Smith, he contends, "first derived his con-
ception of life in the large.   Then he analyzed one of the
great divisions of activity within the whole scheme of life.
On this basis he attempted to decide what human programs
should be adopted with reference to the wealth element
among human interests.   This order and spirit of procedure,
enlarged and specialized, is the methodology for which the
modern sociologists are contending." (pp. 20–21).

In other words, Small pictures sociology as a combination
of science and moral philosophy, in which the process of
setting up social ends is central.   He recognizes this as a
task of philosophy.   Yet because he includes in his subject
attention to the processes by means of which ends are
to be attained, he fails to note in his own terminology where
the one begins and the other leaves off.   In this situation it
is not strange that he should have used "science" and "philosophy" interchangeably.

Confusion of thought is an inevitable concomitant of
confusion in terms.   The social sciences have suffered from
this confusion, and it is quite possible that social philosophy
has suffered as well.   When means and ends are not distinguished in the mind of an observer of social phenomena,
distortions and errors in his thinking may arise in numerous
ways.   He is himself a part of society, and *interested* in the

[3] *Adam Smith and Modern Sociology*.   Chicago: The University of Chicago
Press, 1907, p. 22.

outcome of social processes. He is therefore peculiarly subject to what is sometimes called "wishful thinking." The desire for a particular outcome directs attention to those evidences which point toward this outcome, and away from the evidences which are contradictory to it.

Illustrations are abundant. The confidence with which rival managers predict victory for their respective sides in an election seems to be not wholly a matter of campaign strategy. Unless the result is clearly indicated, both sides expect to win. A national authority on certain phases of city government, connected with the Mitchel administration of New York City, stoutly affirmed to the writer his confidence in Mr. Mitchel's reëlection in 1917 up to the very moment of the disaster which overtook his régime. Professor W. F. Ogburn once related an instance in which he was investigating a strike for the United States Department of Labor. He was informed by the strikers that several hundred of their union members were out. According to the employer, it was but a fraction of the first figure. Both *believed* that they were stating facts, but both were being influenced by their motives, or the ends respectively in view. In more academic circles are to be found the individuals who posit a pattern of social ends which they regard as a "better world," and whose desire for its attainment enables them guilelessly to select those data as evidence of "progress" which do not disappoint them in their hopes.

I trust that no reader will assume that I am condemning such aspirations. Nor am I condemning religion, æsthetics or social philosophies of whatever sort. The contention is merely that *these things are not science;* that clarity calls for a separation, a rendering under Cæsar of the things that are Cæsar's. As a social philosopher, one may be keenly interested in furthering child welfare, good government, and other "reforms." As a social scientist, one is indifferent to furthering them. In the latter capacity one's concern is to give a truthful statement of the exact situation with respect to child labor, corruption in politics, etc., or an estimate of the probable results of proposed social policies with respect to them. It is not one's function to quarrel with fellow-scientists concerning the goals of those policies themselves.

The logical discrimination between social science on the one hand and social and moral philosophy, religion, etc., upon the other, involves at least two corollaries. If social science is really to become science, it must separate itself from religious and ethical endeavor and from all other efforts to set up values or ends of whatever sort. A distinction is important here. These things may be studied scientifically as *data*. In fact, as data they are highly important elements in the proper subject matter of social science. We may study, for example, the religious or political attitudes of people as forces productive of certain results in society. But if our work is scientific we will have the same dispassionate disinterest in directing these attitudes that would be felt in the ideas of the oyster if it should be found to possess any. We should be without any preferences for one attitude as compared with another. We should be as tolerant of, and as interested in, communism, capitalism, fundamentalism, atheism or futurism, as the physicist is interested in alpha rays, molecules or the spectrum. But no more so. The chemist is not intolerant of hydrogen, and engaged in a campaign to regard it as un-Christian or un-American because he prefers the qualities of oxygen.

Once again let me insist that the discussion of values and goals seems desirable. If the present social studies must continue to consist of these things, very well, but would it not be better to stop calling them social science? Let those who so desire promote the acceptance of various ethical, religious, æsthetic, or philosophical views; let them impress their fellow-men with a sense of social, moral, or religious obligation in certain directions. Much of this could be applauded by the scientist in his off-hours as a layman. But let these activities be recognized for what they are, or at least for what they are not, i.e., the scientific study of society. If the distinction were made then those who wish to add to our knowledge rather than to change our belief could proceed to the development of a genuine science of social origins and relationships.

The second corollary relates directly to the function of this book. This is the demand for quantitative method wherever it can be used in the science of society. This demand follows from the logical discrimination that I have attempted to make, and from the human tendency in matters in which we have an interest to engage in "wishful thinking." It will reduce the danger that our "science" may turn out to be mere pious aspiration.

III

A STATISTICAL VIEW OF A PERCEPTUAL WORLD [1]

The existence of differences between natural and social science is unquestioned. Whether these differences relate to method or to subject matter or to both has not yet been clearly and authoritatively stated in a manner to gain general acceptance. The differences in subject matter seem obvious to a casual view. The one, we are inclined to say, deals with material things; the other with social relationships — intangible *somethings* of whose nature we are not sure but which are clearly of psychic rather than of material character. The science of individual psychology, as the college faculty found (see page 13), provides a disturbing case when this distinction is made, for it does not appear to be (at least necessarily) a study of social relationships, while its subject matter is nevertheless intangible and non-material — at least according to traditional ways of thinking.

When differences are sought from the standpoint of method, a dictum by Karl Pearson and others with which the scientific world is in general agreement is confronted: "The unity of all science consists alone in its method, not in its material. The man who classifies facts of any kind whatever, who sees their mutual relation and describes their sequences, is applying the scientific method and is a man of science." [2]

[1] I have presented the same point of view that is here contained in a chapter entitled "The Philosophy of Scientific Social Science" contributed to *Readings in Sociology* to accompany *Introduction to Sociology* by Davis, Barnes and others, D. C. Heath & Co., 1927.

[2] *The Grammar of Science*, Part I, 3d ed., p. 12. In finding the unity of science in its method, Pearson is of course using this term in the sense of

It is to be questioned, then, whether the differences separating the natural and the social sciences are of essential or of incidental character. That is, are they more fundamental than the differences which separate any two individual sciences or groups of sciences which have become distinct from each other? As yet no one knows, and the answer given by any writer will be a statement of his viewpoint. To understand this is to understand its effect upon his work, and, if the reader so chooses, to make allowance for the former in the results of the latter. The present chapter, therefore, like those immediately preceding and following, contains a philosophic argument designed to support the writer's underlying belief in *the essential unity of the universe and of the science which is gradually exhibiting it to human view*. A complete discussion of the questions involved is, of course, out of place here.

The student who is for the first time engaging in original research quickly learns that classification is one of the most perplexing parts of his work. Whatever the things to be classified may be, there are always doubtful cases, while class types frequently shade into each other imperceptibly. Even sex has come to be thought of as a variable, with two distinct modes, but still a variable. This difficulty is encountered when efforts are made to classify the sciences. There seems to be no criterion which can be selected as a basis for making fundamental distinctions. Herbert Spencer made a distinction in subject matter between the "inorganic," "organic" and "super-organic." By throwing the first two together we obtain the vicious verbal distinction between "natural" and "social" science which I have been unable to avoid using in the present discussion. But no one is now

---

logical method. *Cf.* the distinction drawn by Wolf above, page 6. It could scarcely apply to method in the sense of technique.

able to determine where any one of Spencer's classes begins and the others leave off,[3] although we can fix, as it were, modal points of concentration.

Another fundamental distinction which can be attempted is that which separates phenomena, or *percepts*, from *concepts*, together with the sciences thereof.[4] The difficulty here is that every science becomes more conceptual as it becomes more exact, while even mathematics probably has its roots in the perceptual world.[5] There is no sharp line of division among sciences on this basis. Yet the distinction may have equal value as an organizing principle to any other. To me it seems to have greater utility in this respect than the distinction between "natural" and "social," for it does represent a certain difference in motive on the part of the scientist. Pure mathematics and formal logic are not professedly concerned with the actual world of things and events. They deal with an idealized or conceptual world of abstractions, in which two and two always equal four — no more, no less. This world may have no known counterpart or analogue in

[3] In his presidential address before the American Philosophical Society, April 27, 1927, Dr. Francis X. Dercum presented what might be called a biochemical explanation (or perhaps a biochemical-physical explanation) of the manner in which life may have evolved out of non-living matter over a vast period of time. Thus even the emergence of life from the naturalistic standpoint has become an evolutive rather than a definitive concept, having an intermediate zone of doubt.

[4] If I understand him correctly, this is the same distinction which Spykman represents Simmel as finding "in the most general opposition within our knowledge, the opposition between what is *a priori* and what is experience." *The Social Theory of Georg Simmel*, by Nicholas J. Spykman, p. 10.

[5] "It is the merest truism, evident at once to unsophisticated observation, that mathematics is a human invention. Furthermore, the mathematics in which the physicist is interested was developed for the explicit purpose of describing the behavior of the external world, so that it is certainly no accident that there is correspondence between mathematics and nature. . . . But there is always in mathematics a precise quality to which none of our information about nature ever attains." — Bridgman, P. W., *The Logic of Modern Physics*. (The Macmillan Co., 1927) pp. 60–61.

reality, a situation which is found, for example, in the case of at least some parts of non-Euclidean systems of geometry. But in contrast with "mathematical science," "natural" and "social" science alike profess to be concerned with empirical material, with data reaching us through our senses.[6]

It is true that some of the data reported by human sense organs seem more substantial than others. One sees a saxophone and hears the atmospheric disturbances to which it gives rise, but one cannot see or hear or touch or smell the group relationships which in some perplexing manner bind the members of the jazz orchestra together. The first surmise that each member is wholly independent of the others in thought and action eventually breaks down, and it is perceived that they have organization, but the organization seems less tangible than the saxophone.

In actuality the two types of data are not as dissimilar as they seem. The existence of the saxophone is only inferred from sense impressions of it. If the concert patron should become mentally ill and have an hallucination in which the saxophone played a part, the testimony of his senses would later be rejected, if he were restored to sanity, because of the absence of corroboration for the hallucinatory evidence. Corroboration would be required in the form of other sense impressions received directly by the patient, emanating from or relating to the saxophone, or indirectly from other individuals who in turn received sense impressions relating to the instrument in question. When all possible corroboration is secured, belief in the existence of any material thing remains

[6] If two and two are added together in this perceptual world, the result may not be four except within a defined degree of approximation to a conceptual limit. *Cf.* also *The Anatomy of Science*, by Gilbert Newton Lewis, p. 22: "Does one liter of alcohol added to one liter of water give two liters? No, it gives hardly more than one liter and nine tenths."

an inference. Belief in the existence of a group relationship
is of the same character. It is an inference, based upon a
variety of sense impressions concerning the behavior of
individuals who are involved.[7]

All data from the perceptual world turn out to be evidences concerning reality, but not reality itself; or, if
preferred, such evidences are reality and the latter is nothing
more. Whatever the preferred form of statement, it remains
true that what is known of a hypothetical world without
one's own individual mind is universally subject to error and
inexactitude. Scientific method conceptualizes the perceptual data and treats them *as if* they were real and exact
entities. This methodological process, like a great deal more
of scientific method, is essentially fictional. Its justification
is to be found in the results to which it leads. Hence it is as
valid for the scientist to speak of a social group as to speak
of an ounce of ether, provided he can do something further
with the idea. All he knows of either is what he infers
through the mediumship of his own or (by a secondary
process) of an other person's sense impressions.

It may be objected at this point that the physical scientist
has a different kind of situation to deal with, as compared
with the social scientist, because his observations can be
repeated; because, that is, the same material substances
will give him the same sense-impressions when the same
conditions are present. This, it may be held, is not true of
social phenomena. The forms of the latter as we experience
them are always infinitely varied.

It is here that the statistical view prevents us again from

[7] *Cf.* Pearson, *op. cit.*, Chapter II. The argument may, of course, be carried
farther to show that from our sense impressions we *construct* ideas of things,
which are also therefore of a conceptual character. It should be noted, moreover, that I am leaving out of account as social data the content of one's
own individual consciousness. The argument is behavioristic.

finding that basic difference between "natural" and "social" phenomena which our uncritical every-day experience leads us to assume. In any final or absolute sense of the term there are no such things as *repetition* or *identity* in the perceptual world. More correctly, there is no evidence and little presumption for their existence.[8] Precisely the same event never happens twice in the universe of which we know. When the chemist two times in succession performs the experiment of separating water into hydrogen and oxygen, he is not repeating the same event, but rather bringing about two *similar* events. The water used in the experiments is in each case made up of a vast number of molecules. Each of these is an individual, and *may* differ from every other individual molecule in characteristics which the chemist is unable to measure or concerning the nature of which he may be wholly unaware. Because of their vast number these molecules may be *regarded* as all alike. On the *average* the molecules in one experiment will be so nearly like those in the other experiment that they may be treated as if they were identical.[9] We cannot be sure that individual molecules

[8] "There can be no question that the concept of identity is a tool perfectly well adapted to deal approximately with nature in the region of our ordinary experience, but we have to ask a more serious question. Does not the apparent demand of our thinking apparatus to be furnished with discrete and identifiable things to think about impose a very essential restriction on any picture of the physical universe which we are able to form? We are continually surprising ourselves in the invention of discrete structure further and further down in the scale of things, whose sole *raison d'être* is to be found entirely within ourselves. . . . What physical assurance have we that an electron in jumping about in an atom preserves its identifiability in anything like the way that we suppose, or that the identity concept applies here at all? In fact, the identity concept seems to lose all meaning in terms of actual operations on this level of experience." — Bridgman, P. W., *op. cit.*, pp. 93–94.

[9] The possibility of molecules of the same substance differing in mass was denied by Clerk Maxwell, "for if of the molecules of some substance such as hydrogen, some were of sensibly greater mass than others, we have the means of producing a separation between molecules of different masses, and in this way we should be able to produce two kinds of hydrogen, one of which would

differ from each other in this way, nor can we be sure that
they are all alike, but so far as we have experience of nature
through our sense impressions, we find differences existing
among all individuals of the same kind.

It may be that the diversity which seems to exist in human
affairs, and the seeming absence of diversity among smaller
elements of matter, may both be explained by the direction
of human interest and attention. We are interested in
individual human beings *per se* because we ourselves are to
be classed among them. If the same amount of attention
which we give to other human beings were to be directed to
a few individual molecules and their relationships to each
other (assuming this to be possible) it might be that comparable diversity would appear. Such a possibility is suggested
by the well-recognized human inability to distinguish between
individuals of unfamiliar types or species. All members of
an alien people seem strangely alike until we come to know
them, while it is only of recent years that the extraordinary
variations of "personality" existing among the higher animals have come to be recognized.

However this may be, individual differences are customarily
disregarded even in human affairs when we deal with a large
number of individuals. No two persons are alike, yet we
compare Pittsburgh and St. Louis by saying that there is a
certain number of people in each. On the average these
people will be about the same in both cities. Similarly, we
give to every person having certain minimum qualifications

---

be somewhat denser than the other. As this cannot be done, we must admit
that the equality which we assert to exist between the molecules of hydrogen
applies to each individual molecule. and not merely to the average of groups
of millions of molecules." (*Theory of Heat*, 7th ed. p. 329.) On the other
hand, Karl Pearson appears to believe that the sameness of the molecules,
even as to their mass, is a statistical or average sameness only. (*Op. cit.*,
Chap. V.)

a *vote*. It is evident that some citizens are more competent to exercise this privilege than others, but we proceed upon the assumption that in an election one man's opinion is on the average as good as another's. This, it will be seen, is very similar to our assumption in a chemical experiment that all molecules of a certain substance may be regarded as alike. In both cases we obtain a *statistical* statement of a certain situation.

The essential similarity between scientific descriptions of physical and of social phenomena may be still better illustrated by certain scientific laws concerning the action of gases. A gas confined in a receptacle will exert pressure upon the walls which enclose it. The amount of this pressure may be calculated with seeming scientific precision. Yet the physicist is dealing not with a single force, but with the combined forces of an almost infinite number of separate molecules all in violent motion. The motions of these molecules are of almost infinite variety both in speed and direction and are probably in no two cases exactly alike. In two similar receptacles containing the same kind of gas at the same temperature and under the same pressure, it is possible that no molecule in one receptacle is exactly like any molecule in the other receptacle. It is improbable that the *force* being exerted by any one molecule in one receptacle is being exactly duplicated by any molecule in the other. Yet in the *aggregate* (which amounts to the same thing as *upon the average*) the pressure in the two receptacles seems to be precisely the same. It probably is *very nearly but not exactly* the same. In other words, the scientific law which describes the pressure of the gas is *statistical* (a matter of averages) and not *exact*, in any fundamental sense.

Analogously, we have in America a population of individual human beings. As may be true of the molecules, no two of these human beings are exactly alike. As is almost certainly true of the molecules, no two persons are doing exactly the same things — that is, going through exactly the same motions. Nevertheless, it is possible with a certain degree of accuracy to predict what these persons are doing or will do in the aggregate; to predict, for example, the *per capita demand* ("economic pressure") that will be made for food stuffs, or cotton goods or steel. It is a matter once more of statistical averages.

A recent scientific writer points out that the so-called "Second Law of Thermo-dynamics" is based upon statistical probabilities, rather than upon certainties.[10] This important law states that the heat contained in two adjacent bodies is always tending to equalize, by a flow from the hotter to the colder body; that heat, in other words, is "non-reversible," or never "flows up hill." But "never" in this case means "hardly ever." It is *possible*, though so improbable as not to occur once in trillions of years, that a kettle of water placed upon a hot stove would turn to ice. The "law" states merely what is *likely* rather than what is *certain* to happen.

Now again it is statements like these — things likely but not certain of occurrence — which can be made concerning human society. The difference between such statements in the case of social and physical phenomena is mainly one of degree. Likelihood, or *probability*, may vary all the way between certainty that a stated event will take place, on the one hand, and, on the other, certainty that it will not take place. In the perceptual world there is probably no complete certainty with regard to anything. In the case of many physical phenomena, however, the probability is so

---

[10] "Perpetual Motion in the Twentieth Century" by Dr. Paul R. Heyl of the National Bureau of Standards, *The Scientific Monthly*, Feb. 1926. The same point is entertainingly made by Gilbert Newton Lewis, *op. cit.*

high as to amount to certainty for all practical purposes. This is the case with the "Second Law" referred to. We can be "sure" (but not certain) that the kettle on the hot stove will boil. In the case of some social phenomena there can be a fair degree of assurance. Insurance companies can be sufficiently sure, for conservative business purposes, that approximately a certain number of their policy holders will die within a given period. Municipal authorities are warranted in hiring judges and jailers and policemen for long terms, in the expectation that crimes will be committed, although it is *possible* that they will not be. College instructors may *expect* that in a large class a fairly uniform percentage of their students will fail; although it occasionally happens that every student does good work and succeeds in passing. All of these examples refer to sound scientific generalizations; all are based upon probability rather than certainty; each is of a differing degree of probability. In other words, all once again are *statistical* in character.

It must, of course, be admitted that in degree of exactitude, the advantages are usually in favor of the "natural" sciences. There are certain factors that place the development of a science of society under comparative handicaps. I have pointed out above that all data from the perceptual world are in the nature of *indexes*, so to speak, of a hypothetical world of reality beyond the reach of sense impression. But the data of social science are frequently indexes of indexes. That is, they may be one or several degrees farther removed from the "reality," whatever it may be, in which interest actually resides. The phenomena of mental life, for example, can be known in others (and known with approximate precision even in oneself) only as they are expressed in *behavior*. This question will be developed at further length in Chapter VII.

Again, social science cannot become experimental to the same degree as many of the natural sciences. The difficulty inheres, not in any essential difference in subject matter, but in the practical human relationship to the social subject matter. A being which was superhuman in intelligence and power and without ordinary human susceptibilities could presumably experiment with problems of social science as freely as biologists or even chemists experiment with their own materials. Let us examine by two illustrations what the process of experimentation involves.

When workingmen are unemployed, the untrained observer finds a single ready and all-sufficient explanation. The workingmen are "lazy and do not want to work," or "the capitalistic system produces cycles of depression and throws them out of their jobs," or "they are mentally defective," or "they were inadequately trained," or "they are victims of alcohol," or "they are insufficiently nourished to perform the work expected of them." It is seldom considered that all of these factors and many more may have coöperated in bringing about the unemployment of a given individual. What we really want to know is how each of these factors in turn is related to unemployment, independently of all of the others. If, for example, the use of alcohol were reduced or eliminated, what would be the effect? Would employment be wiped out altogether, diminished, or left unchanged? Since neither the first nor the third are probable, to what degree would the elimination of alcohol diminish unemployment?

The problem is not unlike that which confronts the agricultural specialist who is seeking to increase the yield of a certain crop. His problem is to ascertain in turn the relationship between yield on the one hand and, upon the other hand, changes in the quality of the seed, character of soil, temperature, humidity, cultivation, duration of season, and a variety of other factors. All of these factors together produce the result — a crop. But each may change independently of the others, thereby producing a change in the yield. The essence of experimentation is to plan a situation in which all of these changing factors or *variables* will remain constant except one. This one factor is then allowed to change in a predetermined manner and if possible to a predetermined extent. Measurements are then taken of the change in the outcome or total situation. In this way, the comparative significance of each variable can be determined in turn. Thus by planting alternate plots with two qualities of seed and guarding against cross-fertilization, the experimentalist holds constant the variables of soil, weather, temperature, etc., and compares the yield of the two types of seed. Or in another case, the quality of seed, the temperature and the weather may be held constant and two types of soil may be compared as to yield.

The agriculturist can experiment in the manner suggested because he can control, to some degree, the variable factors entering into his problem. The physicist, the chemist and the psychologist, in varying degrees, can similarly control their variables. The meteorologist, dealing with the weather, and the social scientist, dealing with group relationships, have a lesser degree of control over variables. Botanical growth and chemical processes take place in nature without any intervention by man, just as do atmospheric changes and (in a deterministic sense) social activities. There is no sharp line of distinction among natural processes as to the extent to which they may be artificially produced under controlled conditions. The classroom of the teacher of social science may become a laboratory for experiment in a real sense because to some degree the instructor (who now becomes the experimenter) may control the introduction of new variables into the social group situation and to some degree determine the results of their introduction.

But the possibilities of such control are small as compared with the number and variety of social events which take place without control. A science of society in any of its branches must attempt systematic observation, recording, and analysis of these uncontrolled events if it is not to be stilted and fragmentary. This is difficult because they are unforeseen, and the separate effects of the different variable factors cannot subsequently, in most cases, be determined.

The attempt to observe, moreover, either directly or indirectly, may amount in itself to the introduction of new and disturbing variables. People do not readily consent to detailed scrutiny of their personal affairs by others; nor can they themselves provide the scrutiny, however objectively minded, without risk of changing the situation. An extreme but illuminating illustration of the difficulty may be cited from among the research projects now under way by an American sociologist. The problem is to discover the uses to which their time is put by American housewives. Data is to be supplied by the latter themselves for every hour of every day in a certain period. But keeping this record is itself time-consuming, so that an unaltered report upon the time distribution of activities in a "normal" day becomes in the very nature of the case an impossibility.

There are far-reaching implications for scientific theory and for scientific method in the contentions of the *gestalt* psychologists, and in the notion of *creative systhesis* brilliantly expounded in this country by Miss Mary Follette. The whole is always more than the sum of its parts, for it includes not merely these parts themselves but the relationships between or among them. The latter, if the number of parts be numerous, are incomparably more numerous. What this obvious fact is to mean for scientific procedure no one has yet attempted to state. In some quarters it has been taken to indicate the impossibility of extending the older and more usual methods of measurement and analysis to social phenomena. Yet the fact itself is surely as applicable to organic and inorganic as to super-organic "total situations." I am myself inclined to believe that instead of proving that experiment is less possible in social science, Miss Follette's contentions serve merely to show still more clearly the impossibility of complete control, and the inescapable margin of error, in *all* scientific experiment, whatever the field of subject matter.

As if all of the foregoing considerations were not enough to make his task difficult, the social scientist, as the reader was reminded in the preceding chapter, is himself a part of the phenomena to be observed; a social being with prejudices and desires concerning social outcomes. In view of all of his difficulties, he must seek not for *causes* but for *correlations*, or "concomitant variations" among the various factors of the problems with which he deals. Once more it could be shown that the statistical methods which he employs are in all essentials the same as those of the physical scientist. The theory of correlation is well known, and there is no need for illustration of it here.

In concluding this chapter, it should be made clear that no contention is set forth for the fundamental similarity of reality in the social and the physical worlds. I do not know what psychic phenomena are, nor what material phenomena are, *essentially*, or how they differ. All I know of either (apart from my individual consciousness) is what my senses tell me. But I do contend that the scientific method of conceptualizing these sense impressions for purposes of analysis is the same in both instances. Wittingly or unwittingly, scientists adopt the statistical view of the perceptual world, and this gives their work a methodological unity in addition to the unity residing in methods of logical inference, whatever the underlying diversity of subject matter may be. It is this which makes it possible to anticipate a quantitative science of politics, for the difficulties in the way become incidental to our stage of historical development and not inherent in the subject matter itself. They may ultimately be removed by patient and prolonged processes of observation, definition, classification, and recording.[9]

[9] "Nous retrouverons dans les sciences morales tous les caractères des sciences proprement 'scientifigues'. Chacune d'elles comprend, nous le verrons, une branche empirique qui recueille des apparences et exprime, sous la forme de lois, leurs caractères communs, et une branche rationnelle qui en crée les causes ... Nous ne prétendons nullement modifier les sciences morales pour les plier a la forme scientifique; nous affirmons au contraire que, telles qu'elles sont actuellement, elles présentent tous les caractères des sciences dites physiques." .. Jacques Rueff, *Des Sciences Physiques aux Sciences Morales*, Paris, 1922, pp. 89–90.

IV

CASE METHOD AND STATISTICAL METHOD IN HISTORY AND SCIENCE

Among the four subjects in the above title there are six general problems of mutual relationship. With respect to three of these no common agreement seems ever to have been reached. Much has been written concerning the relative functions of case method and statistical method. The former is frequently said to take account of all aspects of one thing or situation, while the latter takes account of one or a few aspects of many things or situations. A number of case studies may thus provide the material from which certain common elements or factors may be abstracted for statistical comparison and summarization. The character of this first relationship, then, seems fairly clear. Nor, in the second place, will there be much disagreement with the contention that statistical method is essential to science. In the preceding chapter I have argued that in the real world of phenomena (as contrasted with the conceptual world of logic and mathematics) certainty has been replaced by probability and exact statement by approximation. These are statistical concepts, and scientific statement is in the last analysis statistical statement.

History, on the other hand, is built upon a description of single unique events. It is, then, a study of cases. Except for some differences with respect to the availability of sources of information, and with regard to the ends sought by the inquiry, a history of the John Doe Family during the Amer-

35

ican Revolution would not differ essentially from a case study of the Richard Roe family by a present day social worker.[1] Hence as to the third question of relationship we may say, with some disregard for differences in the technique of assembling material, that the case method is the usual if not the essential method of history. But how do history and science stand with reference to each other? Are they differing modes of a single coherent process, or of fundamentally separate character? Is case method a method of science? Is statistical method applicable to history?

It is with respect to these three latter questions that difficulty and disagreement are more often found. History, it is true, is often included among the "social sciences." For example, the American Historical Association is a participating body in the Social Science Research Council. Again, the American Association for the Advancement of Science includes "Section L" on "Historical and Philological Sciences," as it also includes Section K on "Social and Economic Sciences." But another representative body of national organizations of which the American Historical Association is a member calls itself the "American Council of Learned Societies." One of America's keenest thinkers, a statistician and philosopher of science, holds that all scientific method must involve relationships between or among variables. If this be so, how can history or the case method qualify as science? [2]

Another American authority on statistics recently expressed the belief that case method cannot be regarded as

[1] Biography may be regarded as a species of history.
[2] Any "case" is of course made up of parts or factors which are in relationship to each other. These parts might be regarded as "variables" in the sense that they will differ from case to case. But when account is taken of these differences we have then to all effects abandoned the case method and adopted the statistical. The concept of variability belongs to statistics.

falling within the domain of science. When this opinion was conveyed to several persons who are versed in case method as a means of inquiry, it evoked their vigorous dissent.

It is difficult to determine to what extent disagreements and obscurities concerning these questions are apparent only — the result of unperceived differences in the definitions of terms — and to what extent they are real. The adjustment of ideas concerning them which is here attempted is not the only adjustment which could be made. As suggested in Chapter I, however, it has met successfully for the writer the important test of a working philosophy, i.e., it has helped to provide order and consistency within the field of attention.

History and science have this at least in common: both attempt to describe the real world of phenomena, including in this the past as well as the present. But whereas the datum or unit of historical inquiry is deemed to be the *event*, the datum of science frequently appears as a material *entity*. The one represents an occurrence in time, the other an appearance in space at a given moment of time. This distinction is more illusory than real. There can be no event without the appearance of change in material entities or things, a description of which is an essential part of the description of the event. The entity or thing, on the other hand, is known to modern science only in its manifestations of change. Inert matter has ceased to exist for the scientific mind.[3] Even from the common-sense or layman's standpoint, moreover, science is usually concerned with occurrences that take place in time, that represent changes of similar or analogous character to those of the historical inquiry. The evolution of species, the transformation of chemical combi-

---

[3] This is illustrated by the discovery that matter and energy are to some extent at least convertible.

nations in a laboratory experiment, for example, are of this character. From the modern relativistic point of view, the *event* has become a "point in space-time," and the distinction between history and science suggested at the beginning of this paragraph tends to break down entirely.[4]

A more persuasive statement of the difference between science and history is found in the contention of historians that the event to which they give attention is *unique*. The events upon which scientific generalization is based, upon the other hand, are said to be recurrent, and in some cases capable of repetition at will. Thus there was but one Franco-Prussian War of 1870, but there have been innumerable repetitions of the event in which hydrogen and oxygen have been combined to form water. This argument will require more extended attention.[5]

The world of reality reported to us by our senses appears to be broken up into things, set off from or distinct from each other. As a matter of fact, it is probable that *discontinuity* or separateness of things, and *continuity*, which carries the opposite meaning, are limiting concepts, nowhere actually found in nature. Under the microscope a smooth metal surface will become broken into irregularities. Were still higher magnification possible, it might be difficult to tell where the metal began and the surrounding atmosphere left off. If sufficient magnification were possible to enable seeing

---

[4] *Cf.* Lewis, Gilbert N. — *The Anatomy of Science*, p. 63. The author says with reference to his own discussion: "It will avoid confusion in our further discussion if we agree to use the word *event* for any episode which has no considerable extension in space or time. For example, if we were dealing with the modern history of Europe, the French Revolution must be treated as affecting a great many square miles of territory over a number of years; but if we were considering the whole history of the solar system, its spacial and temporal extension could be ignored and it could be regarded as an *event* in this technical sense; or, in other words, as a mere point upon our space-time map."

[5] *Cf.* also "the statistical view of the universe" presented in Chapter III.

within the atom, the greater part of that which appears to our unaided senses to be a "thing" would now appear, if modern theory is correct, as unfilled space, and continuity would nowhere be found.

Whatever the nature of the ultimate units of which the world is compounded, of this we are sure: that the things we know with our senses are aggregates of still smaller particles. It is a matter of convenience how much or how little of the world we put together in our mind and agree to consider, for the time being, as a single entity. In thought and probably also in nature every part of reality is involved to a greater or less degree in effective and causal relationships with every other part. The "parts" of the world with which we deal, then, have been separated out from the whole only in a rough, approximate, pragmatic fashion. This pragmatic separation into parts or things has validity of a practical sort, for it is necessary to life, but is without any essential finality.[6]

Another departure from essential reality on behalf of practical results is made when similar but unique "things" are classed together and regarded as so many of the same thing. The individual thing, itself an abstraction from reality, now becomes a *unit* in a series of like things. Every chicken, cow or man is an individual —

[6] Znaniecki, Florian — *The Laws of Social Psychology*, pp. 2-3. "Not only psychological life, but all reality is in a measure a concrete and continuous stream of becoming: every isolation of elements, every rational determination of facts is in a sense an artificial abstraction breaking the continuity of the concrete rush of changes and ignoring innumerable bonds which tie every fact with other facts, simultaneous or successive. This abstraction is, nevertheless, justified in the sciences of objective reality in so far as the concreteness and continuity of becoming are not absolute and uniform: objects stand out from their milieu as relatively stable and connected into relatively isolated systems; facts are determined by certain other facts in a larger measure than by all the rest of the concrete world. This is sufficient to make science possible."

unique. To the census-taker each becomes a unit in a certain class or type of enumerated objects. Because both the "thing" and the class of things are abstractions, they need not be regarded as dissimilar categories. A thing may be treated as a class containing but a single unit. Just as things are compounded of simpler parts into differing orders of magnitude or complexity, so units employed for one purpose are disregarded for another in which a different scale or a different principle of division may be employed. To the taxonomist, the human race as a whole is one unit, *homo sapiens*, among other units in a series of species. The political scientist may be interested in the political state, a unit without necessary or even probable significance to the cultural anthropologist. The sociologist may be interested in social groups or in individuals of specified character. But the "individual" becomes an aggregate to the physiologist who is concerned with the structure and functions of human cells or to the psychiatrist who views personality in terms of complexes and patterns. It has been noted above that according to physicists even molecules have their own velocities and directions of motion and possibly other aspects of "individuality" as well.[7]

The parts into which we divide our world are thus arbitrary classes of arbitrary divisions of reality, both continually changing in reference to the particular purpose in view. Because the selection and classification are arbitrary, a certain definition of the units employed is always implied, even if not stated. The scholar or scientist will elaborate this definition in formal terms and with meticulous care. The student and the layman are less likely to be aware of the need of definition. The presence of the latter in implicit form is often unperceived, and an unnoted change in the

[7] *Cf. Supra*, p. 25

definition may lead to serious errors in reasoning or conclusions. Nor are such errors unknown upon the college lecture platform. For example, in a university course on social problems one of the topics discussed in the reading assignment was prostitution. Authorities were cited for an estimate that the number of prostitutes in the United States was between 200,000 and 500,000. In another paragraph the same authorities were cited for an estimate that the prostitute's male patrons would number from ten to fifteen a day. The two estimates in conjunction lead to the wholly preposterous inference that on an average the entire male population of the nation between fifteen and sixty-five years of age visits a prostitute once every four and one-half to seventeen days. It is clear that the term "prostitute" was tacitly defined more narrowly in the second estimate than in the first.

When phenomena are viewed in the process of development over a period of time, the unbroken continuity of events is even more obvious. Units again are abstracted by the aid of definitions. The definition of an event must include one or more things or classes of things and the changes in connection therewith which occur. (These changes are matters of internal or external relationships.) The founding of the University of Pennsylvania, for example, can be assigned to any one of a number of years. Authorities differ regarding the date of the event because they do not agree in their definition of the University of Pennsylvania. Again, it would be difficult for many people to agree upon the date at which there was resumption of peace between the United States and Turkey. The definition of the "things," i.e., of the two nations concerned would, in this case, be practically the same for all who took part in the discussion, but the differences would be found in deciding between a *de jure* and a *de facto* definition of the changes in relationships which constituted the event of peace.

Perhaps more than anything else, it is the unperceived and uncontrolled changes in definition affecting the classification of things and events, which render difficult the scientific manipulation of social data. It is these changes which sometimes provide justification for that popular arrangement of prevarications in a hierarchical order which has statistics at its apex. While not strictly essential to our discussion of relationships among history, science, etc., therefore, it may be profitable to turn aside at this point and attempt to analyze the nature of these unperceived or uncontrolled changes insofar as they affect the classification of events.

If the definition of the entities involved in a given type of events remains constant, an individual unit in some other classification may conform to the first definition at one time but cease to do so at another. For example, a given "infant" (an entity involved in a type of events known as "juvenile delinquency") has existence according to legal definition for twenty-one years only. The "infant" is also a "human being," i.e., a unit in another and broader classification. The first ceases to exist on the twenty-first birthday of the second, whose derelictions may thenceforth be included in another type of events known as "adult delinquency." Again, *homo sapiens* is believed to be continuous in genetic descent from species to whom that designation could not be given. When did the class of events called "homicide" begin to occur? Clearly, not until (by definition) the genetic stock could be classed as *man*. In both illustrations the definitions of the entities in which or to which changes have occurred in order to constitute events have remained constant. Moreover, the definitions which specify the nature of these changes may also have remained constant. In what manner, then, has the situation been altered? By the transformation of units over a period of time in such a way that whereas they have hitherto been classed as both A and B, they are presently classed as C instead of B, although they remain A.

But the situation is sometimes otherwise. The passing of time may not alter a given unit sufficiently to involve its reclassification. It still remains both A and B. Yet the definition of the changes in which it must be involved to constitute an event of a certain kind may be altered. I.e., while the events now classed together have changed in character, their class name remains the same. For example, in the passage of time, without deviation in his personal habits, the user of intoxicating liquors has recently become party to the event of law-breaking. The almshouse pauper of today is almost invariably an aged person. The almshouse pauper of 1870 might have been a dependent child or a lunatic of younger middle age. The explanation is to be found in the fact that the character of the almshouse as an institution (the implied definition of the changes in personal status necessary for admission) has changed with the intervening years. Yet the name has persisted.

To return to the main thread of argument it has been pointed out that the event involves a definition of the unit of reality in relation to which it occurs, and also a definition of the nature or extent of the changes or occurrences which are to be regarded as the event in a narrower sense. Both definitions may be wide or narrow within boundaries determined by the interest which guides us. The historical case study may extend over the major aspects of American political history (numerous unique events of a defined type in interaction) or it may be confined to the work of poor relief in a single township. A definition of the material units or things (nation or township) and of the types of changes occurring (political or philanthropic) are in both cases implied. The interest, moreover, imposes boundaries *in time* between which the unit events are to receive attention.

Let us sum up the position now reached in the argument. Reality is continuous, both in its spacial and its temporal aspects. "Things" are aggregates of smaller "things," abstracted for pragmatic reasons and by means of definitions from the spacial continuum. "Events" are defined changes in the internal or external relationships of "things," hence, abstractions from the temporal as well as from the spacial continuum of reality. But since no two things, so far as we know, can be exactly alike [8] it follows that no two events can be exactly alike. Nevertheless, again for pragmatic reasons, things and events which are sufficiently alike for the pragmatic purpose, are classified together. The similarity may, and usually does, extend to one or a few only of many characteristics. Classification is a process whereby unique but similar things or events are grouped together and treated *as if* they were all alike. That is, they are called units of the same thing or event. And it may be noted that since things or events which are treated as alike inevitably disclose their individuality in the form of individual differences, sometimes sharply and sometimes in lesser demarcations, we resort for an explanation to the concepts of *attribute* and *variability* each with its appropriate statistical procedure.

The ability of science to find "repetitions" of events, then, depends upon the "scientific fictions" that we have been discussing. It depends in particular upon suitable classifica-

[8] Individuality with respect to spacial position alone will be sufficient to bring about individuality in other respects, for it involves subjection to differing arrangements and magnitudes of the surrounding material "forces." I.e., it brings into being differing sets of relationships. *Cf. Supra*, p. 25.

tion, a wholly pragmatic process. The fiction involved in classification is fundamental to statistical method. Without it, statistical treatment of mass data would be an impossibility. The only available method of procuring knowledge about the world would be the case method. Generalization, because based upon a fiction and leading to truth which is relative and not absolute would be debarred. It is questionable whether even case method could be utilized, for it also involves the fiction of abstraction.

Now classification, as an arbitrary pragmatic process, permits of any degree of generality desired. The class limits may enclose within them many things or events (i.e., individual cases), a few, one, or none at all. If the classes are so defined as to admit many cases in the same class, precise statements concerning these cases are usually deemed to be statistical (i.e., scientific) in character. But if the definitions set up are such as to admit a single item only, the statements concerning this may be regarded as historical in character. In the second instance we might have an exemplification of case method. *The thing or event classified may in both instances remain the same.* The difference is in the classification. It is the contention of the writer that the difference between science and history is fundamentally a matter of the comparative narrowness or width of the definitions by which the unit event is segregated from reality and classified. If so, the difference is not essential but rather a matter of convenience. The two, as suggested in one of the questions raised at the outset above, may be thought of as differing modes of a single coherent process.

Consider an illustration: In the decade 1851–1860, 2,511,060 immigrants arrived in the United States from foreign lands. Class limits have been here defined in such a manner that 2,511,060 cases comply with the definition set up for the individual unit event "Foreign Immigrant Arriving in the U. S., 1851–1860." But the definition may be made more restrictive. For example, three new limiting conditions are introduced when the definition specifies "German Immigrant Arriving at the Port of New York in 1852." The number of cases in the class is now reduced. An enlargement of the number of conditions in the definition of the unit event, corresponding with a reduction in the number of events coming within the class, may be continued until a single event remains: Carl Shurz arrived as an immigrant from Germany at the Port of New York in 1852. Here appears the unique event to which the historian pays attention. But the arrival of every other immigrant from foreign shores has been just as unique. Each arrival in turn has received a certain amount of case study from immigrant officials and others. The arrival of Carl Shurz was a unique event which may be compounded with other unique events into a record of important occurrences in a period, or into a study of the trends and cycles of immigration in relation to economic conditions. The one combination produces history, the other the statistics of social science. The unit occurrence in either case is arrived at by a certain amount of case study.

History and science, then, may be regarded as differing modes of compounding together unique events for the attainment of knowledge. These events are delimited from reality by a preliminary and essential process of abstraction which, if not identical with, is at least an important element in or outgrowth of case study. But there can be no sharp line of demarcation between these two modes, and there must remain intermediate fields of inquiry which are neither clearly historical nor scientific but both. Such, for example, is the present "scientific" field of cultural anthropology.

The culture of a tribe provides the "case" for study. Projected into the past, the methods employed and the results achieved would be regarded as falling within the domain of history. Yet resemblances and differences among contemporary tribes are studied in the same spirit, the beginnings of statistical technique appear, and the work becomes "scientific" in the usual sense.

Whenever "science" focusses its attention upon classes within which it can find an insufficient number of units, it is compelled to fall back upon the case methods of history. Whenever "history" is able or willing to define its "events" in such a manner that they may be classified together, and is able moreover to find a sufficient number of the events in question to generalize, it has by virtue of this fact adopted the statistical methods of science. Consider the manner in which financial depressions, historical events all, have been reduced to equations of trend, indexes of seasonal variation and cycle figures in terms of the standard deviation! But while the case method and history might thus be regarded as merely stepping stones on the road to science, the latter represents merely a limit which will never be actually attained. In the complex world of reality, science and history may be expected increasingly to become transposed and blurred, to merge and separate and merge again in ever more bewildering fashion. And this will be a hopeful thing if our eyes are fixed upon the problems of reality itself, and not upon the vain divisions into which a passing generation attempted to divide it.

V

"Stereotypes" in the Content of Political Attitude

Among the chief concerns of a science of politics are questions involving "public opinion." What this term means precisely, if anything, is not at all clear. At the Second National Conference on the Science of Politics,[1] the members of the Round Table on Political Statistics devoted much time to an effort to agree upon its meaning. The more general term "opinion" was first considered. "It was decided that for the purposes of the problem before this round table the essential points in a definition of opinion could be narrowed to three: (1) opinion need not be the result of a rational process; (2) it need not include an awareness of choice; and (3) it must be sufficiently clear or definite to create a disposition to act upon it under favorable circumstances." The round table was unable to come to a definite conclusion upon the question when is opinion public. It was decided to "proceed to consider the problem of measuring opinion, especially that relating to political matters, and avoid the use of the term public opinion, if possible." [2]

My own preference is to avoid the use of the term opinion and to use instead the word *attitude*, as indicating a disposition or set toward behavior without reference to the degree of rationality that may be present in connection with it.

[1] Held at Chicago, September 8–12, 1924. Reports are published in the *American Political Science Review*, Feb. 1925, pp. 104–162.

[2] *Ibid.*, pp. 123–24.

The reasons which people cite, however sincerely, for their own or others' behavior bear no necessary or even probable relationship to the motives that are really involved. In spite of the conclusions of the round table just quoted, "opinion" and "public opinion" seem to me to connote too much of the rational and conscious elements in the actual motivation. I shall therefore use the word attitude in a somewhat inclusive sense, without endeavoring to determine in any particular case whether the word opinion might be preferable.[3]

I am unable to distinguish in any general way between attitudes which have political significance and attitudes which have not. Almost any question and attitudes toward it may come to have political significance under certain circumstances. Religious affiliation for example, having been nominally eliminated from American politics, is once more prominently in it. Under the impetus of pro-Nordic eugenics, even the color of one's hair may come to assume political importance.[4] As this is written, the morning

[3] In an important article published since this was written, Professor L. L. Thurstone has made a distinction between "attitude" and "opinion" which seems useful, and with which I should agree. He employs the term attitude "to denote the sum total of a man's inclinations and feelings, prejudice or bias, preconceived notions, ideas, fears, threats, and convictions about any specified topic. . . . It is admittedly a subjective and personal affair." The term opinion is reserved to indicate "a verbal expression of attitude." *Cf.* Professor Thurstone's article, "Attitudes Can be Measured," *American Journal of Sociology*, January, 1928, Vol. 33, pp. 529-554. In most instances in which I have used the term in following pages, non-verbal indexes of attitude have been employed in my measurements. It would seem, therefore, that my avoidance of the term "opinion" was consistent with Professor Thurstone's distinction.

[4] Attitudes must not be regarded as single unified and coherent entities. "Our attitudes form complexes which not only are changed internally as various forces are brought to play on us but are so intimately connected that they strongly influence each other and it is frequently impossible to distinguish clearly between them. . . . With our present limited knowledge of attitudes they cannot be dissected and classified with any degree of finality."

paper reports that the Mayor of New York was subjected to espionage on a recent European visit, and that a "political motive is seen." Whether or not the episodes described are political in character depends either upon the motive, which of itself is highly inaccessible to analysis or measurement, or upon the results to which the episodes lead. The latter cannot be foreseen in advance. Neither provides adequate ground for the separation of political attitudes and behavior from those which are non-political.

All political events are immediately determined by the attitudes of individuals. The questions involved may be formalized in such a way as to be decided in an election by means of votes. Or, as is more usually the case, the attitudes of different individuals may contribute informally and with varying degrees of *weight* to the determination of a policy or decision or action. Scenario writers are probably right in assuming that even a "tsar" may cast aside the advice of a minister, and be swayed by the remarks of his barber.

Politics as a science, then, is concerned among other things with the nature, content and distribution of attitudes among individuals, and with the manner in which they have practical effect in the machinery of government. In later chapters various devices for using *votes* as a means of measuring attitudes will be discussed. That is to say, we may infer from votes something as to the attitudes which led to them. This is a backward process. In the present chapter attention is directed to factors relating to the content of the attitudes themselves. This is a forward process, for if we wished, inferences could be drawn concerning the probable character of the votes to which the content of attitude might lead.

Neumann, George B. — "A Study of International Attitudes of High School Students" (*Teachers College, Columbia University Contributions to Education, No. 239*), p. 15.

It is obvious that the factors which affect attitude as here defined are numerous, and that they may be classified in various ways. Thus they may be instinctive or acquired; they may be unknown to the individual or they may be matters of consciously calculated interest; the interests, conscious or unconscious, may be economic, intellectual, religious, and so on. An attempt to develop a classification would be of no especial value here. I wish to deal in this chapter with one group only among the factors which are involved in the determination of attitude, namely, those preconceptions which Walter Lippmann has called "stereotypes," or "pictures in our heads." [5]

While Lippmann has not described stereotypes in technical psychological terms, they are familiar to anyone who is at all observant of his own mental machinery. They provide an economy of attention in the process of cataloging our environment. Only a part of a mental concept of a given thing consists of immediate or stored sense impressions of it. The remainder is "filled out" from stored memories concerning the class to which the thing at hand (perhaps on wholly insufficient evidence) has at once been referred. This composite of real and imputed character is what we "see." The element in the composite which is preëxistent or stored — which does not consist of immediate sense impressions — may be regarded as a stereotype. The individual responds to it as if it were wholly real. Again, we take note of an actual or alleged association, which may be wholly fortuitous, among the attributes of an individual person or thing. From this we generalize and assume a constancy of the association. The appearance of another individual presenting a few of the attributes so associated leads us to

[5] Lippmann, Walter: *Public Opinion*, Parts I and III, passim, especially pp. 15, 29, 30, 79, and 80.

believe that we recognize therein the other attributes as well. Thus a "pseudo-environment" insulates man from reality, and is corrected by the latter only when the divergence becomes so marked as to affect the individual in some intimate or vital manner.

An illustration which is non-political and perhaps somewhat extreme will make the idea clear. A few years ago I was gazing out of my window across a college campus, my mind absorbed in thought. Presently I became dimly conscious of a chicken jumping up and down on the ground in a characteristic manner. In what seemed afterward a leisurely development of reflection, but which must have occupied a very brief moment, it occurred to me that a college campus was an odd place for an old fat hen. With this thought I became more observant and the hen resolved itself into a football which had been punted across the field and was still bouncing. The explanation seems to be something like this: in the course of youthful barnyard observations various characteristics were abstracted from individual fowls and put together in my mental image or stereotype of "hen." Among these were a certain general size and form and certain irregular jumping movements to which individual hens were habituated, perhaps in a hunt for flies. The bouncing of the football reproduced this size, form, and movement. Without waiting to obtain other sense impressions, my mind immediately classified it as *hen* and proceeded to endow it with other characteristics which the hen class should possess. I *saw* a hen. But what I saw was in part an external object and in part a "picture in my head." If I had taken a gun and shot the football in anticipations of chicken dinner, the doctors would have called me a victim of hallucinations. Yet it is questionable whether I would have been less rational than those good citizens who thought of every

German as a murderous brute, who still regard every Bolshevik as a bewhiskered bomb-thrower, or to whom a Tammany candidate is a wearer of tiger's stripes.

The experiments described below [6] have political implications, in that the methods used could be adapted to the analysis of such stereotypes as have been cited in the preceding paragraph. Their prime purpose was to show the existence of stereotypes, and the changes in the latter which might be induced. They were originally undertaken for class-room illustration. They concern the supposed character and appearance in the minds of the subjects (their stereotypes) of persons of various social types, or having defined social functions. The participants in various phases of the experiments were, first, 258 undergraduates of Dartmouth College, in small classes, over a period of two years. Subsequently, the assistance of 31 members of the Norwich Vermont Grange, attending a regular meeting, was procured to provide comparative results.

In an edition of the *Boston Herald* for December 15, 1924, were found nine portraits of persons represented in the day's news. The reproductions were unusually clear and were uniformly about two by three inches in size. They were placed without identification upon a sheet of paper and numbered from 1 to 9. The individuals pictured were as follows: Edouard Herriot, at that time Premier of France; James Duncan, Vice-president of the American Federation of Labor; Leonid Krassin, first Ambassador of the Soviet

[6] The greater part of what follows is taken from an article in *The Journal of Personal Research*, Vol. V, No. 7, November, 1926, entitled "'Stereotypes': A Source of Error in Judging Human Character." The material is used here with the kind permission of the editors of that publication. A further study is now under way in collaboration with a colleague at the University of Pennsylvania, Mr. W. W. Waller. *Cf.* Mr. Waller's and the present writer's paper, in which the methods described below have been elaborated, before the American Sociological Society, Dec. 28, 1927.

Government at Paris; Joseph W. McIntosh, Deputy Comptroller of the Currency; Martin H. Glynn, former Governor of New York; Max Agel, arrested as a bootlegger; Charles M. Schwab, of the United States Steel Corporation; Howard Heinz, manufacturer of food products; and Senator George Wharton Pepper, of Pennsylvania. In the first aspect of the experiment, the subjects were informed that the sheet contained the pictures of a bootlegger, a European premier, a Bolshevik, a United States Senator, a labor leader, an editor-politician, two manufacturers, and a financier. They were asked to identify these individuals by number. Care was taken that no suggestion be given in the instructions concerning the

TABLE 1 — IDENTIFICATIONS BY 141 STUDENTS

Attempted identifications from their photographs of the social type or functions of nine men, the nine types or functions represented being known

Person Pictured	Identified by the Number of Men Stated as									
	Premier	Labor leader	Bolshevik	Financier	Editor-politician	Bootlegger	Manufacturer *	Senator	Total	Chance *
Premier Herriot.......	54	11	55	2	3	4	4	—	133	15
Labor Leader Duncan .	29	25	15	13	14	1	30	9	136	15
Soviet Envoy Krassin..	31	—	9	15	11	—	16	59	141	16
Financier McIntosh ...	7	20	14	15	16	24	33	8	137	15
Editor-Governor Glynn	6	20	5	21	31	2	33	14	132	15
Bootlegger Agel.......	1	6	9	4	11	86	18	2	137	15
Manufacturer Schwab .	1	14	4	18	20	2	56	21	136	15
Manufacturer Heinz...	5	19	6	31	16	6	46	10	139	15
Senator Pepper	—	22	15	16	19	11	35	15	133	15

* The column headed *chance* represents the number of identifications that would be expected in each column on a chance basis. An exception is the column headed *manufacturer*. Since there were two photographs combined under this heading, the chance here would in each case be double the number for the other columns.

order of the photographs, and that each examiner make independent selections for each position. Table 1 gives the result of the attempted identifications by 141 students. The numbers are not uniform in each column for the reason that in a few cases the pictures were known to the examiners, while in a few others no identifications were attempted.

Allowing for the fact that *two* manufacturers were included among the portraits, the total number of correct identifications on a chance basis would have been approximately 168. The actual number of correct identifications was almost exactly double that number, or 337 out of a possible 1224. On a scale between the expected or chance number and the maximum possible number of correct identifications, the excess number of correct identifications was 169 out of 1056, or 16 per cent. However, such a measure as this percentage provides would not give comparable results as between different series of portraits.

Interest attaches to the fact that Herriot, Duncan, Glynn, Agel, Schwab and Heinz were related each to his respective status in a number of cases substantially above the chance number. Krassin, McIntosh, and Pepper were below or equal to chance or expectation.

In the case of Krassin, the Soviet Envoy, a wing collar, Van Dyke beard and moustache contribute to an appearance that may be described as distinguished, and which no doubt led to 59 identifications as the United States Senator, in comparison with 9 as a bolshevik and none as a labor leader. Senator Pepper received as many or more identifications as labor leader, bolshevik, financier, editor-politician, and manufacturer than he received in his own senatorial capacity. The largest number of correct identifications was made in the case of the alleged bootlegger. This individual alone among his associates in the gallery, is pictured in out-door costume.

He is shown in a heavy overcoat with up-turned collar, a cap, tortoise-shell glasses and cigar gripped firmly between his lips. It is interesting that while Mr. Duncan was identified by 25 men as the labor leader, he was selected by 29 as the premier, by 30 as a manufacturer, by 15 as the Bolshevik and 13 as the financier. It is evident that he did not fit definitely into any pronounced stereotype among those called forth by the characters enumerated.

When a comparison of the preceding data is made with

TABLE 2 — IDENTIFICATIONS BY 25 GRANGE MEMBERS

Attempted identifications from their photographs of the social type or functions of nine men, the nine types or functions represented being known

Person Pictured	Identified by the Number of Members Stated as									
	Premier	Labor leader	Bolshevik	Financier	Editor-politician	Bootlegger	Manufacturer *	Senator	Total	Chance *
Premier Herriot.......	8	3	14	—	—	—	—	—	25	3
Labor Leader Duncan .	10	1	3	2	3	—	3	2	24	3
Soviet Envoy Krassin..	1	1	—	1	—	—	2	21	26	3
Financier McIntosh ...	—	8	4	3	4	—	5	—	24	3
Editor-Governor Glynn	2	5	—	3	3	—	9	1	23	2½
Bootlegger Agel.......	—	1	1	1	1	22	—	—	26	3
Manufacturer Schwab .	—	3	1	4	3	—	12	—	23	2½
Manufacturer Heinz...	1	1	—	7	4	2	8	1	24	3
Senator Pepper.......	2	2	1	5	3	2	8	1	24	3

* Consult note to Table 1, which has the same application here.

that obtained from the group of grange members and presented in table 2, the correspondence is seen to be fairly close. Among the latter the total number of correct identifications on a chance basis would have been 29½ out of a possible 219. The correct identifications actually number

58, or again almost exactly twice the expectation. Herriot, Agel, Schwab and Heinz, as among the students, were correctly identified in more than the chance number of cases, while the distribution in other respects shows a close parallel, especially in the high proportions of correct identifications of the bootlegger, and incorrect identifications of the Bolshevik envoy as Senator.

It is evident that some measure of the extent to which opinion has concentrated in the identification of each portrait would be useful. Wherever there is concentration among the identifications, whether these be correct or incorrect, there will be evidence of the existence of a common stereotype concerning the social designation to which the portrait is assigned.

Such a measure has been found by calculating in the case of each photograph the total and the relative differences between the numbers of identifications made for each social designation (i.e., under each column in tables 1 and 2) and the corresponding numbers that would be expected on the basis of chance. For example, the chance number of identifications for Premier Herriot in each column of table 1 would be 15. The differences between the chance and the actual numbers of identifications are respectively 39, 4, 40, 13, 12, 11, 26 and 15. These total 160. But since the chance number in the case of each portrait is derived from the total number of attempted identifications of that portrait and is a function of the latter, the aggregate number of differences so determined may be related in each case as a numerator to the total number of attempted identifications as a denominator. This fraction, when converted to a decimal figure, will provide a relative *index of departure from expectation*. This index will serve one of the purposes of a *coefficient of variation*, for by its use it is possible to compare the relative concentration of opinion concerning each portrait in the two groups providing data.[7]

In table 3, there is shown for each group the total departures from chance expectation, the indexes of departure from expectation, and the rank of the nine portraits according to the latter. It will be noted that a high total departure and a high index within each group, and a high index in either group, denote a relatively high degree of concentration of opinion, i.e., of agreement among the examiners.

When the corresponding indexes shown in table 3 are compared it is observed that in each case those for the grange group are higher. This indicates that within the latter there is a greater concentration of opinion. It suggests that members of the grange are more prone to form their identifications upon the basis of stereotypes than are the students.

The order of rank among the nine portraits in the matter of concentration of opinion is closely similar in the two groups. When correlated by the well-known Spearman

[7] The *index of departure from expectation* is actually a coefficient of variation, based upon a mean deviation. This may be seen by plotting the data in any row of tables 1 or 2. Let the nine numbers of identifications be regarded as nine frequencies, each with a value corresponding to its magnitude. In the case of Premier Herriot in table 1, for example, the X axis will contain values ranging from 0 (number of identifications as Senator), to 54 (number of identifications as Premier). By classes there will be six frequencies of a value 0 to 9 (there are two manufacturers), one frequency of a value 10 to 19, and two frequencies of a value 50 to 59. The mean value will be 15, which corresponds to the chance number of identifications in each column. The departures from expectation will now appear as deviations from the mean. Instead, however, of calculating a mean deviation I have proceeded directly to a division of the total departures by the total values, i.e., nine times the mean, which gives in a form slightly different from the usual formula a coefficient of variation. It appears to the writer that the meaning of a mean deviation and a coefficient of variation derived in this manner would be confusing in reference to the present data, and I have preferred to develop the method and terms that are employed *de novo*, believing that they will have more direct logical significance for the reader.

formula the coefficient of correlation, $r = 0.84$.   Herriot, Krassin and Agel occupy first, second or third position in both groups, though it was only in the case of Agel that the centering of agreement among the examiners took place upon the correct identification.

The appearance of each of these men as portrayed could be described for one reason or another as striking, in comparison with the others.   In the case of each, it is safe to assert, one or more stereotypes, held in common among the

TABLE 3 — TOTAL DEPARTURES FROM EXPECTATION, INDEXES OF DEPARTURE FROM EXPECTATION AND RANK ACCORDING TO THE INDEXES, IN CASE OF IDENTIFICATIONS OF NINE PORTRAITS BY STUDENTS AND BY GRANGE MEMBERS

	Students			Grange Members		
	Departures from chance	Indexes of departure	Rank	Departures from chance	Indexes of departure	Rank
Premier Herriot............	160	1.20	1	34	1.36	3
Labor Leader Duncan	47	0.35	7	17	0.71	5-6-7
Soviet Envoy Krassin	119	0.84	3	37	1.42	2
Dep. Comptroller McIntosh.	34	0.30	8	17	0.71	5-6-7
Ex-Governor Glynn	63	0.48	5	14½	0.63	8
Bootlegger Agel............	140	1.02	2	39	1.50	1
Manufacturer Schwab	78	0.57	4	18½	0.80	4
Manufacturer Heinz........	66	0.47	6	17	0.71	5-6-7
Senator Pepper	36	0.27	9	11	0.46	9

judges, were evoked.   With each stereotype, moreover, it seems likely that characteristic mental and moral qualities supposed in a similar stereotyped fashion to accompany it were suggested to the judges, and seen inferentially in the corresponding features.

In an effort to check this assumption, a further step in the experiment was taken by securing ratings of the sort obtained by Hollingworth.[8] Students who had not hitherto acted as judges were used as subjects.[9] However, it is probable that interest in the previous experiments had already been aroused outside of the classroom among some of the subjects and that a number had an impression in consequence that there was a catch in the directions given. The same group of grange members as before was employed for comparison, all phases of the experiment being carried through upon a single occasion.

In the case of the students, three groups of judges were used. Each was requested to grade the nine portraits, first according to intelligence, second, according to craftiness. The latter was defined as that characteristic, the possession of which would lead to the taking of an unfair advantage in a business negotiation. The first group of judges, 47 in number, were given no statement concerning the identity of the men portrayed. The second group, 31 in number, were misled by a set of false identifications, conforming so far as possible to the major erroneous identifications in the earlier part of the experiment; that is, with incorrect stereotypes. These false identifications were as follows: Herriot as Bolshevik, Duncan as European Premier, Krassin as United States Senator, McIntosh as manufacturer, Glynn as financier, Agel as manufacturer, Schwab as editor-politician, Heinz as labor leader and Pepper as bootlegger. The third group, 39 in number, were shown the portraits accompanied by the real identities.

In the case of the grange members, the group was first asked to grade the nine portraits according to intelligence, without any identifications being given or suggested. After a

[8] Hollingworth, H. L.: *Judging Human Character*, pp. 34 ff., *Vocational Psychology*, p. 43 *passim*.

[9] This part of the experiment was not developed until the earlier part had been carried through. Moreover, reorganization of classes had intervened.

lapse of time during which identifications were attempted by the members they were asked to fold their papers in such a way that the first series of grades would be concealed. The correct list of identifications was then placed beside the portraits and they were asked once more to regrade the portraits in intelligence without reference to their earlier gradings. The circumstances and the time allotted did not

TABLE 4 — PERCENTAGE RATINGS OF NINE PORTRAITS OF INTELLIGENCE BY STUDENTS AND GRANGE MEMBERS, AND ON CRAFTINESS BY STUDENTS, UNDER CERTAIN VARIABLE CONDITIONS CONCERNING IDENTIFICATION

	Percentage Ratings on Intelligence					Percentage Ratings on Craftiness by Students		
	Students			Grange Members				
	No statement	False identity	True identity	No statement	True identity	No statement	False identity	True identity
Herriot........	40.7	54.0	62.2	30.5	73.0	63.5	50.7	49.4
Duncan........	33.4	43.6	25.6	35.5	54.9	52.1	58.9	50.6
Krassin........	69.8	78.3	69.2	79.0	34.0	30.3	29.4	30.4
McIntosh......	53.0	45.6	61.9	52.8	54.9	54.0	56.0	57.4
Glynn.........	65.1	68.2	57.5	41.0	59.0	29.3	39.1	47.8
Agel..........	31.3	30.3	6.4	27.7	13.2	57.5	65.3	68.0
Schwab........	60.2	52.0	70.9	69.5	72.2	46.3	39.1	41.4
Heinz.........	58.8	54.0	58.0	70.2	50.0	54.8	52.0	53.0
Pepper........	36.7	28.8	39.2	45.1	51.2	61.7	61.4	51.0
Mean deviation.	12.8	12.0	17.6	15.8	12.6	10.9	10.5	6.8

permit of gradings upon craftiness, or of gradings upon an erroneous set of identifications. Eighteen papers on which the grading and regrading were both carried through were received.

In aggregating the ratings in each case, an arbitrary system of weighting was employed, in accordance with which the picture rated highest was valued at 8 each time it was placed in this position. The second position in the rating was valued at 7, and so on down to the last or ninth position, which was valued at 0. The possible aggregate rating, therefore, ranged from 0 in the event that a certain picture was in each case rated ninth in the series, to a figure amounting to the product of eight times the number of ratings given — a figure possible of attainment only in the event that a given picture was in each case rated first in the series. The aggregate rating actually received by this method, when related to the maximum possible rating as a percentage of the latter, affords a basis of comparing the valuation placed upon the various portraits under the various circumstances indicated.

The changes in percentage ratings on intelligence when the true identities were disclosed, as compared with those made without statement or suggestion concerning identity, are as follows:

	Students	Grange Members
Herriot	+21.5	+42.5
Duncan	−7.8	+19.4
Krassin	−0.6	−45.0
McIntosh	+8.9	+2.1
Glynn	−7.6	+18.0
Agel	−24.9	−14.5
Schwab	+10.7	+2.7
Heinz	−0.8	−20.2
Pepper	+2.5	+6.1

In table 4 these percentage ratings only are presented, both for the students and for the grange members in the case of intelligence, and for the students alone in the case of craftiness. It should be noted particularly that *three groups of individuals* are referred to in the case of student rating, while the grange ratings are made in both cases by the *same* individuals. However, the variable conditions indicated by the column headings "No statement" and "true identity" are as near as possible alike in both cases.

Table 4 and the changes in rating under variable conditions indicated therein seem to indicate that ratings on intelligence and craftiness from photographs are influenced by the assumed or known identity or social type of the individual portrayed, that is, by the stereotype of such a person in the mind of the judge. Disclosure of the true identities of the nine men portrayed led to changes of rating in the same directions among both students and grange members, except in the case of Duncan, labor leader, and Glynn, ex-Governor. It seems clear that among these nine individuals those whose positions or names in the business or professional world carry prestige, particularly McIntosh, Schwab and Pepper, tend to improve their ratings in intelligence and (except in the case of McIntosh) to decrease them in craftiness as their identities become known. The loss of Heinz in intelligence rating is only an apparent exception to this, for the mistaken identifications in this case were very largely for positions in the series which carry prestige. That is, no added impression of high social position was given by a disclosure of his identity. On the other hand, the declines in intelligence rating for the bootlegger and the bolshevik are striking, the former most noticeably among the students and the latter among the grange members.

Comparisons running counter to *a priori* anticipation include that for Krassin, who among the students rates but slightly higher in craftiness when known as a Bolshevik than when falsely represented to be a United States Senator. Nor do the data always appear consistent, as when the students rate Duncan higher in craftiness when alleged to be the Premier, while Herriot rates lower in the same characteristic when actually identified as the real holder of

this position. But other variable factors of explanation may
enter here; moreover it must be remembered that the
numbers of judges are small.

Some of the more general conclusions suggested by the
preceding data may be summarized:

1. The existence of common stereotypes concerning the
appearance of various classes of persons (senators, boot-
leggers, etc.) is clearly indicated. These led to numerous
errors of judgment.

2. The stereotypes found among students and grange
members were similar, but there appeared to be a somewhat
greater uniformity (concentration of judgment on the basis
of a stereotype) among the latter.

3. Estimates of intelligence and craftiness, presumably
based upon the features portrayed, are in reality influenced
by the supposed identity of the portrait, i.e., by the stereotype of the supposed occupational or social status held in the
mind of the examiner.

This experiment has dealt with stereotypes concerning
the supposed appearance and characteristics of representatives
of certain occupational and social types of persons. It will
not be difficult to discover political situations in which such
stereotypes as these, either favorable or unfavorable, have
been spread widely through an electorate,[10] and have played
a prominent part in the popularity or unpopularity, the
success or failure, of a candidate or official. The following
will illustrate the possibilities of developing stereotypes
artificially concerning persons prominent in politics — all the
more since its paradoxical character in the light of more
recent events is amusing. As a very small child during a

[10] The stereotype is of course different in the case of each individual holding it, but the resemblance may be sufficient to warrant referring to it for the
sake of convenience as an entity, in the metaphysical manner here adopted.

presidential campaign, I was shown a Republican cartoon, portraying the Democratic candidate if elected taking the oath of office with his *foot* upon the Bible. With this clear evidence of irreverence before me, I developed a stereotype concerning this candidate which included a variety of ungodly, wicked and irreligious traits. It was many years before this stereotype was wholly removed from mind, perhaps not until my own valuation upon the traits in question as factors in politics had begun to change. The candidate with whom I had endowed these irreligious qualities was William Jennings Bryan!

Stereotypes of individuals are formed in our face-to-face contacts with them, no less than in the case of estimates made indirectly from photographs, cartoons, hearsay, words spoken over the radio, or otherwise. The distorting effect even upon work which is presumed to be scientific may be given a further illuminating illustration. In his study of the criminal, which followed Lombroso in assuming the existence of an anthropological criminal type, Havelock Ellis presented a series of sketches of criminals made from life by Dr. Vans Clarke, a prison governor. They were alleged to be "by no means very exceptional," representing "at least 10 per cent of the criminals examined." [11]

The widely known Goring report reduced these sketches to a composite portrait, which evidenced features of a highly abnormal appearance.[12] Beside this it placed a composite portrait made from an equal number of photographs selected at random from the official stock of photographs of a prison

[11] Ellis, Havelock: *The Criminal*, 5th edition, London, The Walter Scott Publishing Co., undated, Plates IV–IX. The preface to the 4th edition bears the date 1910.

[12] Goring, Charles: *The English Convict: A Statistical Study.* London. Published by His Majesty's Stationery Office (for sale by T. Fisher Unwin) 1913, Frontispiece and p. 1.

population. The features in the second case show no appearance of abnormality. The report comments: "An
examination of these contrasted outlines shows most strikingly the difference between 'criminal types,' as registered by
the mechanical precision of a camera, and as viewed by the
imagination of an enthusiastic, but uncritical, observer."
In other words Dr. Clarke's sketches were biased in a constant direction — the direction of his stereotype of the men
before him.

Similarly one is made skeptical of attempts to derive
scientific generalizations from biographical data concerning
historical personages. One enthusiastic writer has referred
to biography as "the one ripe and ready field for the study
of physiognomy." "A tabulation of the faces and figures of
eminent personages should long ago have suggested itself as
desirable, if not indispensable." [13] But it is probable that
contemporary biographers are fully as subject to stereotypes
concerning their heroes as was Dr. Clarke with reference to
the prisoners under his charge.

When individuals are in face-to-face contact, however,
there is usually an opportunity for the more erroneous
stereotypes possessed by either concerning the other to be
corrected in the process of becoming acquainted. In this respect the baby-kissing candidate (observe your stereotype of
this person, dear reader!) is productive of political attitudes
which are in closer accord with reality than those built up by
the publicity agents of a front-porch campaigner. First impressions may be modified by conversation and other expressions of personality, and socialization proceeds by direct
inter-stimulation and response.

[13] Kassel, Charles: Physiognomy and Genius, *Popular Science Monthly*,
1911, Vol. 78, pp. 158–163. Also Genius and Hair Color, *Popular Science
Monthly*, 1912, Vol. 81, pp. 284–290.

But stereotypes are not confined to "pictures" of *individuals*. They are closely allied to shibboleths and symbols. They may represent a doctrine, a procedure, a party or some other social institution or agency. In such a case it is probable that the business of stereotype-making for political purposes is even more effective, for in this case further acquaintance with any single individual or any number of individuals does not necessarily dislodge it. "Wall Street," "Socialism," "Evolution," etc., evoke stereotypes in the minds of many people inconsistent with the known personalities of brokers, socialists and scientists. Further research in this direction might be profitable, not only to the political scientist but to the practical politician as well.[14]

[14] The question of stereotypes in the voter's mind is also allied to the question of his information regarding political issues. The latter was made the subject of quantitative study a few years ago by Mr. R. C. Atkinson, then of Columbia University. While the results were not published, Mr. Atkinson informs me that his material tended to indicate the following:

1. The extent of political information increased materially with the extent of formal education, college-educated citizens ranking considerably higher than high-school educated citizens and professionally trained persons higher than the average college person.

2. Men ranked higher than women as a rule in each education group.

3. Professional people as a rule ranked higher than other occupation groups.

4. Almost total ignorance prevailed among all the groups as to minor state offices and judicial candidates. Even among the most highly educated groups there was very little knowledge of lesser candidates and offices which were to be filled at the election.

VI

THE DISTRIBUTION OF INDIVIDUAL POLITICAL ATTITUDES [1]

In the preceding chapter, at least one type of element that must be reckoned with in considering the content of political attitude was subjected to a certain experimental analysis. Even as a study of stereotypes alone, this analysis was fragmentary and incomplete. Moreover it took no account of other factors which have a part in determining this content. Without further formal consideration of the latter, however, we will pass on to the question of distribution of attitudes.

[1] The present chapter is less concerned with the technique of measuring attitudes than with certain concepts and utilizations which illustrate quantitative method in a somewhat wider sense. Consequently, little attention has been paid to much other work which has been done in the same field, and in which the technique of measurement shows higher development than is here exhibited. Some of the more important of these studies have appeared since the present chapter was written. I wish particularly to cite the work of Professor L. L. Thurstone of the University of Chicago which is exhibited in his article already noted, *supra*, page 52, footnote 3. Also, by the same author: "The Law of Comparative Judgment," *Psych. Rev.*, July, 1927; "Psychophysical Analysis," *Amer. J. Psych.*, July, 1927; "The Method of Paired Comparisons for Social Values," *The J. of Abn. and Soc. Psych.*, Vol. 21, pp. 384–400, January–March, 1927. Professor Herbert A. Sturges of Washburn College has presented some of his extensive material in an article, "The Theory of Correlation Applied in Studies of Changing Attitudes," *The American Journal of Sociology*, Vol. XXXIII, pp. 269–275. An unpublished study by Dr. Goodwin B. Watson of Teachers College, Columbia University, is entitled "Orient and Occident — A Preliminary Study of Opinions and Attitudes of Groups of Americans regarding Oriental Peoples and Questions." The studies on "social distance" begun at the University of Southern California fall into the same general class. The pioneer work of Allport and Hartman is discussed below in the present Chapter.

Variability is an outstanding characteristic of social data. Whether we are measuring such physical characteristics as height, weight or chest expansion, or whether we are concerned with intellectual capacities or performances, a sufficiently large number of measurements upon homogeneous individuals seems to point invariably to a *continuous* distribution from the lowest measures to the highest, with a massing of cases at some point on the scale which is usually about mid-way between the two extremes.

It is assumed that if the number of individual cases could become infinite, every position on the scale, however small the gradations, would be represented by frequencies. In practice, frequencies are assembled together during classification around *mid-points*, so that a distribution which is theoretically continuous is actually presented in any given series as if it were discontinuous or discrete. The measurements given *approximate* the actual dimensions. This process of classification, it should be noted, is an artificial one in the sense that the number of classes, together with the location of mid-points or class limits, depend entirely upon the will of the classifier, who is presumably guided by the purposes for which the data are to be employed.[2]

The *normal frequency distribution* of the individual cases represented by the familiar "bell-shaped curve," results from the operation of a variety of unrelated or slightly related factors which determine the dimensions of the individual case. The effect is to render the combination of factors operating with respect to any individual a matter of chance. In determining a man's height, for example, an indefinite number of hereditary and environmental influences are at work. In the case of a single individual, most of these may make for tallness. They reinforce each other and an excep-

[2] *Cf.* page 40.

tionally tall individual is produced. In the case of another a large majority of the factors may make for shortness. But it is much more likely that while some factors may make for tallness others are making for shortness. These cancel out each other's influence. Hence it is nature's custom within any variety of individuals to give the larger number a medium height.

It appears to be traditional among writers on such subjects as this to assume that readers are familiar with the arts of flipping coins and throwing dice. I shall here follow in the beaten track in offering an illustration. In flipping two coins at a time let us assume that the head of each stands for a factor making for tallness, while the tails represent shortness. In every four throws there is one chance that both will come heads (tallness), one chance of both coming tails (shortness) and *two* chances of one being heads and the other tails (i.e., of tall and short influences cancelling, leaving medium height). But this will be true only if each coin is equally likely to fall either way. That is, there must be no connection between the way in which the two coins fall, nor must either be more likely to fall one way rather than the other. If the two coins are soldered together at the edge with the same face up, we could get two heads or two tails but never one of each. Or, if the head side of each coin were made of lead and the tail side of aluminum, both coins would come heads together more frequently than they would come tails, or even than they would come one head and one tail. In this case we would call the distribution *modal* but *skewed*. If the coins were soldered it would be *bi-modal*. The three types of distribution referred to would in tabular form be somewhat as follows assuming that two coins were thrown together eight times:

	Number of chances there will be thrown		
	Both coins heads	One head One tail	Both coins tails
Both coins genuine and unrelated, producing the normal frequency distribution....................	2	4	2
Coins soldered together at the edge, producing a bi-modal distribution.	4	0	4
Both coins loaded with lead on the head side and aluminum on the tail side, producing a skewed distribution, which might be as indicated..	4	3	1

It will be apparent that skewness and departure from a single mode will be indications that the fundamental influences determinative of our measurements are not a set of numerous, equi-potent and independent factors.[3] The question in which we are here interested is to discover the nature of the relationships in these respects among the factors productive of attitudes. There seems to be no obvious *a priori* reason to suppose that the political attitudes of individuals do not follow the normal frequency distribution which is characteristic of more easily measurable mental characteristics or products. As was pointed out above (p. 53) the factors which are directly or indirectly, consciously or unconsciously, determinative of attitudes seem to be numerous. Moreover, each of us seems to encounter constantly a wide variety of attitudes or expressed opinions on the part of others. Considering the political group as a whole, and

[3] A multi-modal distribution may indicate that the data are not homogeneous, as when the heights of men and of women are thrown together in a single distribution. This may be regarded as a special case of the situation here described. That is, *male sex* or *female sex* may be regarded as names which indicate in each case a collection of *associated* factors, the one set making for greater height than the other.

the opportunities of each individual to be influenced by those of differing opinion with whom he comes in contact, there appears to be a situation similar to that which produces the normal distribution in the case of heights.

We are in fact accustomed to recognize variability of attitude. We distinguish between opinions on either side of a given issue which are lightly or strongly held, between those which are predominantly emotional and those which are predominantly intellectual in character, between those which are moderate and those which are extreme. However, we neglect to note the intermediate positions along these various scales of opinion, because it is difficult to do so.[4] Moreover, the democratic concept, in which, according to Bryce,[5] the idea of "one man one vote" is central, has tended to direct attention away from qualitative differences between individual opinions.

It is conceivable that with the development of the technique of mental measurements, qualitative differences in individual opinions might be valued in the process of measuring the collective decision on a given political issue. With respect to the collective decision on prohibition, for example, we might assign greater value to the opinion which was based on scientific analysis of the physiological, social or economic effects of the liquor traffic than to the opinion which represented prejudice, self-interest or casual impression. We might even be willing to weight the opinion which represented strong conviction, relative to the opinion which was weakly held and very near the point of indifference. According to any one of the possible lines of classification, an average opinion might theoretically be obtained, in which

---

[4] In particular, it is difficult to procure *equi-distant* "steps," or positions along the scale. Professor Thurstone's ingenious method of meeting this difficulty is portrayed in his articles, noted above on page 71.

[5] Bryce, Viscount James: *Modern Democracies*, pp. 20–23.

each opinion was weighted according to its place along the scale in the entire distribution.[6]

While the fact of variability in political attitudes is recognized and even has certain utilizations in systems of plural voting, little effort has been made to discover the form of distribution. Arguing from analogy, it would be logical to set up the hypothesis that the attitudes upon a given question of individuals in a given group are distributed normally. It would have to be assumed that this question was one which did not affect all members of the group alike in opposition to some other group; further, that the group was sufficiently homogeneous to provide all members thereof with some interest or concern in the outcome. For example, the hypothesis would not cover the distribution of attitudes among German-Americans on the question of declaring war upon Germany; nor would it cover the attitudes of New York voters upon the detailed controversies concerning the Colorado River improvement. It would cover the question of American relations with Germany within the American electorate as a whole (in which case German-Americans might be expected to comprise the more atypical individuals at one end of the distribution) and it would cover the larger aspects of flood control in the Mississippi valley, in which the entire nation, presumably, has a humanistic interest and a material stake.

Such an hypothesis was set up by the present writer a few years ago, but without experimental verification.[7] Its fate

---

[6] An approximation to this idea is contained in the system of plural voting which is based upon property ownership. Where such a system exists, *any* opinion held by the plural voter is accorded greater value than the corresponding opinion of the citizen with a single vote. The hypothetical system here suggested would grade the *opinions*, rather than the person who held them.

[7] "The Political Vote as a Frequency Distribution of Opinion," *Journal of the American Statistical Association*, March, 1924. The present chapter contains some of the material there presented, with the kind permission of the editors.

affords an interesting illustration of the value and the dangers of analogical and deductive reasoning in social science. It was contended that the *vote* provides a crude measurement of attitudes or opinions which are complex and variable. With this device, opinions which would normally be distributed continuously are consolidated into a discrete series, containing but two classes. That is, opinions which would normally fall at all values along the X ordinate are grouped into two classes of *pro* and *con*. Instead of smoothing the histogram into a curve, the reverse process occurs; out of the curve is constructed a histogram of two classes containing all of the frequencies in the series.

The class limits, as in the case of every other series, are fixed arbitrarily; but since there are but two classes, each extends in one direction to the extreme value included in its side of the distribution. Hence there is but one class limit to be arbitrarily defined — the point at which the issue shall be drawn for presentation to the voters. According to the location of this limit on one side or the other of the mode of opinion, the verdict of the electorate will be "for" or "against." Statesmen and politicians are successful according to their ability to estimate this modal opinion and define the issues accordingly. It follows that no genuine issue is likely to remain drawn at a point which is far removed from the central massing of opinion. Extremists, sensing the futility of getting their views adopted, or even voted upon, decry political methods and call for "direct action" to secure their ends.

This hypothesis was illustrated and to a certain extent tested by its application to some leading political issues before the American people, among these the tariff. It is possible to distinguish five positions in order along a scale which would represent differing views upon this question.

These views would be (1) absolute free trade; (2) tariff for revenue only; (3) low protection; (4) high protection; (5) complete isolation, or embargo on imports. These views may be represented graphically and in wholly hypothetical form in Figure I. That each position is relative and shades

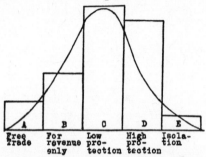

FIG. 1 — HYPOTHETICAL FREQUENCY DISTRIBUTION OF OPINIONS RESPECTING THE TARIFF

imperceptibly into the position adjoining, will be apparent if we consider the differences between high protectionists and low protectionists.

Let us assume a legislative body, each member of which is in favor of a tariff, but uninfluenced in his vote by party considerations or factors other than his own attitudes. Assume further that this legislature is confronted with the task of fixing the duty upon a specified commodity. Suppose that proposals for an ad-valorem duty are brought before this body, each proposal in turn representing an increase of five per cent in the tariff contemplated. We should expect with each proposal to find a number of legislators who would desert the high tariff side of the division and go over to the low tariff side. Thus the number of high protectionists and low protectionists, so far as the tariff is judged upon its merits alone, depends entirely on the point at which the issue is drawn for decision.

In the American Congress the tariff issue has usually been drawn within the ranges of attitude which we have characterized as "low protection" and "high protection." The Republican and Democratic parties, as represented in Congress, have stood for "higher" and "lower" tariffs, respectively. It is obvious that American attitudes, as distributed between free trade on one extreme and national economic isolation on the other, tend to mass within a range calling for some kind of tariff protection for American industries. Too great a departure from this central mass of opinion in either direction by the party in power will throw the mode of the distribution into the class represented by the opposition party, and create a party turnover at the next election.[8]

In Figure 2 the frequency distribution of attitudes or opinions respecting the tariff which was postulated graphically in Figure 1 has been broken up into a series of bi-segmented histograms to represent the probable result of a vote, if the issue were drawn in turn between each two consecutive positions of the five that were distinguished. Thus if the vote were upon the question of free trade (histogram 2) it would be expected that the persons whose attitudes were represented by A (in Figure 1) would vote in the affirmative, and those represented by B, C, D, and E in the negative. If the vote were upon the question of low protection vs. high protection (Histogram 4) we should expect A, B, and C to unite in the affirmative against D and E.

[8] In actuality, the departure of governmental policy from modal opinion must be sufficiently great to overcome the tenacity with which voters cling to the party habitually supported. Party regularity, in other words, is a factor which tends to check or slow down the tendency here described. The latter is presented in its hypothetically pure form, abstracted from the political reality.

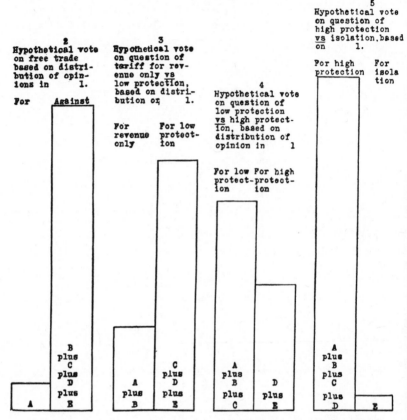

FIG. 2. — HYPOTHETICAL DISTRIBUTION OF VOTES UPON THE TARIFF WHEN
THE ISSUE IS DRAWN IN CERTAIN FORMS INDICATED IN FIGURE I.

The continuous distribution of attitude on another question was indicated by a poll on prohibition taken by *The Literary Digest*.[9] The histogram in this case contained three classes rather than the conventional two presented by an "aye" and "nay" vote. The voter could be recorded either

[9] *Literary Digest*, July 8, 1922. Final returns, Sept. 9, 1922.

(1) for continuance and strict enforcement of the Eighteenth Amendment and the Volstead Act; (2) for modification of the Volstead Act to permit light wines and beers; (3) for repeal of the Prohibition Amendment. The fact that no one of these classes was represented by a majority of the votes led to claims by the propagandists on both sides that the results represented a victory for their own extreme point of view. "Drys" called attention to the majority against a return to "wet" days. "Wets" called attention to the majority against the existing stringent enforcement laws. Each drew the issue at a different point along the scale.

As still a third distribution of attitude there were cited the various positions taken upon the question of public ownership. At one extreme the anarchist holds for complete individualism, at the other the extreme socialist would place all industry under state control. In the middle ranges are to be found those who would nationalize the railways; those who would add coal mines to railways; those who would add to these the packing plants and the flour mills. Individual and class interests help to determine the particular industries or services which the individual would be willing to have publicly owned. Hence as to any particular industry, attitude might be multi-modal or skewed. Still it was thought probable that the thoroughgoingness of public-ownership opinion in the abstract would remain normal in distribution.

The general hypothesis just described, together with some further corollaries which will be cited later, was advanced by the writer at about the same time that substantially the same notions were independently suggested by Professor Floyd H. Allport in collaboration with Mr. Dale Hartman. There was, however, this difference: Allport and Hartman proceeded to test their ideas by actual inductive experiment, whereas in my own case the hypothesis in its general form was not tested, and was supported only by logical analysis of deductive character. As will presently appear, the experimental procedure tended to substantiate the belief that attitudes can be thought of as distributed along a scale; but it tended also to discredit the hypothesis that they are distributed normally.[10]

The technical procedure that they adopted is worthy of careful attention by the students who are now experimenting along similar lines. Upon various phases of seven concrete issues of current political interest, sixty upperclassmen at Syracuse University were asked to write their personal views. "The resulting opinions on each issue were then carefully sifted and the distinct and relevant views were assembled. Keeping the issues separate, these views were printed on slips of paper and arranged independently by six judges, teachers of political science and psychologists, in order of their logical position in a scale ranging from one extreme on the issue in question to the opposite extreme. The average rank assigned to each statement was taken as its final rank in the completed scale." Students (freshmen in the college of liberal arts) were instructed to check the one statement regarding each of the seven issues which most nearly coincided with his or her view. "With each issue

---

[10] I am greatly indebted to Messrs. Allport and Hartman for permission to use freely their studies dealing with this topic. I use here an article on "The Measurement and Motivation of Atypical Opinion in a Certain Group," by Floyd H. Allport and D. A. Hartman, *The American Political Science Review*, Vol. XIX, November, 1925, pp. 735–760. Unless otherwise noted, quotations are from this article. The authors' interest in this study was directed primarily to atypical opinion or attitude, while mine at this point is directed to the distribution of attitude. Hence I am assuming the responsibility for employing some of their results for a somewhat different purpose than that for which they were published.

there was provided a place for the student to check the *certainty* of his opinion on a graphic scale of five steps ranging from 'extremely uncertain' to 'extremely certain.' A similar scale was provided for checking the degree of *intensity of interest* or *feeling* upon the question concerned." [11]

An average of 367 opinions upon each issue were obtained in this manner. Their distribution is shown in Figures 3 to 9

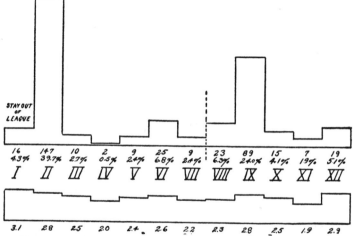

FIGURE 3 — Distribution of Opinions upon League of Nations

inclusive, which are reproduced here from the Allport-Hartman study. It will be seen from these charts that all of the three forms of distribution mentioned above on page 73, i.e., approximately normal, multi-modal, and highly skewed, are present. Thus attitudes toward the League of Nations (Figure 3) were decidedly bi-modal, a division occurring

[11] The technique represented by these scales was supplemented by individual detailed studies, psychological and otherwise, of "the motives and traits of their personalities which give rise to the opinions they hold" in the case of individuals whose opinions were atypical.

"possibly upon party lines." Twelve positions on the attitude scale were distinguished upon this issue, ranging from the extreme policy of isolation at position I to the opposite extreme, calling for a world-state, at position XII. Position II, calling for non-adherence to the League but for friendly coöperation with other nations, represented the opinions of 147 students or 39.7 per cent of the number; but position IX, calling for adherence with subsequent adjustment of

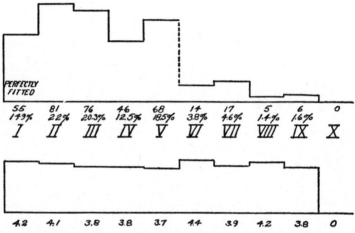

FIGURE 4 — DISTRIBUTION OF OPINIONS UPON QUALIFICATIONS
OF COOLIDGE

defects, expressed the opinions of 89 students and represented a second modal point upon the scale.

Two or possibly three modal points are similarly found among proposals, eleven in number, respecting Congressional control over Supreme Court decisions upon matters of constitutionality. (Figure 5.) With respect to the qualifications of Coolidge for President (Figure 4) the distribution of attitudes appears to have a single well-defined mode, but the preponderance of opinions was favorable and the distribution was skewed. In the case of the Ku Klux Klan (Figure 9) at least three modes seemed to appear. On the distribution of wealth and the question of graft in politics (Figures 7 and 8) a tendency toward normal distribution of attitude was apparent, although both were skewed. The prohibition question (Figure 6) develops what is perhaps the most curious distribution of attitudes of all, for while the sentiment for prohibition is overwhelming, the small pro-licence minority

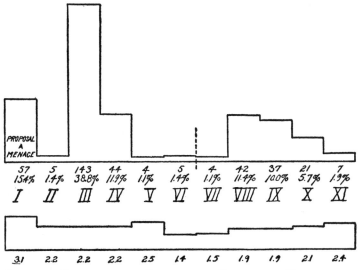

FIGURE 5 — DISTRIBUTION OF OPINIONS UPON LEGISLATIVE CONTROL OVER SUPREME COURT

arrange themselves in "a little distribution curve of their own" which at most points is "practically normal."

On the whole, then, the hypothesis that political attitudes tend to be distributed normally has fared rather badly in the light of experimental verification. It must be recalled that the subjects were freshman students in a university — a group much more homogeneous in most respects than a random sample of the electorate. Since heterogeneity and variability mean substantially the same thing, the electorate would undoubtedly be even more diverse in its distributions of attitude than were these students.

In another particular, however, my hypothesis survived the Allport-Hartman experiment. As a corollary I made this suggestion: "If political opinions are distributed in the normal manner, it is probable that radical changes in public

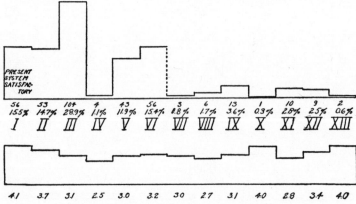

FIGURE 6 — DISTRIBUTION OF OPINIONS UPON PROHIBITION QUESTION

opinion occur less frequently than is usually supposed. The relative strength of parties at election time may be changed in either of two ways. In the first, the points at which the issues are drawn may remain constant. Hence, a comparatively slight shift of the modal opinion may bring about a transfer of power from one party to another that appears superficially as a 'sweeping verdict at the polls.' Nevertheless, the shift is most likely to have taken place within the central quartiles of the distribution where opinion most nearly approaches indifference. Subsequent events usually prove in such a case that the changes of opinion were not profound or thoroughgoing. Opinions lightly held are easily changed. Thus the fickleness of public opinion that is so frequently observed may be a phenomenon representing the comparative indifference of the central portions of the distribution of opinion.

"In the second case, opinions may remain distributed in the same way, but the points at which the issues are drawn may be shifted. When this occurs, it is usually the result of manœuvering for advantage on the part of politicians and party leaders. Old issues are presented in a new light, so that in effect the opinions of the electorate are reclassified and new class limits are established. Any shift of party strength between two elections in which the same issues are presented probably involves both of these occurrences."

By a somewhat different line of reasoning, Allport and Hartman arrived at a similar hypothesis: "It is suggested that the atypical extremists are actuated in their thinking by partially repressed emotional drives, and that they develop a method for concealing from themselves and others the fact that their opinion is

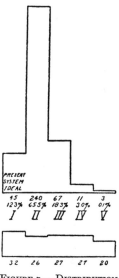

FIGURE 7 — DISTRIBUTION OF OPINIONS ON DISTRIBUTION OF WEALTH

determined rather by wishes than by the process of reason.[12] Dogmatic certainty and moral conviction are the means adopted to offset, of course unconsciously, the challenge that so extreme a view as theirs should be carefully analyzed. To put it another way, if one wishes to hold a certain belief

[12] I took a comparable view in a paper on "Motives in Radicalism and Social Reform," *The American Journal of Sociology*, March 1923.

which happens to be of an extreme sort, one must have a strong conviction. Otherwise, one can not feel justified in holding the view in the face of the great majority who think differently.   On *a priori* grounds we should expect, therefore, that those who stand at the atypical extremes would express the greatest degree of certainty in their opinions."

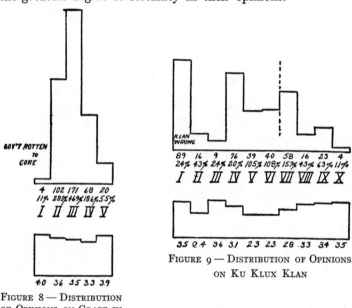

FIGURE 9 — DISTRIBUTION OF OPINIONS ON KU KLUX KLAN

FIGURE 8 — DISTRIBUTION OF OPINIONS ON GRAFT IN POLITICS

Let us again look at the actual evidence which the authors found.   Below each curve of distribution in Figures 3 to 9, they have plotted in a flat-shaped graph, beneath each step in the scale, the average certainty which was felt by the persons who chose the view represented by the step in question. "The possible range of certainty scores is from 1 to 5; and the units of vertical distance express the position of the average point of certainty upon this scale."   Thus, with regard to the League of Nations (Figure 3) the two extremes, positions I and XII, "show the highest certainty of opinion, the averages being 3.1 and 2.9 respectively. At the reactionary end we also find three successive certainty steps upward in direction opposite to the decreasing extremeness of views I, II, and III."

Without going into the details of each distribution, it may be said that the authors found evidence in the case of each of the seven issues that persons taking the more atypical positions on the attitude scale held their opinions with a higher degree of certainty than those whose opinions fell near the modal points. Moreover, the ratings for intensity of feeling were correlated closely (coefficient above 0.90) with the ratings for certainty. "Intensity and certainty go together."

To the extent, then, that attitudes were shown to be normally distributed, support was given to my contention that the fickleness of public opinion might be "a phenomenon representing the comparative indifference of the central portions of the distribution of opinion." The manner in which a subsequent study of my own has run counter to this aspect of the hypothesis is shown in Chapter XIX.

On the whole, I am still inclined to believe that there is "something in" the hypothesis that individual attitudes are distributed normally, *apart from some distorting situation.* Scientists customarily reason in this manner. Thus the law of gravitation states what *would* happen under certain ideal conditions which are never exactly attained in actuality. But there is little more than futility in employing an hypothesis based upon ideal conditions unless the latter are sometimes approximated in actuality. Such procedure in economic theory was largely responsible for giving it the "dismal" reputation that it once possessed.

If normality of distribution should be established as an

ideal situation frequently approximated there would be practical and theoretical implications. To cite one of the former, it could be shown that movements for political reform are more likely to succeed when proceeding step by step, than when presenting their complete program. The mode may be shifted, but slowly. If the political change which is made as a result of the first distribution of attitude proves satisfactory to the voters, the modal shift is likely to continue in the same direction, and successive steps may prove possible.

For example, a distribution of attitude three decades ago with regard to the political rights of women would probably have disclosed the following points along the scale: (1) Women should have no voice in public matters; (2) women should have a voice in voluntaristic organizations, as in church societies, but in no other; (3) women should have the suffrage with respect to school elections; (4) school and municipal suffrage should be given; (5) all suffrage except for national elections should be allowed; (6) complete national suffrage as well as local; (7) women should unite in politics, attempting to secure sex dominance in public matters. With many minor variations, the issue of woman's rights has been drawn in turn between each consecutive pair of these various positions on the scale. The mode of individual attitudes has been shifted constantly in the same direction until it is now to be found, quite clearly, within the group of attitudes which sanction all forms of *voting* equality between men and women. It has not yet shifted to the point at which *office-holding* for women is regarded with equal favor, nor to the point at which woman's dominance in politics can be regarded as a practical possibility.

Further research upon the distribution of individual attitudes might disclose under what circumstances it may be "normal." If the distribution is not normal, it is because the factors determining individual attitudes are not numerous, equi-potent and independent. Here, even if the results were wholly negative from the standpoint of establishing normality of distribution as a typical or approximated ideal situation, it might still be possible to discover the circumstances which produce non-normal distributions. It is not impossible that this would be of even greater value, for it might disclose information concerning *the modes of association and interaction among the factors which are creative of our individual attitudes and states of mind.*[13]

[13] Professor Allport has written me as follows concerning the discussion in this chapter: "I think an analysis for the reasons why distributions will often be skewed or bimodal would be illuminating. I suppose it is due to the fact that political opinions are usually created by special movements or agencies of propaganda and an opinion scarcely becomes public in this sense until it is biased or has a bi-partisan split. It would be interesting to test your hypothesis upon a question the rudiments of which lie in attitudes of the masses, but which has not yet been made an issue. A situation of this sort might have been the question of prohibition about thirty or forty years ago. I am inclined to think that the distribution upon such subjects would much more nearly resemble the normal. Possibly also this would suit your idea of the gradual steps required in political reform. I seem, however, to detect a trace of the old group mind theory in the hypothesis of a normally distributed public opinion. We must remember, of course, that we are measuring not the mind of a public but the alignments of attitudes upon specific questions which may concentrate in almost any manner according to group stimulus and pressures. I believe we are dealing with two different things in public opinion, before and after an issue has been raised, though to be sure the former has something to do with the latter. 'Apart from the distorting situation,' however, it is doubtful whether the opinion one is measuring would really exist. When such propaganda enters one would expect skewing and bimodalism to be the inevitable result."

VII

OBJECTIVE INDEXES OF SUBJECTIVE VARIABLES: WITH AN ILLUSTRATION

In Chapters V and VI, mental states have been discussed in a manner very much as if they were objective realities which could be defined and measured. Now attitudes and motives in themselves offer a valid subject of scientific inquiry, but they are not susceptible of measurement. It is only when they find expression in behavior that they yield to quantitative analysis. One of the main tasks of a quantitative science of politics, therefore, is a search for behavioristic materials representative of the intangible subjective elements of political activity. Thus in the experiments by Allport and Hartman described in the preceding chapter, each student was asked to select and check a previously prepared statement which most nearly approximated his own opinion. The investigators could not determine how competently their subjects could appraise their own opinions. Nor were they able to guard against deliberate error in the appraisals. More than one would-be wag may have falsified his statement with some humorous intent.[1] The investigators were dependent upon the behavior of their subjects for inferences concerning its source. They were forced to *assume* that the former bore some close and direct relationship to the latter.

There are numerous forms of political behavior which

---

[1] This is alleged to have been common among recruits who took the army alpha psychological tests by several of the number to whom I have talked. In class-room experiments I have found it a possible source of error against which it was necessary to guard.

might be measured, at least in theory. There is one, however, that seems most easily obtainable, that is characteristically associated with American politics, and that is clearly related to the underlying attitudes. This is the *vote*. Votes are by no means certain or universal indicators of political attitudes or political activity. There is overlapping both ways. Many political activities neither consist in nor lead to voting. On the other hand, there are many votes which have no connection with agencies of organized government. There are beauty contests, for example, elections to scientific societies, and the choice between oranges and grape fruit in a coöperative boarding house. Professor Catlin [2] would possibly regard all of the latter as political questions. Without agreeing or disagreeing with his theoretical position, I wish to accept it as a methodological convenience at this point. Since I find it difficult to distinguish between political and other questions, it is likewise difficult to distinguish between political and other votes. And there is no need for the distinction. The voting process has the same general form and the same general value as an indicator of attitude wherever it is employed.[3]

Votes are useful indexes of political attitudes, then, because they are the most tangible and measurable units of political behavior. They are tangible because simple and precise. They are measurable, for although each is really a *gross* measure of attitude, the value of which may differ widely in different individuals (see page 75), they are nevertheless assumed to have equal value and are counted and recorded officially. They provide the closest analogy within the field of politics to the monetary unit in the quantitative

[2] *Op. cit.*, *The Science and Method of Politics.*

[3] The differences among various voting systems, wide as they are from certain standpoints, do not negate this statement in the light of the interpretation given in this book.

analyses of economic statisticians.   Just as one of the major
tasks of the latter is to convert the raw indexes in terms of
dollars into refined indexes of economic conditions, in the
same way the political statistician must manipulate and combine his raw indexes, the votes, into expressions which are
indicative of the political situation in which he is really interested.

Like a newly invented tool in the physical sciences or the
mechanical arts, an index may permit of observations or may
facilitate the determination of relationships which have
hitherto been obscured.   Perhaps the most significant
suggestions to be found in this book are devices consisting
of indexes of this kind.   However, the purpose of this short
chapter is to emphasize the necessity, if one is to engage in
quantitative political research, of being constantly on the
alert to devise indexes *suited to the purpose at hand*.   General
or advance instructions as to procedure can no more replace
ingenuity in this respect than can the legendary manual
upon ways of killing a cat.   I shall therefore give no rules
for devising indexes, but shall instead cite here an illustration
of the manner in which one required index was fashioned.
This may serve not as a pattern for identical use in other inquiries, but as suggestive of ingenius possibilities.

In making my study *Farmers and Workers in American
Politics*,[4] I desired to secure an index by means of which the
varying degrees of "progressivism" to be found in various
parts of the state of Nebraska might be determined.   No vote
for a single candidate or upon a single issue in a state election seemed available for the purpose, especially since the
aggregate vote for a recognized old-party candidate at a

---

[4] *Columbia University Studies in History, Economics and Public Law,*
Whole Number 253, New York, 1924.   The material which follows is taken
from pp. 174–177, with the permission of the editors of the Studies.

general election always contains the unknown effect of "straight party voting." A peculiar situation in the election of 1922 provided the basis for devising the index desired.

In the primary election of 1922, R. B. Hôwell, a "Progressive Republican" won the Republican nomination for United States senator in the State of Nebraska. C. W. Bryan, a "Progressive Democrat" won the Democratic Party nomination for governor. As a result, a "progressive" and "composite slate," headed by Howell and Bryan, and containing candidates nominated by the Progressive Party as well as by the old parties, was "officially endorsed by the Nonpartisan League, the local labor organizations and the Committee of 48." [5] Both Howell and Bryan were elected, the former receiving 59.8 per cent of the combined vote of the Republican and Democratic candidates for senator, the latter 56.6 per cent of the combined Republican and Democratic vote for governor.[6]

A measure of the extent to which voters of any group *split their votes* on behalf of the "progressive slate" will serve as an index by which the progressivism of the group may be gauged. It is obvious that if every Republican and Democrat had voted a "straight party ticket" the percentage of the total Republican and Democratic vote received by Howell would have varied inversely as the percentage of the vote received by Bryan, and *vice versa*. Each percentage would be the reciprocal of the other, for added together they would equal 100 per cent, i.e., all of the Republican and Democratic votes. Where Howell, Republican, was strongest, Bryan, Democrat, would be weakest, and so on. Hence the

---

[5] According to campaign literature of the last-named organization. A leading Democratic Party politician in Nebraska has recently described the alignment to me as having been almost wholly spontaneous in character.

[6] All election figures in this chapter are taken from the *Nebraska Blue Book*, 1922.

correlation between the percentage of Bryan votes and the percentage of Howell votes in the various counties would in such a case be negative and perfect; i.e., r would $= -1.0$.

On the other hand, if every Republican supporter of Howell voted likewise for Bryan, and if every Democratic supporter of Bryan voted likewise for Howell, the correlation between the percentages of the vote received by each would be positive and perfect; i.e., r would $= 1.0$. In this case Bryan and Howell would each receive 100 per cent of the combined Republican and Democratic votes.

A simple measure of progressivism is thus obtained by averaging the percentage of the senatorial vote received by Howell with the percentage of the gubernatorial vote received by Bryan. If the average is 100 per cent, then it is clear that *all* Republicans and Democrats *split their votes in support of both progressive candidates.* If the average is 50 per cent it is clear that all Republicans and Democrats cast *straight party ballots.*[7] If the average is 0 per cent it is clear that all Republicans and Democrats split their votes *by the rejection of both progressive candidates.* Thus an average above 50 per cent indicates a tendency for voters to split ballots in behalf of the progressive candidates; the higher the average the greater the tendency. Conversely, an average of less than 50 per cent indicates a tendency for voters to split ballots in behalf of the conservative candidates on both tickets.

While in fact both Howell and Bryan were elected, it is nevertheless probable that each received a comparatively poor vote in the counties in which the other received a comparatively good vote. This is suggested when the percentages of the vote received by each in the various counties are

[7] Conservatives and progressives may both have split their votes, but in equal numbers so that they balance.

correlated.   The coefficient of correlation is found to be

$$r = -.228 \pm .038$$

Of 93 counties in Nebraska, Howell carried all but 6, while Bryan carried all but 10. There were no duplications among the 16 counties. Two counties only showed an average percentage of votes for Bryan and Howell of less than 50 per cent. Thus the state as a whole was quite uniformly progressive in its vote, although some sectional variations were discovered. The nature of these variations is of interest in another connection, and they will be described in detail below, on pages 133-134.

VIII

The Social Density of Attitude and its Distribution

The distribution of individual political attitudes has been examined in Chapter VI. It was pointed out that if the forms of that distribution can be ascertained, various theoretical and practical uses can be made of the knowledge. There is another respect in which political attitudes can be regarded as variable, and as conforming to modes of distribution. This is closely related to the particular manner in which political activities are organized. The party manager, for example, cares little about the variations of attitude among his individual supporters at election time. What he wants to know is whether his candidate can carry such and such a ward, or city or state, and by what plurality. If his party can secure no more than forty per cent of the votes in County A, can it offset the deficit by securing at least sixty per cent in County B? That is, he is concerned with variations in the tendency of certain attitudes to be generally prevalent in units of the electorate.

For convenience this may be called the social density of attitude. By social density, then, is meant the comparative prevalence of a given type of individual attitude, or the extent to which it is held, within a given portion of the population — in this case, of the electorate. When votes are used as indexes of this distribution, the *individual* attitudes involved are, of course, consolidated into two crude and seemingly discrete classes of "generally favorable" and "generally opposed" with respect to any particular issue. (See page 77.) It should be noted that the units which are to be classified are no longer the attitudes of single persons upon a given issue. They are rather stipulated parts of the electorate, geographical or otherwise, within which varying degrees of social density of attitude are to be found. The nature of this stipulated unit will necessarily depend both upon the interest of the investigator and upon the availability of data.

In theory it would be possible to study the social density of attitude concerning a given issue as distributed among age groups, religious sects, occupational groups, or any other recognized segments into which the electorate might be divided. In practice, American methods of casting and recording votes at elections render it impossible to distinguish, say, between the votes of a Presbyterian and a Methodist, or between the votes of a man of sixty and one of twenty-five. Under an occupational system of representation it might be possible to note the variations of attitude as between, for example, carpenters and farm laborers. But the American basis of representation is geographic and we are accustomed to think of geographical distinctions. "The Fourth Ward goes Democratic," "Upstate is overwhelmingly Republican," "Harding invades the Solid South," are all expressive of interest in geographical variations in social density of attitude.

Several of the studies described in following chapters employ as an index of progressive attitude the vote cast for Robert M. La Follette for president of the United States in the election of 1924. The same data may be used illustratively here. The states in which this candidate was acknowledged to have a chance of success included Wisconsin, Minnesota, Iowa, North Dakota, South Dakota, Nebraska,

Montana and Idaho. To find the variations in density of progressive attitude in the area within these eight states it was necessary to select some small geographical unit into which the entire region could be divided. Moreover, it was necessary that data should be available by means of which these units could be placed upon a comparable footing. Townships would not serve these purposes for many reasons, but especially because of the fact that they do not divide up the entire area. City wards and rural townships or precincts might be employed in some states together as units which between them exhaust the area. But the number would be large, and to comply with the second requirement of comparability the amount of calculation involved would be exorbitant. The *county*, however, is a universal political subdivision thruout the region, its numbers are neither too great nor too small, and election returns on a county basis were in all instances procurable. It was therefore selected as the unit of inquiry.[1]

Slightly more than 566 counties are to be found in the eight states named. In a very few, election returns were unavailable. In the case of 566, however, the La Follette vote was calculated as a percentage of the aggregate vote for Coolidge, Davis and La Follette, the three major candidates. The votes for the remaining candidates were disregarded as negligible. This percentage within each county provides a very close approximation, therefore, to the index desired

---

[1] A variety of sources was used. When available the official returns as recorded in the official "Legislative Manual" or "Blue Book" (appearing under various names) of a given state were accepted as authentic. However, past experience has disclosed numerous errors even in these official documents. The state election returns appearing in the 1925 *World Almanac* were carefully corrected in the 1926 issue (correspondence with the editor), and were again checked by the present writer with the figures appearing in the *Chicago Daily News Almanac*. In some cases this led to correspondence with the appropriate state officials concerning doubtful figures.

within each county.[2] Whether, as I have called it, this is an
index of *progressive* attitude does not greatly concern me.
Some people regarded La Follette as a reactionary. Progressivism is anything we wish to call it. A La Follette vote is
really an index of the attitudes which lead an individual to
vote for La Follette — and nothing more. But it may be
assumed that similar votes are the result of similar attitudes,
and that high densities of La Follette votes in two communities are indicative of corresponding attitudes, similarly dense,
within them.

The distribution of percentages for 566 counties is shown
in tabular form in Table 5 and Graphically in Figure 10.[3]
In the latter the solid irregular line connects the points
actually plotted from the table. The broken bell-shaped
curve which roughly synchronizes with this represents the
distribution that would be mathematically normal for the
same data.[4] The two smaller curves represent the actual
distribution of counties in the separate states of Minnesota
and Iowa. No normal curve was superimposed in the case of
the latter. It will be seen that the curve which includes all

[2] I am in effect using *rates* or *ratios*, a practice which has become familiar
in the case of mortality and morbidity statistics. That is, *attitude density*
is a concept similar to that of the *prevalence* or *incidence* of a disease in vital
statistics. The legitimacy of employing rates in statistical distributions is
discussed by G. Udney Yule, "On the Interpretation of Correlations between
Indices or Ratios," *Journal of the Royal Statistical Society*, June, 1910, pp.
644–647.

[3] Both of these, with some of the related exposition have been taken from
my paper before the American Political Science Association in December,
1925, which appeared in the American Political Science Review for May,
1926, under the title "Some Applications of Statistical Method to Political
Research."

[4] Curve fitting is a familiar statistical procedure, which need not be discussed here. A method of superimposing the ideal normal frequency curve
upon actual data is given in Chaddock's *Principles and Methods of Statistics*,
pages 222 ff. which is to be supplemented by the standard table of ordinates
of the curve given in his Appendix C. The other measures mentioned in the
next few paragraphs are likewise fully treated in all textbooks on statistics.

of the counties approaches in form the normal frequency distribution, and that the same is probably true of the separate curves for two states as well.

TABLE 5 — DISTRIBUTION OF COUNTIES IN EIGHT "LA FOLLETTE" STATES, ACCORDING TO THE PERCENTAGE OF THE VOTE GIVEN LA FOLLETTE AMONG THE THREE MAJOR PRESIDENTIAL CANDIDATES IN THE ELECTION OF 1924.

Percentage for La Follette	No. of Counties
0.0— 4.9	1
5.0— 9.9	5
10.0—14.9	11
15.0—19.9	45
20.0—24.9	47
25.0—29.9	63
30.0—34.9	79
35.0—39.9	75
40.0—44.9	67
45.0—49.9	53
50.0—54.9	43
55.0—59.9	38
60.0—64.9	24
65.0—69.9	12
70.0—74.9	3
	566

Since this is the case, it is legitimate to employ the same recognized statistical technique in answering further questions concerning the distribution in Table 5 that might be employed in the case of a table showing the heights of college students. Thus it may be asked, What was the *most representative* expression of La Follettism among these counties? The percentage of the La Follette vote over the area as a whole does not answer this question because of the wide differences in population. Resort may be had to a procedure which is often illegitimate, namely, the averaging of the individual percentages. For the 566 counties of the eight states under examination the three averages in most common use are found to be as follows: arithmetic mean, 37.9 per cent; median, 37.1 per cent; mode 35.5 per cent. The relatively close correspondence between these three average values again confirms the approximate normality of the distribution. Any one of the three gives a closer representation of the usual or typical county situation than does a single percentage which uses the state or the region as a base. Having calculated average values, one of these may be used from which to measure variability. The concept of

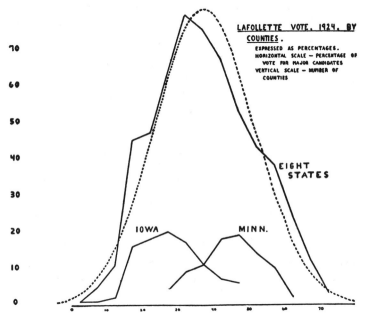

FIGURE 10 — LA FOLLETTE VOTE, 1924, BY COUNTIES IN EIGHT WESTERN STATES AND IN IOWA AND MINNESOTA.

variability itself may be illustrated. Assume that the men of Zeta College possess a mean height of 68 inches and that we wish to compare their heights with those of the members of a circus troupe. The latter will include a number of midgets and several side-show giants. The average height of the circus may turn out to be the same as that of the Zeta students, namely 68 inches. Yet it is obvious that the two groups differ widely in the extent to which the individuals in each approach the average height. That is, they differ in variability. Similarly, it is possible that of two states giving approximately the same support to La Follette so far as aggregate returns are concerned, one may have the density of "progressive" attitude quite evenly spread over the entire state, while in the other it may be strongly developed in some counties and substantially absent from others.

To take an actual case, the variation in the percentage of La Follette votes in the state of Montana is from 15.0 in Meagher County to 67.3 in Mineral. The range is thus 52.3 per cent, or more than half of the possible variation. In Minnesota, although there are half again as many counties as in Montana, the range of variation is but two-thirds as great. It extends from 25.7 in Rice County to 64.6 in Pennington. The range is 38.9 per cent. It might be suspected that certain factors connected with the social or economic homogeneity of the two states, with the comparative extent of their areas, or with their facilities for communication, had something to do with the greater homogeneity in radical opinion that is indicated in Minnesota.

The range, however, is an inadequate measure of variability. For accuracy of comparison, we must utilize measures which take account of the values of *all* of the individual measurements. This necessitates the calculation for each state of either the average deviation or the standard deviation, and the reduction of either of these to a coefficient of variation. The latter permits of the direct comparison as to variability of series having different kinds of units or, as in the present case, similar units but averages of differing value.

TABLE 6 — PERCENTAGE OF THE VOTE RECEIVED BY LA FOLLETTE IN CERTAIN STATES AND AREAS, BASED UPON THE COMBINED VOTE FOR THE THREE MAJOR PRESIDENTIAL CANDIDATES IN THE ELECTION OF 1924

A few counties, for various reasons, are missing.

State or Area	Number of Counties	Mean of County Percentages	Standard Deviation	Coefficient of Variation
I	II	III	IV	V
Wisconsin................	71	54.3	10.35	19.1
Minnesota................	87	45.0	8.60	19.1
Iowa....................	98	28.5	9.53	33.4
North Dakota............	53	49.4	11.59	23.5
South Dakota............	68	34.9	12.47	35.7
Nebraska................	93	25.5	10.16	39.9
Montana................	55	35.6	11.38	32.0
Idaho...................	44	35.3	7.93	22.5
The above 8 states combined	566	37.9	13.98	36.9
Maine..................	16	5.07	2.067	40.8
North Carolina..........	100	1.145	1.347	117.6
Michigan................	83	11.4	6.576	57.7

Using the same data as before concerning the La Follette vote, coefficients of variation have been calculated for a number of individual states, including Michigan, Maine, and North Carolina, and the eight states previously mentioned in which his prospects were regarded as favorable, together with the combined area of the latter. These are included in Table 6. It should be remembered that a low coefficient of variation is indicative of a high degree of homogeneity with respect to the La Follette vote.[5]

The table is suggestive. In Wisconsin and Minnesota, where La Follette sentiment was strongly developed, the coefficient of variation was in each case 19.1 per cent. In

[5] This is not equivalent to political homogeneity in general, which is not of present concern.

Michigan, where the candidate was somewhat less successful than in the country at large, it was 57.7 per cent. In North Carolina, where La Follette support was practically confined to isolated railroad centers, it was 117.6 per cent. In Idaho, a state in which geographical and cultural homogeneity are strikingly low, the coefficient was 22.5 per cent; while in Iowa, which is exceptionally homogeneous in the same respects, it was 33.4. In both of the latter states La Follette received moderately strong support, although this support was stronger in Idaho.

These figures indicate that La Follette strength was positively related to low relative variability among these percentages. It is not clear whether this relationship is due to anything more than the fact that the coefficient of variation is itself a function both of the standard deviation and the mean.[6] If there is a relationship in addition to that involved in this dependence, it would suggest that economic and social homogeneity may not be so essential for the diffusion of political attitudes as is the strong development of the latter at the points from which they spread. It is possible that an equation could be calculated from data of this sort which would express what might be called the *velocity* of diffusion, as a function of the comparative degree to which the attitude had already been accepted. The relationship, assuming its existence, might be expected to prove non-linear, the velocity accelerating up to a certain point, after which deceleration would set in.[7] The meaning and use of the coefficient of

[6] The coefficient of variation equals 100 times the standard deviation divided by the mean. The relationship in the case of the 11 states included in Table II, ascertained by the method of correlation by grades, is expressed by the coefficient of correlation, $r = .94$.

[7] "Diffusion" as here used implies something more than the mere spread of acquaintance with an attitude, or the ideas upon which it is ostensibly based. That which is being spread is an acceptance of the attitude by individuals. It is regarded as a process which may still be going on after some

variation in such a connection are not sufficiently understood to give more than suggestive value to such a hypothesis here. I confine myself at this point merely to suggesting one direction in which statistical methods of determining variability may yet throw light upon an important social and political phenomenon.

The preceding calculations have been justified by the obvious approach of the data in form to the normal frequency distribution or, as it is perhaps more legitimately called, to the probability curve. But it must not be supposed that the distribution of attitude densities has always this form. When the percentage vote for La Follette by counties is distributed state by state separately, a majority of the states which have been mentioned in this chapter do seem to show frequencies having more or less closeness of approximation to the normal form. But *certain tendencies toward skewness in a direction away from the end of the scale toward*

---

individuals in a given community have adopted the attitude. This use of the term may seem objectionable, but the term itself is the most appropriate that has been found to express the meaning. The term "velocity" is used because it implies the *rate* at which this acceptance of attitude is taking place. The rate of acceptance within a group of individuals is obviously dependent upon the speed with which acceptance is taking place within individual members of the group. This, it may be supposed, is to no small degree dependent upon the frequency with which the attitude is exhibited to one individual by other individuals, that is, upon the reiteration of its expression. That is, when A and B express the same attitude to C, the effect upon C's attitude is probably greater than the mere sum of the effects of A's and B's attitudes, each taken independently. As the number of individuals having the same attitude increases, the number of separate contacts between those and other individuals will increase in some non-linear ratio. The probable number of duplicate or reinforced contacts with these other, non-infected, individuals will, however, increase at some rate greater than that of the total number of contacts. It follows from this that the rate of acceptance will for a time accelerate, because of the proportionately greater chance of reiteration. Deceleration would result from the principle of diminishing returns from reiteration. Continued reiteration of an attitude by others, that is, might eventually cease to have any effect upon the unconverted individual. These suppositions, reminiscent of Gabriele Tarde's "Laws of Imitation," are, of course, wholly speculative at present.

which the mode inclines are to be observed. This will be illustrated in table 7, where the distributions in Wisconsin and Michigan are compared. In the former La Follette was unusually strong; the attitudes leading to La Follette votes were dense, and the mode is high along the scale. In the latter, La Follette did not seem to "cut much of a figure" in the election, and the mode is low in the scale.

TABLE 7 — DISTRIBUTION OF COUNTIES IN WISCONSIN AND MICHIGAN, AC-
CORDING TO THE PERCENTAGE OF THE VOTE GIVEN LA FOLLETTE AMONG THE
THREE MAJOR PRESIDENTIAL CANDIDATES IN THE ELECTION OF 1924

Percentage for La Follette	Number of counties	
	Michigan	Wisconsin
0.0– 4.9	12	
5.0– 9.9	33 Mode	
10.0–14.9	22	
15.0–19.9	6	
20.0–24.9	6	
25.0–29.9	2	1
30.0–34.9	1	4
35.0–39.9		3
40.0–44.9	1	6
45.0–49.9		7
50.0–54.9		11
55.0–59.9		14
60.0–64.9		16 Mode
65.0–69.9		8
70.0–74.9		1
Total	83	71

(Michigan: Skew; Wisconsin: Skew)

Further illustrations of this tendency appear in a tabulation of the number of votes cast for the first presidential elector on the Democratic ticket in 1924 in 1470 election districts of the city of Philadelphia. The number of votes cast for a candidate in a district is not a good index of the density of the attitudes favorable to him, for it takes no account of the number of votes cast for other candidates. It is the relative rather than the absolute number of votes for a given nominee which is significant. Nevertheless,

TABLE 8 [8] — NUMBERS OF ELECTION DISTRICTS IN THE CITY OF PHILADELPHIA, SEGREGATED IN VARIOUS COMBINATIONS OF WARDS, DISTRIBUTED ACCORDING TO THE NUMBER OF VOTES RECORDED FOR THE FIRST PRESIDENTIAL ELECTOR ON THE DEMOCRATIC TICKET IN THE ELECTION OF 1924.

(The modal group in each distribution is indicated by *Mo*)

Number of Democratic Votes Recorded	Number of Election Districts				
	Wards 1–20 Inclusive	Wards 21–48 Inclusive	"Machine" Wards: 1, 2, 3, 4, 5, 7 and 13	"Independent" Wards: 21, 22, 23, 33, 34, 35, 37, 38, 40, 41, 42 and 43	Entire City
I	II	III	IV	V	VI
0–4	85	10	61 *Mo*	1	95
5–9	92 *Mo*	21	47	4	113
10–14	67	46	23	19	113 *Mo* *
15–19	45	68	6	19	113
20–24	26	82	6	40	108
25–29	34	69	2	41	103 *Mo* *
30–34	23	110	6	62	133
35–39	22	83 *Mo* *	3	39 *Mo* *	105
40–44	13	83		47	96
45–49	9	84		44	93
50–54	5	67		33	72
55–59	8	65		37	73
60–64	4	47		27	51
65–69	4	46		25	50
70–74	1	28		16	29
75–79	1	29		13	30
80–84	2	24		9	26
85–89	1	13		7	14
90–94		10		3	10
95–99	1	5		3	6
100–104	2	9		2	11
105–109		4		2	4
110–114		6		2	6
115–119		5		3	5
120–124		1			1
125–129		2			2
130–134		5		3	5
135–139					
140–144	1				1
145–149					
150–154	1				1
155–159					
160–164					
165–169					
170–174		1			1
Total	445	1025	155	501	1470

* According to a three class moving average

[8] Source: *Pennsylvania State Manual*, 1925-1926, pp. 529-551.

election districts are much more uniform in size than are, for example, states or counties. The labor of calculating percentages for each district would have been prohibitive and it is believed that the raw totals here used have sufficient validity for the illustrative purposes for which they are used.

The tabulations referred to, appear in Table 8. Election districts are there distributed according to various groupings of wards which have been segregated in the light of well-known characteristics of Philadelphia politics. In a general way, the first twenty wards of Philadelphia are regarded as the particular stronghold of the Republican or Vare organization. They have been placed together in column II with the remaining wards of the city in column III. Among the first twenty wards, however, are some which more prominently than others seem susceptible to the domination of a Philadelphia Republican political machine. Numbers one to five inclusive are along the waterfront in South Philadelphia and are generally known as the "river wards." Ward seven extends westward in a narrow strip along South Street, and contains a large portion of the city's most densely populated colored section. Ward thirteen includes the heart of "Hobohemia," to employ Nels Anderson's apt designation. These wards have been grouped together in column IV. In column V, on the other hand, have been aggregated twelve wards which appear to represent most strongly the opposing "anti-machine" tendency. Each was carried in the primary election on September 20, 1927, by former-Mayor J. Hampton Moore, who sought to wrest the Republican mayoralty nomination from the nominee of the Vare organization. We may for convenience refer to them as "the independent wards." All districts in the city are aggregated in column VI.

It has frequently been charged that anti-organization candidates in various districts of the first twenty wards have been "zeroed," i.e., reported by election officials in their returns as receiving no votes; and that in some other districts, presumably for the sake of appearance, such candidates have been allowed a few votes only of those which were actually cast for them. Particular interest attaches, therefore, to the distribution in columns II and IV, and the manner in which the asymmetry there disclosed has affected the distribution for the city as a whole shown in column VI. It would appear superficially, that the distribution in column IV was "J-shaped." It is really not "J-shaped" but rather extremely asymmetrical.[9]   In Table 9 this is made

TABLE 9 — ELECTION DISTRICTS IN FIRST THREE CLASSES OF COL. IV, TABLE 8, REDISTRIBUTED INTO A DISCRETE SERIES, SHOWING ACTUAL NUMBER OF VOTES RECORDED.

Number of Democratic votes recorded	Number of election districts
0	2
1	10
2	12
3	24 Mode
4	13
5	12
6	11
7	13
8	3
9	8
10	2
11	6
12	3
13	6
14	6

[9] Cf. Statistical Analysis, by Edmund E. Day, Chapter IX. The author classifies frequency distributions according to "the position of the class of maximum frequency in the range of the variable," and from this standpoint finds four types: 1, Symmetrical; 2, moderately asymmetrical; 3, extremely asymmetrical; 4, "J-shaped." This classification does not of course include the bi-modal or multi-modal distributions of which I have spoken on page 73. Professor Day observes (p. 124) "Though the symmetrical distribution is of great theoretic importance and is commonly encountered in some fields — notably biology and anthropology — it is not of frequent occurrence in economic and business research. Far more common in business and economic material are asymmetrical distributions."

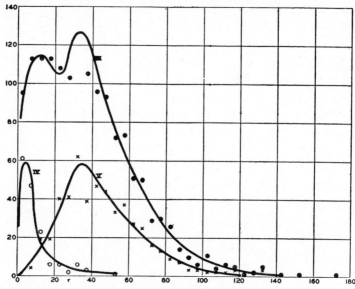

FIGURE 11 — DISTRIBUTION OF ELECTION DISTRICTS ACCORDING TO VOTES CAST FOR FIRST PRESIDENTIAL ELECTOR ON DEMOCRATIC TICKET, PHILADELPHIA, 1924.

Vertical Scale — Number of districts.   Horizontal Scale — Number of votes cast.   Free-hand curves are fitted to points plotted:

IV. Districts in "Machine Wards"
 V. Districts in "Independent Wards"
VI. All districts in city.

clear by redistributing the first three classes under column IV of Table 8 into discrete classes according to the actual number of Democratic votes recorded; i.e., from one to fourteen.

In Figure 11 the frequencies in each class of Table 8 in columns IV, V, and VI have been plotted according to a uniform scale. Through the plottings in each case has been drawn a free-hand curve which seems approximately to describe the data and which is given the same identifying number as the column of the table. No effort has been made to "fit" a curve by mathematical means to any one of these series. Curve IV (the "machine" wards) seems to bear superficial resemblance to that which represents the distribution of incomes.[10] A curve such as this may be obtained by plotting the terms in the expansion of the binominal $(p + q)^n$, when $p + q = 1.0$, and p is given a small value relative to q.[11] Curve IV (of Figure 11) also bears some resemblance to curves described by Professor Kelley.[12]

The distribution in the "independent" wards (col. V and curve V) shows a much closer approach to "normal" than does that for the "machine wards" (IV). The divergence between the two distributions is striking. Together these two groups of wards contain about forty-five per cent of the election districts in the city. The result of their divergence is seen in the distribution for the city at large (column VI of Table 8) and in the corresponding curve in Figure 11. The distribution is clearly bi-modal, and remains so when it is smoothed with a three class moving average.

Now bi-modality is invariably regarded as evidence of absence of homogeneity in the data which is distributed. It usually indicates some concealed line of demarcation among the cases. For example, if one were given a series of measurements of heights of college students and should find two modal points of concentration, he would suspect that the measurements referred to both men and women, or to students of two distinct races, or that some other similar distinction among the cases was to be found. So with the

[10] Cf. Day, op. cit., Chart 29, p. 127.

[11] These terms are given by G. Udney Yule, *An Introduction to the Theory of Statistics*, Seventh Edition, p. 294, for the binominal series 10,000 $(p + q)^{20}$ for values of p from 0.1 to 0.5. This table is reproduced in Day, op. cit., p. 124, with the corresponding graphs on his p. 125.

[12] Truman L. Kelley, *Statistical Method*, Chart IX, pp. 131 and 133, Type V. Our Curve V likewise bears resemblance to Professor Kelley's less asymmetrical Type III.

distribution of election districts in the city of Philadelphia as a whole (col. VI) *heterogeneity of data is evidenced. Its source is apparently to be found in differences of opportunity for a free expression of attitudes and a correct tabulation of votes at the polls, which distinguish the "machine" wards and the "independent" wards.* There is no reason to suppose that bi-modality would be due to other factors. Philadelphia is probably more homogeneous in its population and its habits than any other large American city of more than half a million population.

Attention to the frequency distribution (in the ordinary statistical sense) of the social density of attitudes as indicated by election returns appears to me to be a highly significant subject for further research in quantitative politics. It may set up as one important objective for possible attainment nothing less than *a method for determining mathematically whether an election has been a free and unhampered expression of attitude on the part of the electorate.* Little more has been done here than to advance a first suggestion in that direction. We need to know more about the forms of distribution and the amounts and directions of variation which are to be expected if an election is conducted freely and without manipulation, before we can measure departures from expectation and make inferences concerning their cause.[13] But this is only one of the possible results to be

[13] I have in mind the possibility of something analogous to a study made by Karl Pearson on "The Scientific Aspect of Monte Carlo Roulette," *Fortnightly Review*, February, 1894; republished in vol. I of a series of Pearson's collected papers entitled *The Chances of Death and Other Studies in Evolution*, pp. 42–62. Pearson used the *standard deviation* as a tool with which to examine the results of a large number of turns of the roulette. By comparing the actual with the mathematically probable distribution he arrived at the conclusion that "Roulette as played at Monte Carlo is not a scientific game of chance." (p. 55.) "If judged by returns which are published without apparently being repudiated by the *Société*, (it) is, if the laws of chance rule, from the standpoint of exact science the most prodigious miracle of the nine-

achieved when the legitimacy of using common statistical
concepts and methods in the analysis of data such as this
becomes better attested.[14]

---

teenth century." (p. 61.) I do not understand that Pearson regarded the
game or the returns as subject to artificial manipulation, such as might be
the case in a set of election materials. I am suggesting that some political
statistician in the future may be able to say precisely what the practical politician now says on the basis of inside knowledge and a "hunch," concerning
the freedom from dishonest manipulation or otherwise of a given election.

[14] The political importance with which this form of variability is credited
among politicians is evidenced in a news despatch from Washington appearing in the first right hand column of page 1, *The New York Times*, November
20, 1927, in which the results of a poll of editors and political leaders throughout the country upon presidential possibilities is described. The aggregate
votes on the Republican side gave Hoover 844 and Lowden 766. But *The
National Republic*, a political magazine in which the results appeared, was
quoted by the *Times* as saying: "The reports indicate that Governor Lowden's strength is chiefly concentrated in a dozen states, while that of Hoover,
Hughes and Dawes is more widely scattered." Further, "The poll indicates,
the magazine says, that the political situation, so far as the Republican candidates are concerned, is 'exceedingly spotted.'" This phraseology embodies
in popular form the concept of the social density of attitude and its distribution.

IX

ATTITUDE DIFFERENCES: AN APPARENT CONTRADICTION ANALYZED

Political scientists and laymen alike refer frequently to differences in attitude among individuals or between social classes in terms which suggest great diversity. Between reactionaries or conservatives and the radical there is presumed to exist a wide gulf. Both are frequently dubbed *extremists*. The pronouncements of radicals and the doctrinaire utterances of the capitalist press often make it appear that opposite poles of thought and attitude completely dominate certain groups in modern political society. What attitudes can there be in common between a Lenin or Trotzky on one side and a Coolidge or Hughes upon the other?

Within narrower realms of conflict are to be found the political issues which separate the body politic into contending groups. Those who follow the news despatches from Washington or from state capitals are accustomed to think of Democrats and Republicans, of "ins" and "outs," of the "organization" and the "reformers" or "insurgents" as in perpetual conflict, in disagreement upon almost every issue that may arise.

Seemingly inconsistent with these viewpoints are logical considerations and considerable data which suggest that while attention is directed to differences a much larger amount of *agreement* is overlooked. Conflict in itself is interesting. It makes "news." Agreement generally does not, except as it may end a period of conflict, or except as the subject of agreement is itself a matter of concern. Thus "human nature" seems to provide a foundation for a distorted version of the importance of differences as compared with agreements between and among individuals and groups.

If Mr. Charles E. Hughes and Mr. Leon Trotzky were compelled to week-end together among native Africans, they would undoubtedly discover a surprising number of common interests and attitudes. In habits of dress, in preferences as to food, in linguistic thought-patterns, in assumptions as to time and space and natural order, in intellectual interests and emotional reactions concerning literature, plastic art, music, yes, even in their interests concerning the political order, they would doubtless find themselves the sole members of a like-minded group drawn together by "consciousness of kind." That most of these elements of relative like-mindedness would be assumed rather than discussed would but testify to their reality.

Within the narrower regions of party and bloc conflict peculiar to this nation and the several states, suspicion that disagreements are over-emphasized need not depend on speculation. In his study, "The Influence of Party upon Legislation in England and America," which was based upon analyses of roll-call votes in American legislatures, Lowell decided to exclude those which were unanimous. He says:

". . . To insert them seemed unnecessary, and in fact, they occur only in consequence of a peculiar procedure. No one would, of course, care to insist upon a call of the roll when there was no opposition; and hence the names of the persons voting in such cases would not be recorded were it not that in a number of states the constitution requires a yea-and-nay vote on the final passage of every bill. Under these circumstances the quantity of unanimous votes is sometimes prodigious. In the Senate of New York, for example, there were in the session of 1899, 1,235 yea-and-nay votes, of which 961 were unanimous. Except for the provision in the constitution there would have been no roll call on these votes and to include them in our list would merely swell the tables inordinately without any corresponding advantage."[1]

Yet the number of occasions altogether on which unanimous agreement occurred must have been several times that in which it was yielded on the final passage of the bills.

A similar finding has been reported by Leonard P. Ayers in a survey of school administration in Cleveland.[2] During twenty months from the first of 1914 through August, 1915, the roll was called in the Cleveland Board of Education, made up of seven members, 2,069 times. In 2,018 instances the vote was unanimously "aye." That is, there was failure to agree only fifty-one times, or once in each forty-one roll calls. The total number of individual negative votes was sixty-nine. These were distributed among the seven members as follows: 3,5,5,5,6,12 and 33.

My own analyses of roll-call votes in state legislatures, taken at a later date than those examined by Lowell and at a time when the pressure of legislative business had undoubtedly increased, showed even higher proportions of unanimous agreement than he has indicated.[3] In fact, it is safe to generalize: *In every public "deliberative" body disagreement upon the final disposition of a question is the exception rather than the rule.*

Turning to the electorate itself, Ogburn and Peterson have noted a similar situation.[4] On the basis of their

[1] Lowell, A. Lawrence: The Influence of Party upon Legislation in England and America, Annual Report, *American Historical Association*, vol. i, 1901, pp. 321–542.

[2] *School Organization and Administration*, 1916, a volume in the Cleveland Foundation Survey of Education. A portion of page 36 is here paraphrased.

[3] *Farmers and Workers in American Politics*, Chapter VI. My methods are discussed here in Chapter XV.

[4] "Political Thought of Social Classes," William F. Ogburn and Delvin Peterson, *Political Science Quarterly*, Vol. XXXI, pp. 300–317.

analyses of popular votes on initiative and referendum measures in Oregon they conclude that:

The figures indicate that the differences between the social classes are not so great as many have been led to suspect. Capital (the upper class) and labor agree in eighty pairs out of every one hundred on the most radical and progressive legislation that has come before the Oregon voters during five years. The points of agreement far outweigh the points of difference. The heterogeneity of Oregon society does not seem to have proven a serious obstacle to the problem of government. The figures show little indication of class conflict nor do they point to a revolution. They rather point toward harmony and show a considerable ability on the part of the social classes to get along together.

Between these evidences, and the opinions of those who hold that great gulfs are to be found between social classes, there is evidently a contradiction. How is it to be resolved? Are we justified in talking of political *extremes* and *extremists*, of *opposing* parties, when the similarities are found so greatly to outweigh the differences?

The contradiction can be resolved by regarding the differences of attitude between individuals and classes as *relative*. Those who feel the differences to be large in absolute terms are the victims of a fallacy not unlike that which sometimes appears when comparative magnitudes are represented by bars in a diagram. The fallacy resides in the failure to place the bases of the bars at zero. However slight the difference, one can be made to appear any number of times greater than the other (visually, that is) by moving the base line away from zero toward but not beyond the lesser of the two magnitudes. This is illustrated in Figure 12. On the left of the figure, two salaries of $9,000 and $10,000 respectively are compared. Although the first is nine-tenths of the second in magnitude, it is made to appear but half as great by placing the base line at the point on the scale which would represent a salary of $8,000. This device is often used to give a false impression of growth in sales or newspaper circulation.

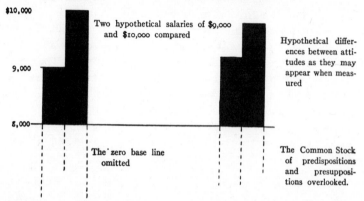

FIGURE 12 — A FALLACY IN THE GRAPHIC COMPARISON OF MAGNITUDES, WITH A SUGGESTED ANALOGY IN THE COMPARISON OF ATTITUDE DIFFERENCES

Similarly, the vast common stock of predispositions and presuppositions, stretching backward as it were to an indefinite and hypothetical zero line, tend to be overlooked in our discussions of differences among individuals and groups. This is suggested on the right side of Figure 12. It is out of this common stock that the relatively slight variations which we observe develop. It is impossible to escape from our biological predispositions. Mr. Clarence Day, Jr., in his delightful and illuminating little book, *This Simian World*, has presented some fanciful pictures of an earth dominated by intelligent but non-Simian beings — super-felines, for example. Between such "men" and our own Simian stock there would be a chance for real differences of attitude!

Our common presuppositions also are far more numerous than we often assume. It is doubtful whether, even apart from inherited biological make-up, any man or woman *can* be radical, in any genuinely radical sense. In the greater part of attitude and conduct, twentieth-century western mores and folkways will survive any vicissitudes of communistic, futuristic or fundamentalist ecstacy. The most confirmed political or economic crystal-gazer could not acquire the mental imagery of primitive man or the pre-Copernican cosmical outlook of our own ancestors. It has sometimes seemed to me amusing that fundamentalists should ride in Fords, as well as make use of other refinements of civilization. The answer to the paradox is that they are *not* fundamentalists in much the larger part of their attitudes and behavior. As a feat of radicalism, the changes of attitude necessary to achieve genuine fundamentalism should be relatively easy, for the patterns are available for guidance. But fundamentalists have not accomplished it. Their assumptions sometimes contribute to the exasperation which their assertions produce. How difficult it would be, then, for a rational individual of today to achieve an attitude not based upon social patterns of the past or present, but upon those of the future. The genuine futurist, like the genuine radical or fundamentalist, is an impossibility!

All of this is speculation, yet I think it justified to emphasize an hypothesis that might easily be subjected to experimental verifications. In analyzing political differences we are dealing, again to use analogy, with *surface indications,* demarcations within a relatively slight possible range of variation. As to the ultimate possibilities of more fundamental deviations, not sanctioned by our present folkways and mores, we are scarcely aware. All of this is to be kept in mind in the discussions of "difference" and "likeness" among groups, both in the chapters which immediately precede this one and in those which follow in Parts IV and V.

X

Regionalism and Diffusion of Political Attitudes

A. the hypothesis

A few years ago the writer made an analysis of election statistics in a number of American states.[1] In the case of each, one or more elections were selected for examination in which some evidence concerning the distribution of *progressive* political attitudes seemed to be obtainable. The immediate object of search concerned differences or similarities in attitude that might be discovered among farmers and workingmen. It seemed to become apparent, however, that while occupational cleavages existed and might in some cases be measured, the more outstanding differences occurred among *regions* into which a state was politically divided. These regions were not demarcated with any precision, and the term itself was not entirely adequate to express the situations disclosed. It seemed rather that attitudes (as indicated by the votes employed as an index) changed gradually as one passed from one section of a state to another. The direction and extent of these changes was complicated by another tendency toward pronounced differences between urban and rural constituencies and by several other variable factors. The impressions which were obtained of these interrelated forms of attitude variation were only in part verified by analysis, since they were not in the immediate focus of interest. Some of the situations where analysis was

[1] *Farmers and Workers in American Politics*, Chapter V, pp. 143–183. The citations which follow are from this chapter, together with Tables 10 to 13 inclusive.

attempted, however, led to the following classifications of data and the attendant descriptions.

In Minnesota distinct concentrations of the radical and conservative vote along geographical lines, with their correlated areas of crop specialization, were noted. The index here consisted of two state elections in which Henrik Shipstead, subsequently elected United States Senator on the Farmer-Labor Party ticket, was a candidate. In Table 10 counties have been grouped in a number of ways to emphasize the cleavages referred to. The corn counties are situated mainly in the southern part of the state, the wheat counties are in the northwestern section, in the Red River valley; the oats counties are scattered, falling partly in both of the other areas. From the geographical and crop standpoints, it is evident that Shipstead received heavy support from northwestern wheat counties and very light support from southern corn-growing counties.

In North Dakota two lines of cleavage among the voters have been apparent throughout the successive electoral contests between the Nonpartisan League and its opponents. The first has been drawn between farmers on one side, and the voters of the towns on the other. The second has been geographical, separating the conservative eastern counties from the more radical western counties. The latter distinction corresponds also to areas of comparative rural prosperity within the state. A referendum election on June 26, 1919, offered several clearly defined expressions of opinion by the voters, illustrative of these lines. In Table 11 the cleavages may be seen in the vote on House Bill 18, a cornerstone of the Nonpartisan League program at that period, calling for the establishment of a state-owned bank.

The vote in favor of the state bank is seen to be half again as great, proportionately, on the western border of the state as in the Red River counties on the eastern border. It is in the western counties that the low average values of farm property are found, and these low values appear to be associated with the pro-bank vote. Of the six counties

Table 10 — Vote of Henrik Shipstead in Minnesota, 1920 and 1922, by Certain Groupings of Counties According to Geographical Location and Crop Specializations [2]

Area Segregated	Vote received as Independent candidate for Governor, 1920		Vote received as Farmer-Labor Party Candidate For U. S. Senate, 1922	
	Number of votes cast	Per cent of total vote	Number of votes cast	Per cent of total vote
The State of Minnesota	281,402	35.3	325,372	45.5
Two rows of 19 counties on the southern border of the State	31,601	23.9	41,666	36.0
Seven counties bordering on the Red River of the North	18,414	43.7	19,360	53.6
Block of 8 northwestern counties generally two deep from the Red River	19,999	48.1	20,912	57.6
Thirty counties producing one million or more bushels of *corn* and more corn than any other cereal crop, exluding Hennepin	70,518	31.7	65,036	42.6
Seventeen counties producing one million or more bushels of *oats* and more oats than any other cereal crop	50,986	40.0	55,169	50.1
Thirteen counties producing one-half million or more bushels of *wheat* and more wheat than corn. (Includes 7 of the oats counties)	35,965	44.7	36,969	53.1

[2] Sources: *Fourteenth Census*, Agriculture, Minnesota, County table iv, and *Legislative Manual of Minnesota*, 1921 and 1923.

TABLE 11 — VOTES CAST FOR AND AGAINST HOUSE BILL 18, ESTABLISHING THE BANK OF NORTH DAKOTA, IN REFERENDUM ELECTION, JUNE 26, 1919, BY VARIOUS GROUPINGS OF COUNTIES [3]

County Groupings	"Yes"	"No"	% "Yes" of total
The State, 53 counties	61,495	48,239	56.0
Bordering Red River, eastern boundary of State, 6 counties	9,241	11,959	43.6
Eastern Block, extending westward to include Rolette, Pierce, Wells, Kidder, Logan, McIntosh, 27 counties	30,981	29,779	51.0
Western Block, all counties not included in preceding item, 26 counties	30,514	18,460	62.3
Bordering Montana, western boundary of State, including Billings, 7 counties	7,091	3,900	64.5
Containing "urban" population (not wholly "rural") 12 counties	20,831	20,714	50.1
Cass, single county more than 50% "urban" containing City of Fargo	2,339	2,421	49.1
Grand Forks county, containing City of Grand Forks	1,755	2,623	40.1
Wholly "rural", 41 counties	40,664	27,525	59.6
Counties grouped by average value of all farm property per farm:			
$10,000–$15,000, 6 counties	7,590	3,813	66.6
$15,000–$20,000, 23 counties	25,418	15,831	61.6
$20,000–$25,000, 4 counties	4,311	4,634	48.2
$25,000–$30,000, 8 counties	9,635	9,205	51.1
$30,000–$35,000, 10 counties	11,061	11,153	49.2
$35,000–$40,000, 1 county	1,146	1,182	49.2
$40,000–$45,000, 1 county	2,339	2,421	48.4
Counties producing 2,000,000 or more bushels of wheat each in 1919, 11 counties	17,433	18,479	48.5

[3] Source: *Legislative Manual of North Dakota*

facing the Red River every one returned a majority vote
against the bank bill. Of the eight counties along the southern border, facing South Dakota, five returned a majority
against the bill.[4] Thirteen of the sixteen counties voting "no"
are in the eastern half of the state, and two of the remainder
face the South Dakota boundary.

In South Dakota the vote cast for the paradoxical "Non-
Partisan Party" candidate for governor in 1920 provided a
suitable index for the disclosure of differences in attitude
with respect to the Nonpartisan League program. Some of
the classifications of this vote that were made in the search
for lines of cleavage are contained in Table 12.

Careful study of the data upon which Table 12 is based
leads to the conclusion that the vote in this election was
determined by sectional influences associated with crop-
producing areas, rather than by occupational or class distinctions. Of seventeen counties in which thirty per cent or
more of the vote for governor was polled by the Non-
Partisan candidate, thirteen lie in the eastern third of the
state, while sixteen lie in the eastern half of the state. Of
the five counties which cast forty per cent or more of their
votes for the Non-Partisan candidate all are in the eastern
one-third of the state. The wheat-producing areas are in this
eastern section, especially in the northeastern corner at the
southern end of the Red River valley. The corn section is
also in the eastern half of the state, but concentrated in the
southeastern counties along the Missouri River, where the
vote for Bates was very light.

In view of the sectional lines of cleavage, there appears to
be little occupational significance in the low vote cast for
Bates in the mining regions in the Black Hills and the comparatively high vote which he received in Brown County,

[4] This does not appear in Table 11.

TABLE 12 — NUMBER AND PERCENTAGE OF VOTES CAST FOR BATES, NON-
PARTISAN PARTY CANDIDATE FOR GOVERNOR OF SOUTH DAKOTA, 1920, BY
VARIOUS GROUPINGS OF COUNTIES [5]

County Groupings	Total vote for Governor	Vote for Bates	
		Number	Per cent of Total vote
The State.................................	183,888	48,426	26.3
Lawrence County (Metalliferous miners).......	8,427	504	6.0
Four Black Hills Mining Counties............	11,804	797	6.8
Brown County (R. R. labor).................	10,167	3,459	34.0
Minnehaha (Sioux Falls)....................	12,943	2,895	22.4
Eight counties containing cities of 5000 or more population...............................	50,403	12,167	24.1
Three counties more than 50% urban (included in preceding item)........................	22,466	6,027	26.8
Sixteen counties in which farmers comprise 15% or more of total population.................	24,902	4,772	19.2
Thirteen counties in which the wheat production exceeds one-half million bushels and in which wheat is the largest cereal crop............	44,922	14,803	33.0
Twenty-four counties forming an irregular three-county column on the eastern border of the State, but omitting the three which border on the Missouri River......................	87,779	27,269	31.1
Three counties bordering on the Missouri River.	10,131	1,494	14.7
Fourteen counties in the north and east border of the State, including Harding but not Union, that is facing North Dakota, Minnesota and a small portion of Montana..................	55,808	16,896	30.3
Thirteen counties on the south and west border including Union but not Harding and not including the unorganized counties of Shannon and Todd (that is, facing Nebraska, Wyoming and a corner of Iowa)	39,522	6,552	16.2

[5] Sources: *Fourteenth Census*, Volumes on Population and Agriculture, and *Legislative Manual of South Dakota*.

the railroad center in the wheat belt. Nor does the comparatively low vote which the candidate polled in the counties inhabited most largely by farmers have greater significance, for the latter tend to be found in the western half of the state's area.

A similar conclusion was forced upon me in the case of Iowa, when I examined the important contest between Brookhart, the radical, and Cummins, the conservative, for the Republican senatorial nomination in 1920. The alignments appear to have occurred not upon occupational or class but primarily upon sectional lines. These appeared to run north and south as well as east and west. Out of forty-five southern counties, nineteen, more than two-fifths, gave a plurality for Brookhart. In the remaining fifty-four northern counties, nine, one-sixth only, gave Brookhart a plurality. Brookhart's vote was stronger on both the northern and the southern boundaries of the state than in the central regions, but along the Missouri River, which forms the western border of the state, he failed to carry a single county and received but little more than one vote for every two given his opponent. These tendencies are shown in slightly different form in Table 13.

In addition to the geographical cleavages, the association of another factor with the Brookhart-Cummins vote is indicated by Table 13. This is the factor of average farm values. The conservative Cummins vote appears to have been proportionately greater in those counties in which the average value of all farm property was the highest. But these counties are found for the most part in the Missouri River valley, running north and south, and in the central area of the state, running east and west, precisely those sections in which Brookhart was weakest, according to the sectional analysis.[6] It is in these areas, moreover, that the

[6] This may be seen graphically in the *Yearbook of the Department of Agriculture*, 1921, pp. 493 and 492.

Table 13 — Votes Cast for Smith W. Brookhart and Albert J. Cummins in Republican Senatorial Primary, Iowa, 1920, with Percentage of Vote Received by Brookhart of the Combined Vote, by Various Groupings of Counties

County Groupings	Votes			
	For Brook-hart	For Cum-mins	For Brook-hart and Cum-mins com-bined	Brook-hart's as a percent-age of the com-bined
The State of Iowa..............	96,563	115,768	212,331	45.5
Southern counties; 45 in 4 southern rows, including Cedar, Scott and Clinton......................	45,962	48,492	94,454	48.7
Northern counties, 54 in 5 northern rows........................	50,601	67,276	117,877	42.9
Southern border counties, 19 in two rows, excluding those touching the Missouri River............	18,931	17,629	36,560	51.8
Northern border counties, 19 in two rows, excluding those touching the Missouri River............	17,800	19,806	37,606	47.3
Missouri River counties, 9 on western border touching the river....	6,999	11,618	18,617	37.6
Urban counties, 15 in which 50% or more of the population reside in cities of 10,000 or more population, 5% or more of whose population are wage-earners in manufacturing enterprises...........	26,412	30,300	56,712	46.6
Counties grouped by average value of all farm property, per farm:				
Less than $20,000, 2 counties....	3,189	3,125	5,314	60.0
$20,000–$25,000, 5 counties.....	4,008	4,433	8,441	47.5
$25,000–$30,000, 16 counties....	16,662	18,667	35,329	47.2
Over $55,000, 12 counties.......	8,108	12,553	20,661	39.2

maximum production of corn occurs [7] and that the maximum expenditures are made for feed[8] and for farm labor.[9] The southern counties in which Brookhart was strongest show relatively lower average values of farm property and of average values per acre. They likewise show a slightly higher tendency to the production of winter wheat in place of corn.[10]

The means whereby an index of progressivism was procured in the case of Nebraska has been described in Chapter VII. The existence of sectional variations of attitude in that state was also there mentioned. The average vote received by Howell and Bryan in the state at large amounted to 58.2 per cent. Exclusive of Douglass County, containing the city of Omaha, the average is 59.5 per cent. Counties in which this average exceeded 65 per cent, and which may therefore be regarded as unusually progressive, number eight. Six of these are in a compact geographical area in the central part of the state. Counties in which the average falls below 55 per cent, and which may therefore be regarded as "conservative" or "least progressive," number twelve. Seven of these form a consecutive belt bordering the Missouri River above its confluence with the River Platte. This is a region of corn, high farm values, and high expenditures for farm labor, corresponding to the conservative regions on the opposite side of the river in Iowa and South Dakota.

The evidence seems to indicate that in this Nebraska election the non-party lines of political cleavage were sectional rather than occupational. In Douglass County, containing the industrial population of Omaha, and 93.7 per cent urban, the percentage vote for Bryan and Howell

[7] *Ibid.*, p. 437, fig. 27.
[8] *Ibid.*, p. 495, fig. 108.
[9] *Ibid.*, p. 496, fig. 110.
[10] *Ibid.*, pp. 438 and 437, figs. 29 and 27.

averaged was 49.3 per cent — less than in any other county of the state. In Lancaster County, containing the city of Lincoln, the percentage vote for these candidates averaged nearly 60 per cent. The first is one of the northeastern Missouri River group of counties which appear to be conservative regardless of whether they are urban or rural. The second is one of a group of twenty-two counties between the Missouri and Platte Rivers and the Kansas border, which are above the average for the state in the support which they gave to the progressive and Nonpartisan slate.

The particular sectional variations in political attitude that were disclosed in the preceding analyses have not in most cases been checked by subsequent work with new data. Nor is this essential to the present problem, although it might be desirable. The fact that these sectional differences did exist at one time or another in the period from 1919 to 1922 offers material for an attempted scientific explanation of equal importance to one which might be based on similar data for the current year. Our interest, in other words, is directed to finding an explanatory concept under which particular regional variations may be subsumed rather than toward any particular arrangement of regions at a given time in a given state.

From this standpoint, a number of curious circumstances have been disclosed in the preceding evidences of this chapter. None of the theories already suggested serves to explain all of them, and in fact each is contradicted by some part of them. What is needed is *a generalization which will harmonize all of the data*. Two of these curious and seemingly inconsistent sets of facts may be examined.

The Missouri River valley, containing counties in the three states of Iowa, Nebraska and South Dakota, appears as a conservative region with reference to the remainder of each of these states. The indexes employed do not permit direct comparisons across state lines; but in each of the three states the Missouri River counties are the more conservative. Together they comprise a homogeneous geographical and economic area in the heart of the corn belt. It is plausible to suppose, therefore, that contiguous areas of similar economic interests have similar political complexion. This becomes an hypothesis.

It is contradicted, however, by the situation in the Red River valley to the north, which falls in the two states of Minnesota and North Dakota. This is the heart of the wheat belt, another homogeneous geographical and economic area. Politically the situation is very different from that in the Missouri River valley. The counties on opposite sides of the river bear directly opposite relationships to the political geography of their respective states. The counties which lie on the east bank of the river were found to be among the most radical in Minnesota. Those on the west bank of the river are properly regarded as the most conservative in North Dakota. Nor are these distinctions due to the comparative proportions of urban and rural population in each. The wholly rural counties of Pembina and Traill are conservative relative to other North Dakota counties. The partially urban counties of Clay, Polk, and Pennington, across the river in Minnesota, are radical with reference to that state.

At least one hypothesis would serve to explain this anomaly, so far as North Dakota and Minnesota are concerned. North Dakota *as a whole* may be a more radical state than Minnesota. If there were some accepted standard of radicalism applicable alike to both states, we might find radical sentiment constantly decreasing in intensity as we traversed an arc, extending from western North Dakota, through that state and northwestern Minnesota to the Iowa border. But such a situation would not readily be explained on the basis of the hypothesis set up in the case of the Missouri River valley. On the other hand, it would be explained by a still more general hypothesis, namely, that the concepts of *culture areas* and *culture diffusion*, developed by American anthropologists out of their studies of the culture traits of primitive peoples, might be applied to the origin and spread of political attitudes.[11]   This more general culture-area hypothesis would also reconcile and harmonize with the data respecting the Missouri River valley, for the latter might then be regarded as a culture center of conservatism, or, conversely, an outer fringe of some culture area of radicalism. The hypothesis that I was dealing with various aspects of a "middle western 'culture area' of political discontent" in this manner emerged.   In addition to the North Dakota–Minnesota–Iowa line of diffusion already suggested, its general characteristics upon the basis of available evidence were summarized as follows:

"But the lines of diffusion from North Dakota appear to run southward as well as toward the Minnesota boundary. Southern North Dakota is more conservative than northern North Dakota and northern South Dakota is more radical than the southern portions of that state.   A relatively conservative area is discovered in the Missouri River counties in the southeastern corner of South Dakota, and running

---

[11] The concepts named have become so familiar to social scientists in recent years that it seems needless to recapitulate them.   I have included a theoretical statement concerning their application here in a chapter on "Political Attitudes as Elements of Culture Diffusion" contained in a testimonial volume now in preparation by students of Professor Franklin H. Giddings. Material excerpted from this article appears in the following pages of the present chapter, although in less complete form than in the article itself. The concepts themselves, with others related thereto, are defined and elaborated in *Man and Culture*, by Clark Wissler.

southeasterly along both banks of the river in Iowa and Nebraska. . . .

"In Nebraska, a separate center of progressive political opinion appears to exist in a cluster of counties about the middle of the state. The tendencies toward progressive political behavior appear to lessen as the eastern, northern or western borders of the state are approached. Thus, another line of diffusion appears to run from North Dakota, through South Dakota into Nebraska, where, as in the case of Iowa, it encounters another center of diffusion spreading outward to meet it."

B. EFFORTS TO TEST THE HYPOTHESIS

To test the hypothesis in its more limited application to the northwestern states, it was necessary to await an occasion in which the traditional party alignments should be broken down in such a way that a uniform index might be secured over the entire area effected. The quadrennial vote for president does not provide such an index because of the factor of "party regularity." That is, the vote for the Republican presidential candidate in some states, particularly in the north, and the vote for the Democratic candidate in others, represent primarily the traditional party regularity of the 'states involved. They have no clear general meaning as indicators of conservatism, radicalism, or anything else when states are -compared. An occasion of the kind required was presented by the La Follette campaign of 1924 and the index of "progressive" attitudes that it afforded.

The percentage received by La Follette of the total vote for the three major presidential candidates was again, as in Chapter VIII, the index employed. The area covered by the distribution recorded in Table 5, however, was extended to include in addition to the eight states named on pages 99-100 all or a portion of the counties in the states of Michigan, Illinois, Missouri, Kansas, Wyoming, Colorado, Utah, Washington, Oregon and Nevada. The counties to be employed were divided according to the percentage of La Follette votes in each into fifteen classes, the total range being from 0.0 per cent to 74.9 per cent and the class intervals being in each case (as in Table 5) five per cent. These classes were numbered from one to fifteen and each county assigned its class number on a standard county outline map of the region affected. In comparing counties, differences in class were designated as differences in *rank*, a difference of one rank representing an assumed difference in the La Follette vote amounting to five per cent of the total vote for Coolidge, Davis and La Follette. If we adopt here the terminology employed in Chapter VIII the rank is a measure of the *density* of the attitudes supporting La Follette's candidacy.[12]

For purposes of detailed investigation two problems involved in the hypothesis were separately considered. The first concerned the part played by state boundaries as barriers to similarity of attitude with respect to such issues as those which La Follette's candidacy presented. It has been held by Professor Wissler[13] that political boundaries have slight relationship to the diffusion of culture. If political attitudes be regarded as culture elements, however, it would be expected, *a priori*, that, in this case at least, an exception would be found; i.e., that diffusion of political attitudes would occur more freely within a set of recognized political

---

[12] In the article on "Political Attitudes as Elements of Culture Diffusion" referred to in footnote, page 136, these ranks have been assembled into still broader classes and are shown graphically on a county outline map of the region involved.

[13] *Man and Culture*, pp. 13, 18, 136 and passim.

boundaries.[14] The second detailed problem concerned the geographical distribution of La Follette sentiment. The two questions may be stated as follows: (1) Is there evidence, susceptible of numerical summarization, of greater similarity in the La Follette vote between adjacent counties within given states than between adjacent counties on opposite sides of the boundaries between these and other states? If greater similarity can be shown to exist generally within the state, this fact would strongly support the contention that the state boundary is a barrier to the diffusion of political attitudes. (2) Is there evidence of the existence of "centers" or localities of special density of La Follette sentiment, surrounded by areas of decreasing density as the distance from the center increases?

Only an exhaustive investigation, geographically extensive, detailed, and taking into account a variety of economic and social factors in the population involved, would give satisfactory answers to these two questions. Several modes of attack upon them are represented in the evidence which follows, but this is given with full appreciation of its limited conclusiveness.

Several technical perplexities in the procedure of inquiry presented themselves. I wished to compare the rank (in density of La Follette attitude) of adjacent counties. But when are counties adjacent? The following criteria were arbitrarily employed: if separated by a water boundary, the latter must be of such a character that the counties are presumed to divide the stream between them. Thus, counties facing each other across the Mississippi River are regarded as adjacent, while counties facing each other across

[14] This view is developed at greater length in the article on "Political Attitudes as Elements of Culture Diffusion" for the testimonial volume to Professor Giddings referred to above.

Lake Michigan or its bays are not. To be regarded as adjacent, two counties must share the same boundary for a distance of one-fourth or more the length of that boundary of each which extends in the same general direction. In a few cases these criteria required arbitrary interpretation.

In comparing the ranks of counties across state lines, it seemed desirable at the outset to segregate the comparisons in which the state boundary was a "natural" barrier such as a river or mountain ridge, from those in which it was "artificial," as a line of latitude or longitude. In Table 14, aggregate differences in rank between adjacent counties across natural state boundaries are compared with aggregate differences in rank between each set of border counties and adjacent counties within the same state. All possible comparisons between individual counties permitted by the criteria of adjacency are included, except that a comparison between the same two counties is made but once. For example, in the case of the Red River boundary between North Dakota and Minnesota, running generally north and south, interstate comparisons can be made only between counties lying east and west with reference to each other. In the intrastate comparisons, on the other hand, a particular North Dakota border county is compared with other North Dakota counties lying north, west and south. It is obvious that the intrastate comparisons will be more numerous than the interstate. The comparison in each case is made with reference to that part of the state boundary only in which the particular boundary feature cited prevails.

In Table 15, the data given is analogous to that in Table 14, except that the comparisons apply to state boundaries of "artificial" character.

It is apparent from the summary lines at the foot of both

TABLE 14 [15] — DIFFERENCES IN COUNTY RANK, LA FOLLETTE VOTE, 1924, INVOLVING NATURAL STATE BOUNDARIES

(All possible comparisons made)

Across State Boundary				Within State			Within State		
Boundary	Barrier	No. of comparisons	Av. dif. in Rank	State	No. of comparisons	Av. dif. in Rank	State	No. of comparisons	Av. dif. in Rank
Minn.-Wis.	Miss. & St. Croix R.	12	3.16	Minn.	24	1.87	Wis.	24	1.79
Minn.-N.D.	Red River	8	3.50	Minn.	17	1.00	N.D.	17	2.06
Iowa-Ill.	Mississippi River	10	2.30	Iowa	22	1.50	Ill.	17	1.64
Iowa-Neb.	Missouri River	12	1.67	Iowa	14	1.78	Neb.	18	1.67
Neb.-S.D.	Missouri River	7	1.57	Neb.	13	0.85	S.D.	13	2.23
Mont.-Ida.	Bitter Root Mts.	12	2.92	Mont.	17	1.88	Ida.	25	1.76
Wash.-Ore.	Columbia River	4	1.50	Wash.	7	3.00	Ore.	5	1.00
Summary across boundaries		65	2.48	Summary within states				233	1.71

tables 14 and 15 that the differences in rank between adjacent counties (i.e., differences in attitude toward La Follette) are greater when a state boundary intervenes than when this political barrier is lacking. The character of the boundary, whether natural or artificial, however, does not appear to affect the result. In fact the difference referred to is greater in the case of the artificial boundaries. This seems to suggest that the obstacle to diffusion which is interposed by the boundary is a function of the social or political organization of the states involved, rather than a function of any geographical characteristic.

There is, however, a possibility of error in these tables due to the application of the criteria of adjacency within each

[15] Consult text for additional explanation not given in table headings.

Table 15 — Differences in County Rank, La Follette Vote, 1924,
Involving Artificial State Boundaries

(All possible comparisons made)

Across state boundary			Within State			Within State		
Boundary	No. of comparisons	Av. dif. in Rank	State	No. of comparisons	Av. dif. in Rank	State	No. of comparisons	Av. dif. in Rank
Minn.-Iowa	13	2.00	Minn.	22	1.32	Iowa	24	2.50
Minn.-S.D.	6	2.17	Minn.	12	1.33	S.D.	13	2.08
Iowa-Mo.	16	3.31	Iowa	20	1.05	Mo.	23	0.52
Wis.-Ill.	9	2.44	Wis.	16	2.38	Ill.	12	1.08
Neb.-Kas.	17	0.88	Neb.	27	1.15	Kas.	28	1.03
Neb.-Colo.	7	1.43	Neb.	13	1.46	Colo.	12	1.33
Neb.-Wyo.	5	2.00	Neb.	8	2.33	Wyo.	8	1.12
Neb.-S.D.	8	3.50	Neb.	16	2.06	S.D.	14	2.50
S.D.-N.D.	9	3.00	S.D	20	1.80	N.D.	20	2.15
S.D.-Wyo.	5	1.80	S.D.	14	2.50	Wyo.	7	2.00
N.D.-Mont.	7	6.29	N.D.	12	1.50	Mont.	16	2.62
Mont.-Wyo.	6	1.50	Mont.	12	2.33	Wyo.	14	2.00
Wyo.-Ida.	4	2.75	Wyo.	7	2.28	Ida.	12	2.08
Wyo.-Colo.	7	4.71	Wyo.	12	1.83	Colo.	14	1.28
Wyo.-Utah	4	6.25	Wyo.	8	2.75	Utah	8	1.00
Ida.-Utah	4	3.76	Ida.	12	1.50	Utah	5	2.00
Ida.-Wash.	6	0.67	Ida.	12	1.33	Wash.	10	2.10
Wash.-Ore.	4	1.50	Wash.	7	3.00	Ore.	5	1.00
Summary across boundaries	137	2.63	Summary within states				495	1.72

state. As noted above, comparisons within the state are made between a given county and its neighbors on three sides, the neighbor or neighbors on the fourth side furnishing the comparison across the boundary. It is possible that this method has resulted in a longer average boundary contact in the comparisons within than in the comparisons across the state lines. This might be true especially where a high degree of geometrical regularity in the shape and size of counties exists, as in the counties on the Minnesota border of Iowa.

While it was thought that the general irregularity of county boundaries was sufficient to neutralize such a tendency, it nevertheless seemed desirable to pay attention to differences across state lines in relation to differences between border counties and those in the "next tier back." [16] Such comparisons were made in the case of both "artificial" and "natural" boundaries.[17] It is by no means clear which of the modes of comparing interstate with intrastate differences between adjacent counties is the more satisfactory. In the case of natural state boundaries the use of first and second tier counties for the intrastate comparisons increases the average excess of the interstate comparisons from 0.77 ranks to 0.96 ranks, an increase amounting to about one per cent of the entire vote for president. In the case of the artificial state boundaries, on the other hand, this average excess is decreased from 0.91 ranks to 0.75 ranks. If the distinction between natural and artificial boundaries be dropped, and the comparisons of Table 14 aggregated with those of Table 15, we have:

Across state boundaries: Comparisons, 202: Av. difference in rank, 2.58
Within states: Comparisons, 728: Av. difference in rank, 1.72
                                        Excess   .86

Similarly, when the "second tier" type of comparisons are

[16] I.e., between the border county and those which lay adjacent to it but in an opposite direction from the border state. If all counties were rectangular and equal in shape we could refer to this last comparison as one between the first and second tiers of counties next to the border, and for convenience they are so termed. Objective criteria for defining the "second tier" were impossible and much arbitrary classification was required. In a number of cases no comparison could be made because of extreme irregularities in size and shape.

[17] The detailed tables of the second set of comparisons appear in the paper already referred to, Note 11 page 136.

aggregated for both "natural" and "artificial" boundaries we have:

Across state boundaries: Comparisons, 186: Av. difference in rank, 2.52
Within states: Comparisons, 317: Av. difference in rank, 1.70
                                         Excess   .82

The preceding data indicate that in those northwestern states where the La Follette candidacy received its chief support, *differences in the votes of adjacent counties were more marked where state boundaries intervened than where this was not the case, to an average extent greater than four per cent of the total vote for president.* The average difference was from forty-eight to fifty per cent greater in the former case as compared with the latter.

Let us next proceed to check the assumption that economic factors will promote or retard the diffusion of attitudes. For this purpose, "retail shopping areas" compiled by the J. Walter Thompson Co., and consisting with a few exceptions of aggregates of one or more undivided counties, have been regarded as units within which a degree of economic homogeneity might be presumed to exist.[18]   No effort has been made to ascertain whether this homogeneity is in the nature of common economic interests. It is clear, however, that there will be within each such area a relatively large number of economic contacts, as represented by the tendency of retail purchasers to trade at a common center.[19]   Within the northwestern mountain and Pacific states to which attention has previously been directed, a number of shopping

---

[18] *Population and Its Distribution*, The J. Walter Thompson Co., 4th ed., 1926, Part IV. No attempt is made here to criticize the districts as presented, although some of them are probably unsuited to the present purpose, or to the purpose for which they are designed. *Cf.* the writer's note on this book, *Political Science Quarterly*, June 1927.

[19] *Cf.* my article on "Political Attitudes as Elements of Culture Diffusion," op. cit. It is there argued that diffusion of attitudes may be considerably dependent upon face-to-face contacts.

areas are composed of four or more counties in two or more states, and these have been selected for analysis. They are as follows:

Grand Forks, N. D.	(N. D., 5	counties:	Minn., 7	counties)		
Fargo, N. D.	(N. D., 6	"	: Minn., 3	"	)	
St. Paul, Minn.	(Minn., 4	"	: Wis., 5	"	)	
Sioux Falls, S. D.	(S. D., 15	"	: Minn., 4	"	)	
Lead, S. D.	(S. D., 3	"	: Wyo., 1	"	)	
Dubuque, Iowa	(Iowa 8	"	: Ill., 1	"	; Wis., 2	counties)
Burlington, Iowa	(Iowa, 3	"	: Ill., 1	"	)	
Sioux City, Iowa	(Iowa, 15	"	: S. D., 10	"	; Nebr. 19	counties)
St. Joseph, Mo.	(Mo., 4	"	: Kans., 2	"	)	
Spokane, Wash.	(Wash., 14	"	: Ida., 4	"	; Mont. 4	counties)
Boise, Ida.	(Ida., 9	"	: Ore., 2	"	)	
Ogden, Utah	(Utah, 4	"	: Wyo., 2	"	)	
Pocatello, Ida.	(Ida., 16	"	: Wyo., 2	"	)	
Portland, Ore.	(Ore., 10	"	: Wash., 4	"	)	

The size and arrangement of these shopping areas is such that it would be difficult to take account in any systematic fashion of the factor of adjacency as defined in preceding pages. The problem has been attacked as if all counties within a given shopping area were adjacent to each other. The only variable factor dealt with has been that of the state boundary, or boundaries, dividing the counties into two or more groups. One aim, then, is to ascertain whether differences in rank among these counties are affected by the state boundaries which separate them. Another aim is to learn whether differences in rank are greater or less than would be expected according to some criterion of chance difference. Chance difference is regarded as that which existed between counties under similar relationship with respect to state boundaries but which are not affected by inclusion in the same shopping area.

Inasmuch as the factor of adjacency is neglected, the

expression "differences in rank among these counties" in the preceding paragraph refers in the case of a given grouping to all possible combinations of counties, taken two at a time. The mean difference in rank between each county and every other has been calculated.[20] That is, the unit is a *comparison between two counties,* and the differences in rank found in these comparisons have been averaged. For some purposes, the mean difference between the single county containing the trading center and other counties in the shopping area has been determined. The averages in both cases have been treated as comparable with each other, and with the average differences in rank ascertained above between adjacent counties.

Table 16 is presented with reference to the first aim. I.e., are differences in rank within shopping areas affected by the presence of state boundaries? For each shopping area, the possible comparisons have been segregated into two classes. In columns B and C the number of comparisons and the

[20] The number of combinations of n things taken r at a time is usually expressed by the following formula:

$$C_{nr} = \frac{n(n-1)(n-2) \ldots (n-r+1)}{r!}$$

in which $r!$ represents factorial r or $(1 \times 2 \times 3 \ldots r)$. Readers who are familiar with the enormous number of possible combinations among a relatively small number of cases may assume that the task as stated in the text would be an insuperable one. However, when n is large and $r = 2$, C is relatively much smaller than when r takes higher values. Thus Minnesota has 87 counties. The number of possible comparisons of rank among them taken two at a time is found by substitution in the above formula as follows:

$$C_{87.2} = \frac{87 \cdot 86}{1 \cdot 2} = 3,741$$

The calculation of differences in rank in such a number of combinations is not difficult when advantage is taken of the fact that these counties have been arranged in a frequency distribution, and hence may be compared by whole classes at one time. In practice, two computing machines were employed simultaneously, one for the calculation of products and the other for summation. The whole task is not unlike that of totaling product-moments in a correlation table.

average differences in rank pertain to counties which (in the case of each comparison) are separated by a state boundary. In columns E and F, the comparisons pertain in each case to a pair of counties within the same state. For any given shopping area, the entries in columns B and E, when totaled, represent the possible number of combinations, two at a time, between the counties in the area. When counties in three states are involved, the interstate comparisons are shown in three lines and the area total given in a fourth. Columns G and H indicate whether, in the case of a particular set of comparisons, the interstate differences have a higher (+) or a lower (−) average than the state differences. All interstate and intrastate comparisons are aggregated in the final line of the table, with the average difference for each aggregate.

Table 16 indicates that within the shopping district there is a slightly greater average difference between the counties in different states (2.25) than between those in the same states (2.04). The difference is about one per cent of the aggregate presidential vote. Apart from the question of state boundaries, such a result would be expected, for the counties in the first case are on the average at a greater distance from each other than in the second case.

By comparing the summary on page 143 and the summary line of Table 16 it will be seen that there is less interstate difference among the counties of shopping areas (2.25) than among counties opposite each other across state boundaries in general (2.58). This difference is equivalent to 1.65 per cent of the aggregate presidential vote. Again the factor of adjacency, which has been neglected, would operate to produce a contrary result. That is, in the case of the shopping areas many of the counties compared are at considerable distance from each other. Other things being equal,

Table 16 — Mean Differences in "Rank" (in Percentage of La Follette Votes) Among Counties of Interstate "Shopping Areas"
(Mean differences across state boundaries are compared with corresponding
differences among counties of the area which are comprised entirely within
the state indicated.)

Comparisons Across Boundary			Comparisons Within State			Excess of Interstate Dif. (C – F)	
Shopping Area	Number	Mean Difference	State	Number	Mean Difference	+	–
A	B	C	D	E	F	G	H
St. Paul	20	2.25	Minn.	6	1.50	0.75	
			Wis.	10	2.20	0.05	
Grand Forks	35	4.37	N.D.	10	1.20	3.17	
			Minn.	21	1.14	3.23	
Fargo	18	1.78	N.D.	15	2.60		0.82
			Minn.	3	1.00	0.78	
Sioux Falls	60	2.18	S.D.	105	2.44		0.26
			Minn.	6	0.50	1.68	
Lead	3	1.00	S.D.	3	2.00		1.00
Dubuque							
(Ia.-Ill.)	8	1.62	Ia.	28	2.11		
(Ia.-Wis.)	16	2.25	Wis.	1	2.00		
(Wis.-Ill.)	2	2.00	Ill.	0			
(Area Total)	26	2.04		29	2.10		0.06
Burlington	3	3.00	Ia.	3	1.33	1.67	
			Ill.	0			
Sioux City							
(Ia.-S.D.)	150	2.11	Ia.	105	1.65		
(Ia.-Neb.)	285	1.86	Neb.	171	2.10		
(S.D.-Neb.)	190	2.56	S.D.	45	2.55		
(Area total)	625	2.14		321	2.02	0.12	
Spokane							
(Wn.-Ida.)	56	1.82	Wash.	91	2.55		
(Wn.-Mt.)	56	2.68	Ida.	6	1.17		
(Mt.-Ida.)	16	2.12	Mont.	6	3.50		
(Area Total)	128	2.23		103	2.52		0.29
St. Joseph	8	0.75	Mo.	6	0.50	0.25	
			Kans.	1	0.00	0.75	
Boise	18	3.72	Ida.	36	1.00	2.72	
			Ore.	1	1.00	2.72	
Ogden	8	5.25	Utah	6	3.16	2.09	
			Wyo.	1	1.00	4.25	
Pocatello	32	2.62	Ida.	120	2.07	0.55	
			Wyo.	1	4.00		1.38
Portland	40	1.40	Ore.	45	2.04		0.64
			Wn.	6	0.00	1.40	
Summary	1024	2.25		858	2.04	0.21	

they would be expected to show larger differences than between counties sharing the same boundary.

At first glance, the inference would seem to be warranted, then, that state boundaries are of less significance as barriers to the diffusion of political attitudes when the counties concerned are in the same shopping area. While suggested by the data, this conclusion is, nevertheless, hazardous, because of the possibility that a disproportionately large number of interstate shopping districts fall within regions of comparatively low difference between counties. Moreover, it will be observed that there is greater intrastate difference among the counties of shopping areas (2.04) than between intrastate adjacent border counties in general (1.72). A possible explanation of this fact is to be found in the factor of adjacency, already dwelt upon, which operates in the case of the latter.

Table 17 presents an arrangement of comparisons similar to that of Table 16. In this case, however, all possible comparisons between counties in the shopping area and the single county containing the trading center are included. The number of comparisons is necessarily much reduced.

When compared with Table 16, the summary line in Table 17 shows tendencies in the anticipated direction. The average differences between the county containing the trading center and other counties of the shopping area are less than the corresponding differences between these counties when all are compared together. This is true both for interstate comparisons (2.15:2.25) and for intrastate comparisons (1.81:2.04). This suggests that the counties containing the trading center occupy a *mediate position* with reference to other counties of the respective areas. Moreover, the intrastate differences are less on the average by more than two per cent of the aggregate presidential vote than the average differences in general between adjacent counties on opposite sides of state boundaries (2.15:2.58, in terms of ranks of 5 per cent each).[21]

Another aspect of the general problem of diffusion of

TABLE 17 — MEAN DIFFERENCES IN "RANK" (IN PERCENTAGE OF LA FOLLETTE VOTES) BETWEEN COUNTY CONTAINING TRADING CENTER OF INTERSTATE "SHOPPING AREA" AND OTHER COUNTIES OF THE SAME AREA WITHIN AND WITHOUT THE SAME STATE.

Shopping Area	Comparisons with Counties in other States			Comparisons with Counties in Same State as Trading Center		
	State	Number of Comparisons	Mean Difference	State	Number of Comparisons	Mean Difference
St. Paul	Wis.	5	2.40	Minn.	3	1.00
Grand Forks	Minn.	7	5.43	N.D.	4	1.25
Fargo	Minn.	3	4.33	N.D.	5	4.20
Sioux Falls	Minn.	4	2.75	S.D.	14	2.00
Lead	Wyo.	1	0.00	S.D.	2	3.00
Dubuque	Ill.	1	2.00	Iowa	7	2.14
	Wis.	2	1.00			
Burlington	Ill.	1	4.00	Iowa	2	1.50
Sioux City	S.D.	10	1.70	Iowa	14	1.21
	Neb.	19	1.58			
Spokane	Ida.	4	0.75	Wash.	13	1.69
	Mont.	4	2.25			
St. Joseph	Kans.	2	0.00	Mo	3	1.00
Boise	Ore.	2	3.50	Ida	8	0.75
Ogden	Wyo.	2	1.50	Utah	3	5.00
Pocatello	Wyo.	2	3.00	Ida.	15	1.80
Portland	Wash.	4	0.00	Ore.	9	1.56
Summary		73	2.15		102	1.81

[21] If the "rank" and percentage differences given here and elsewhere could be stated as a percentage of the La Follette vote they would of course appear more striking. They are stated in terms of the aggregate vote for president polled by the three leading candidates, because the proportion received by La Follette is itself variable — a ratio which differs for every county.

political attitudes concerns the part played by transportation and mail routes. As a working hypothesis it might be assumed that counties which are adjacent and served by the same line of railroad (so far as important centers of population in the respective counties are concerned) or which are similarly adjacent and connected by regular postal mail routes, would tend to differ less in the percentage of La Follette votes than would adjacent counties without such contacts. Back of the hypothesis is the supposition that mail and rail connections would bring about more frequent personal contacts and a greater opportunity for the diffusion of political attitudes.

In testing the hypothesis, a standard Rand-McNally commercial atlas of the United States was employed for the determination of railroad connections, mail routes, and population of communities. Intrastate comparisons of counties only were attempted. In six states, comparisons of all adjacent counties were made and the differences in rank were listed in one or another of three classes: (1) Comparisons in which mail or rail contacts between substantial parts of the population of both counties were clearly present; (2) comparisons in which such contacts were clearly absent; (3) doubtful cases. It was found impossible to make this classification in the other states studied for the reason that greater density of population had resulted in mail or rail contacts between practically all adjacent counties.[22]

Table 18 gives the result of the comparisons.

The average difference in rank is less between adjacent

---

[22] For the present purpose a slight modification in the criteria of adjacency was employed, as follows: when a mail or rail route led directly from a population center in one county to a population center in another county, a comparison was entered under class (1) even though territory in another county intervened, provided the two counties touched at a common point or a boundary of a length however short.

TABLE 18 — AVERAGE DIFFERENCES IN THE LA FOLLETTE VOTE BETWEEN
ADJACENT COUNTIES WITHIN STATES, CLASSIFIED ACCORDING TO THE PRES-
ENCE OR ABSENCE OF RAIL OR MAIL CONTACTS BETWEEN THE COUNTIES
COMPARED.

State	Contacts present		Contacts Absent		Contacts Doubtful	
	Number of Comparisons	Mean Difference	Number of Comparisons	Mean Difference	Number of Comparisons	Mean Difference
Wyo.	19	2.00	14	1.50	4	0.75
Mont.	51	1.94	45	2.42	8	2.12
N.D.	50	2.40	44	2.14	16	1.62
S.D.	79	1.68	46	2.37	18	2.39
Ida.	32	1.69	48	1.52	7	0.86
Wash.	42	1.43	36	1.80	4	1.50
Summary	273	1.85	233	2.02	57	1.77

counties having mail and rail contacts (1.85:2.02) than
between counties without such contacts. This result is in
the anticipated direction, but the difference is slight, amounting to less than one per cent of the total vote for president.

In Table 19 there are brought together all of the summary
data from the preceding paragraphs, together with certain
other comparisons including average differences among the
counties of all of the states for which complete data were
secured.

Another method of attack upon the general problem will
be indicated, although adequate results from its use cannot
be given here. If the hypothesis of culture areas of political
attitude be sound, there should be a demonstrable relationship between similarity of attitude and distance of separation.
This has already been touched upon on pages 147 and 149.
One illustration of the method can be given.

On the county outline map previously used, a dot was
placed by inspection at the geographical center of every

TABLE 19 — SUMMARY: NUMBER OF COMPARISONS AND AVERAGE DIFFERENCES IN RANK (IN PERCENTAGE OF LA FOLLETTE VOTES) AMONG COUNTIES IN VARIOUS RELATIONSHIPS

Basis of Comparison	Number of Comparisons	Average Difference
Minnesota — all counties	3741	1.97
Wisconsin — " "	2485	2.33
Montana — " "	1485	2.58
Idaho — " "	946	1.79
Michigan — " "	3403	1.47
N. Dakota — " "	1378	2.54
S. Dakota — " "	2278	2.05
Iowa — " "	4851	2.15
Nebraska — " "	4278	2.31
Wyoming — " "	253	1.92
Washington — " "	741	2.13
Summary — All counties within each of 11 states	25839	2.10
Minnesota-Wisconsin, across border	6177	2.69
Adjacent counties — across state boundary	202	2.58
Adjacent border counties — within state	728	1.72
Shopping areas — all comparisons across state boundary	1024	2.25
Shopping areas — all comparisons within state	858	2.04
Shopping areas — trading center with counties across state boundary	73	2.15
Shopping areas — trading center with counties in same state	102	1.81
Mail & Rail contacts, adjacent counties in six states: Contacts present	273	1.85
Do: Contacts absent	233	2.02
Do: Contacts doubtful	57	1.77

county in North Dakota. Employing the county of maximum percentage of La Follette votes as a center, the distance between the center of this county and the center of every

other county in the state was measured.[23]   At the same time,
the difference in rank between the two counties was noted,
and the two series thus established were correlated. By the
standard Pearson formula, the coeffecient of correlation
obtained was

$$r = .549 \pm .066$$

This indicates clearly that so far as the vote for La Follette
in this particular election in North Dakota was concerned,
there was a high and negative relationship between La Follette
"strength" and distance from the center of his strongest
support. As far as this goes it supports the culture area
hypothesis. But it is not clear what influence economic
and cultural differences between different sections of the
state may have in producing the result, and the next step
would be to determine the corresponding degree of relationship with respect to some of these other factors.

The argument and conclusions of this chapter may be
briefly recapitulated. Certain comparisons among state
election returns in the Middle West showed the need of a
broader generalization than any which had been developed
in connection with individual states, to account for certain
regional distributions of attitude density, and to subsume
otherwise contradictory evidence. This led to an hypothesis
that political attitudes could be regarded as elements of culture
and that they developed the phenomena of *culture areas* and
culture diffusion. The hypothesis seemed useful in inter-
preting the particular midwestern situations that had been
disclosed. Subsequent efforts to subject the hypothesis to
inductive verification warrant the following conclusions:

  1. The hypothesis of culture areas of political attitudes

[23] Since relative distances only were desired, the distances as given in
millimeters on a ruler were employed. These could if desired be translated
into actual miles.

has strong *a priori* support and is consistent with the data assembled, but has not yet been established empirically.

2. The present data point toward the existence of four relationships with reference to the distribution of the La Follette vote in the election of 1924. These bear upon the hypothesis:

(*a*) State boundaries interpose a real barrier to similarity in the vote (i.e., to diffusion of attitude) within contiguous areas.

(*b*) The influence of state boundaries is reduced within areas in which retail shopping relationships prevail with reference to a common trading center.

(*c*) There is slight indication that diffusion may be furthered by the presence of regular lines of rail or mail communication.

(*d*) Analysis in one state indicates lessening intensity of La Follette support as the distance from a center of La Follette "strength" increases.

In a word, the most that I can claim is that the hypothesis still promises to be fruitful, and that it merits much further inductive efforts at verification.

XI

Stability of Regional Differences in Political Attitude [1]

Everyone is familiar with the tendency of political attitudes of a given nature to wax and wane. American history is replete with illustrations of the rise and decline of political movements. Translating this expression into the terms used in Chapter VIII, the tendency may be described as the rise and decline in *density* of political attitudes. For example, the density of the pre-war "insurgent" attitudes seemed to reach a maximum with the Rooseveltian progressive movement of 1912. Post-war reaction appears to have reached its climax with the Harding "sweep" or "landslide" of 1920. Some of these variations in point of *time* will be analyzed in the chapters of Part VI.

The question for consideration in this chapter concerns the *location of these changes* in density. Does the change take place proportionately among all portions of the voting population, or is it "spotted"? *What, in other words, is the stability of the distribution pattern of attitudes?* For a statistical answer to this question it is necessary to find for some constant collection of political sub-divisions two or more elections at different times in which there was an occasion for approximately similar attitudes to find expression. Such a situation, with the backgrounds and general characteristics

[1] Much of the material in this chapter was originally gathered for a paper read at the semi-centennial meeting of the National Conference of Social Work, Washington, D. C., May 16–23, 1923. A synopsis of this paper appears in the *Proceedings*, pp. 508–510.

of which I had some personal familiarity, was presented in a series of popular elections and initiative and referendum votes in the state of Washington in the years from 1914 to 1920 inclusive.

The outstanding characteristic of the state of Washington is its division into two contrasted geographical areas. The state is cut from north to south by the Cascade Mountains which condense the moisture from trade winds warmed by contact with the Japan Current and precipitate it over the western third of the state. As a result western Washington is humid, heavily timbered and dependent upon the lumber industry for its main source of support. This fact, in conjunction with its harbors and fishing interests, has given it a thorough industrial and urban character. Farms must usually be cleared of stumps at heavy expense and in consequence are small. Eastern Washington comprises two-thirds of the state. Deprived of moisture it has but one-third of the population and is largely rural and agricultural. Farms here, except in the irrigated valleys, are large. These differences of physiographical character are reflected in political behavior.

Washington adopted its initiative and referendum amendment in 1912, at the "peak" of the movement. The legislature of 1913 provided the necessary legislation to carry the amendment into effect. It was not until the general election of 1914 that the first measures under the amendment could go before the voters at the polls. In other words, Washington's experience with the referendum started at the precise time that general public interest in it began to decline in the country at large.[2]

Forty-six initiative measures were filed with the Secretary of State at Olympia prior to 1923. In the case of about

[2] *Cf.* Chapter XVII.

two-thirds of these, no petitions were presented, and only eleven actually found a place on the ballot, of which three only were adopted. Sixteen referendum measures were voted upon, of which two only were adopted. The voters of Washington, that is, turned down twenty-two of the twenty-seven measures upon which they voted, sixteen of these measures having been originally passed by the legislature, and eleven having been initiated by some group of voters. We might epitomize this experience by saying that the initiative seldom won and the referendum seldom lost. The attitude of the voters might thus be regarded as one of *laissez faire*, as protest against legislation *per se*. The character of the five measures that were approved, on the other hand, indicated a tendency to approve state interference in certain matters. These measures were: a state wide prohibition law, a stringent "bone dry" enforcement act, a law abolishing commercial employment agencies, the repeal of an onerous poll tax law, and a soldiers' bonus measure.

Of the twenty-seven measures voted upon, there were a number which would be classified as labor legislation. These included a measure calling for a legal eight-hour day, another which represented the demands of organized labor for the legal abolition of private employment offices, and a third which would have abolished a poll tax which was especially odious to radical and labor groups. In addition there were five measures which might be construed as "social legislation" in a moderately strict sense. These were, first and second, the prohibition and "bone dry" acts referred to; third, an act creating a teachers' retirement fund; fourth, the so-called "School Medical Inspection" measure; fifth the "30–10" measure, providing increased state support for public schools.

Several of the initiative and referendum measures, then, seem to provide an excellent index of political attitudes upon a variety of "labor" and "social" legislative proposals. Attention may now be turned to an election in which some of these same attitudes appear to be expressed.

In November, 1920, the Farmer-Labor Party of Washington, formed jointly by a number of economic and political organizations, including the State Federation of Labor, the Nonpartisan League and the Committee of Forty-Eight, and informally supported by the Socialist Party organization, made a serious effort to capture control of the state government.[3] While affiliated with the national party of the same name, little attention was paid to the latter or its candidates. Mr. Robert Bridges,[4] former chairman of the Port of Seattle Commission, as the Farmer-Labor Party candidate for governor received 35.7 per cent of the votes in the nineteen counties of western Washington and 19.6 per cent only of the votes in the twenty counties of eastern Washington.

There are thirty-nine counties in the state of Washington. For each the percentage of the total vote cast for Bridges in this election and the percentage of the vote cast for the several initiative and referendum measures among those voting upon each have been calculated. The counties have then been *ranked* according to these percentages, and according to a variety of other social data recorded for each in the United States Census of 1920. By correlating these several series together in pairs according to rank, inferences may be drawn (1) as to the character of the support given the measures enumerated; (2) as to the stability of the distri-

[3] For a concise and accurate historical summary of the Farmer-Labor Party's activities in the state of Washington from 1920 to 1922, *cf.* article by John C. Kennedy (secretary of the state party organization) in the *American Labor Monthly*, June, 1923, entitled "The Outlook for a Labor Party."
[4] Now deceased.

bution pattern.[5] A very large number of possible paired correlations might be calculated. A few of these only are presented in Table 20.

It should be noted that the number of votes received, whether large or small in the aggregate, is disregarded by the method according to which the coefficients in Table 20 were obtained. The results merely enable us to say whether a given measure tends to be relatively strong or relatively weak in the counties where another measure or characteristic is relatively strong. We find, for example, a high negative correlation between the order of support given to prohibition and the order of support given to measures sponsored by organized labor. This means that where prohibition sentiment was relatively strong, labor sentiment was relatively weak, and *vice versa*.

It is interesting to note that prohibition was originally adopted by the vote of the conservative eastern section of the state, and against the majority vote of western Washington. The negative correlation of −.39 between the order of support given to a radical Eight Hour Day measure in 1914, and the order of support given to prohibition on the same ballot, is some indication of the opposition originally shown toward prohibition by labor and radical interests generally.

An interesting shift of public opinion on this question is

[5] The formula used was derived by Karl Pearson, and is explained in most of the elementary textbooks on statistical methods, in particular by Harold O. Rugg, "Statistical Methods Applied to Education," pp. 286–289. Rugg's Table VII for r, given ρ (rho), has been used by the present writer in the formula

$$r = 2 \sin \left(\frac{\pi}{6} \rho \right) \text{ where}$$

$$\rho = 1 - \frac{6 \, \mathrm{S} \, \mathrm{D}^2}{\mathrm{N}(\mathrm{N}^2 - 1)}$$

No *probable error* is ascertained by this method.

TABLE 20 — CORRELATIONS BY GRADES BETWEEN CERTAIN VOTES AND CERTAIN POPULATION CHARACTERISTICS ACCORDING TO THE CENSUS OF 1920 IN THE 39 COUNTIES OF WASHINGTON

Vote: Prohibition, 1914, & Vote: Teachers' Retirement, 1914   −.51
  "   "   " & " Eight Hour Bill, 1914, promoted
                              by Socialist group   −.39
  "   "   " & " "Bone Dry" Bill, 1918   .08
  "   "   " & " Bridges, radical Farmer-Labor
                              Party candidate for governor, 1920 −.28
  "   "   " & Rank of counties in order of pop.   .13
  "   "   " & Proportion of farmers to total population, .33
  "   "   " & Value of farm property per farmer   .46

Vote: "Bone Dry" 1918 & Vote: Eight Hour Bill, 1914   .05
  "   "   "   " & Rapidity of decennial population increase
                              1910–1920.   .11

Vote: Teachers' Retire- & Anti-employment office bill, 1914 (Federa-
  ment, 1918   tion of Labor measure)   .66

Vote: School Medical
      Inspection, 1922 & Vote: Prohibition, 1914   .09
  "   "   " & " "Bone Dry," 1918   −.35
  "   "   " & " Bridges, radical, 1920   .385
  "   "   " & " Repeal of poll tax, especially
                              odious to labor and radical
                              groups, 1922   .29
  "   "   " & Rank of counties in order of population −.15
  "   "   " & Rapidity of population increase, 1910–1920 .28
  "   "   " & Proportion of farmers to total population −.30
  "   "   " & Value of farm property per farmer   −.43

Vote: "30–10" School
      Act,   1922 & Vote: Teachers' Retirement, 1914   .57
  "   "   " & Vote: Bridges, radical, 1920   .68
  "   "   " & Proportion of farmers to total population −.55
  "   "   " & Value of farms per farmer, 1920   −.59

Vote: Bridges, radical
      1920   & Vote: Eight Hour bill, 1914   .80
  "   "   " & Rapidity of population increase 1910–1920 .57
  "   "   " & Proportion of farmers to total population, −.37
  "   "   " & Value of farm property per farmer, 1920   −.55

Vote: Anti-employment office bill, promoted by State Federation of
      Labor, 1914, and Eight Hour bill, promoted by Socialists, repudi-
      ated by Federation of Labor leaders, 1914   .80

disclosed, however, by the vote four years later on a stringent "Bone Dry" Act. Not only is there no significant
correlation between the vote for the prohibition law and
that for the "Bone Dry" act, but the negative correlation
between "dry" sentiment and labor sentiment had in 1918
disappeared. There had been little shift between counties
in the relative strength of labor and radical sentiment during
these same years, for we find the high positive correlation of
.80 between the Eight Hour vote of 1914 and the Farmer-
Labor Party vote of 1920. Hence the statistical evidence
substantiates the common opinion that Washington labor
ceased its opposition to prohibition in the years immediately
after the law was adopted.

The Teachers' Retirement Act, passed by the legislature
in 1913, was beaten on referendum in 1914 by a vote of four
to one. Little effort was made in its behalf. The vote
indicates that what strength it had was drawn more largely
than elsewhere from the same counties that supported most
vigorously the victorious anti-employment office bill, fathered
by the State Federation of Labor, and sponsored by the
"Joint Legislative Committee" of the Federation, the
Grange, the Farmers' Union and the Direct Legislation
League. Opposition was greatest where the movement for
prohibition was strongest, i.e., in the rural counties.

The "School Medical Inspection" measure was passed by
the legislature of 1921 and came to popular referendum in
November 1922. Under its terms, parents or guardians in
first- or second-class cities might prevent the physical
examination of their children by filing an annual written
refusal of consent. If a contagious or infectious disease was
suspected in good faith by the school physician or nurse, the
child might be examined for this disease alone, sent home if
infected, and the parents notified. No form of vaccination

"or other medication" might be made a condition for entrance to the schools, either as pupil, teacher, or employee. An earlier law had provided that no child might be vaccinated "against the will" of its parents or guardian. The proposed law changed this provision to permit vaccination only with the "written consent" of parents or guardian.

This measure, when it was before the legislature, was commonly said to have the support of Christian Scientists. When it went to the referendum no arguments, either pro or con, were filed with the Secretary of State for circulation among the voters, although this is legally permissible and is usually resorted to. The measure is reported to have been opposed in the campaign by persons interested in public health, by various Protestant religious groups, and by some commercial bodies, among the latter being the Spokane Chamber of Commerce, whose trustees unanimously recorded their opposition. About 70,000 names were obtained on the referendum petitions, as compared with the 24,000 legally necessary. The measure was defeated by a vote of 156,000 to 97,000. Seventy and two-tenths per cent of the voters in eastern Washington and sixty-eight and five tenths per cent of the voters in western Washington opposed it.

The support for this measure tended to be stronger in those counties which have been increasing more rapidly in population, in which likewise the radical vote is heaviest. Opposition tended to be greatest in the prosperous rural counties, where the "dry" sentiment likewise finds its greatest strength.

The "30–10" school fund equalization measure, defeated in 1922 by a vote of three to two, had the endorsement of the state Parent-Teacher Association, the Washington Education Association, the State League of Women Voters, the State Federation of Women's Clubs, and the State

Federation of Labor. It proposed to raise by state taxation thirty dollars, and by counties an additional ten dollars a year, for each child of school age, the two funds to be apportioned to local districts maintaining school for at least 160 days, according to school attendance. It was estimated that the bill would have thrown about half of the cost of local schools upon the state. The measure was opposed by the State Federation of Taxpayers' Associations, a conservative organization formed ostensibly to reduce the tax burden.

An interesting aspect of the vote on this measure is that it received its heaviest support from the very counties which would be called upon, under the measure, to meet an increased burden of taxation. The rural counties, which would have benefited by its enactment, opposed the measure, on the whole, more than the industrial counties having a relatively heavy assessment roll. This appears to have been a case in which conservatism and caution outweighed in the minds of voters the dictates of enlightened self-interest.

Let us sum up the evidence as to the stability of regional patterns of attitude. There are two types of situation in this respect which stand out: (1) Assuming that the attitudes which led to a vote for prohibition in 1914 are similar to those which supported the "Bone Dry" measure in 1918 (an assumption supported by surrounding evidence), it is clear that an important change in the regional distribution of "dry" sentiment occurred between the two years named. Moreover, the direction of this change is indicated, and is again confirmed by the evidence accumulated in "common knowledge." *Between 1914 and 1918 the sentiment of organized labor in the state of Washington changed from "wet" to neutral or "dry."*

(2) The second type of situation is dissimilar, and perhaps more usual. This is indicated by the high positive correla-

tion (.80) with respect to the relative distribution of the labor vote in 1914 and in 1920. The size of the vote with reference to the total in either case is immaterial. *Where Labor's general attitudes were concerned, changes in the density of attitudes affected the entire state in a moving equilibrium.* Gains or losses were proportionately distributed. They were not "spotted."

Thus it appears that no single answer can be given to the question raised at the outset of this chapter. Changes in attitude are sometimes distributed evenly throughout an area or population, leaving the original distribution pattern of attitudes apparently unchanged. But at other times the attitudes characterizing particular parts of an area, or particular segments of its population may change, in a direction or at a rate which is not balanced by corresponding changes elsewhere. In the latter event, the distribution is altered, and a new configuration of social groupings, with respect to their attitudes, results.

XII

URBAN, VILLAGE, AND OPEN-COUNTRY DIFFERENCES IN
POLITICAL ATTITUDE, WITH SOME CONSIDERATION OF
ECONOMIC CLEAVAGES

It may be well at this point to re-state the plan upon which several of the preceding chapters have been organized. This may aid the reader in relating the present chapter to them and to those which follow. The term "distribution" was used in Chapters VI and VIII in its more common statistical sense. That is, in Chapter VI interest was centered upon the numbers of individuals or "frequencies" to be found at each successive point along a scale which represented the type, whether radical or conservative, or the intensity, of individual attitudes upon a given topic. When data were plotted, the base line (or X axis) was presumed to extend from the extreme of individual attitude in one direction to the opposite extreme in the other. The vertical plottings in each case showed the number of individuals holding the attitude represented on the base line scale. Thus we had a "frequency distribution." The same meaning was given the term "distribution" in Chapter VIII. The base line there extended from one extreme representing no votes (i.e., no attitudes) favorable to a candidate, to the opposite extreme representing all votes favorable to him. The items plotted were no longer individuals but electoral units, i.e., counties or election districts.

In the chapters beginning with Part IV, however, the concern is with distribution in a different and less statistical sense. The question might be asked in the form: how is the vote for a candidate or a cause divided among various discrete units of the electorate which may be distinguished? Or, still better, how do different groups within the electorate *differ* in their votes? In answering any such questions the technique of discovery will involve some form of *classification*. Theoretically the electorate might be divided up in a well-nigh infinite variety of ways. In reality narrow limits to inquiry are imposed by official modes of grouping, recording and reporting votes and voters, and by the possibilities of statistical analysis of records.

The present chapter deals with groups which have been segregated from the electorate according to two modes of classification. Primarily it is concerned with differences in the political attitudes of urban and rural voters, and between two fundamental sub-groups to be distinguished among the latter. In my own inquiries no systematic attention has been paid to attitude differentials along economic lines although these appeared to some extent in Chapter X. Charles A. Beard and Arthur N. Holcombe have shown some of the possibilities in this direction. Another important study was by Ogburn and Peterson.[1] However, some evidences of economic class distinctions are contained in the data of the present chapter and form the second mode of classification referred to. The following chapter deals with a number of other stratifications within the electorate.

Rural sociologists have frequently called attention to the inadequacy for purposes of social research of the distinction drawn by the United States Census Bureau between "urban" and "rural" territory. It is contended that within the category "rural," including as it does the residents of small incorporated places as well as the farming population, important differences in social and economic status are

[1] *Op. cit.*, p. 118.

TABLE 21 — VOTE OF HENRIK SHIPSTEAD IN MINNESOTA, 1920 AND 1922, BY
CERTAIN POPULATION UNITS INCLUDING FARMING AND WORKING-CLASS
AREAS [1]

Population Unit	Vote received as Independent candidate for Governor, 1920		Vote received as Farmer-Labor candidate for U. S. Senate, 1922	
	Number of votes cast	Per cent of total vote	Number of votes cast	Per cent of total vote
The State of Minnesota............	281,402	35.3	325,372	45.5
St. Louis County [2]...............	15,430	29.6	19,903	43.6
City of Duluth................	7,021	25.6	7,511	37.6
Towns and villages (iron ranges) .	8,409	34.1	12,392	48.2
Entire state except St. Louis County	265,972	35.7	305,469	45.7
"Urban" by Census definition...	98,974	32.0	121,740	44.2
Minneapolis [3]................	47,488	35.7 [3]	53,898	45.4
"Eight labor wards" [4].......	29,535	50.6 [3]	32,868	60.6
Minneapolis [3] and St. Paul....	71,442	35.4 [3]	81,120	46.1
Eleven "working-class" wards (among 25) in both cities [5].	33,758	50.7	35,265	63.3
7 cities, 10,000–25,000 population.................	7,496	22.9	10,580	42.1
14 cities, 5000–10,000 population.................	10,698	29.5	15,171	41.9
29 incorporated place of 2500–5000 population...........	9,338	24.2	14,869	39.2
"Rural" by Census definition: Incorporated places of 1000–2500 population [6]..........	12,362	19.1	19,873	32.0
"Rural" area outside of places of 1000–2500 population.....	154,636	41.6	163,856	49.4
40 counties wholly "Rural" by Census definition.........	76,223	38.6	86,054	47.0
Incorporated places of 1000–2500 population [7]........	7,043	18.8	12,271	32.7
Incorporated places of less than 1000 population [8]....	7,539	20.1	13,116	33.0
Area mainly unincorporated [9]	61,641	50.2	60,667	57.4

concealed. Striking confirmation of this contention was obtained in connection with the analyses of state election returns which have several times above been cited.[2]

In two states, Minnesota and Wisconsin, election returns were available on a precinct basis. This made it possible, with the aid of the Fourteenth Census, approximately to segregate the vote cast in all incorporated places of stated sizes, whether within or without "rural" territory, and also in the area outside of incorporated places. Some overlapping

[2] Especially Chapters VIII and X. The tables and some of the descriptive material concerning them in the present chapter are taken from my *Farmers and Workers in American Politics.*

[1] Sources: *Legislative Manual*, Minnesota, 1921 and 1923, General Election Returns; and *Fourteenth Census*, Population, vol. i.

[2] St. Louis County is separately classified for two reasons: (*a*) It contains the Mesabi and Vermillion Iron ranges, and hence, has a unique industrial character within the State; (*b*) Much of the iron areas are urban in character but unincorporated.

[3] The base used for Minneapolis in determining the percentage of the Shipstead vote in 1920 is the total vote for Governor, rather than the total number of ballots cast.

[4] The 1st, 2d, 6th, 7th, 9th, 10th, 11th and 12th. — so designated by John Lord, a writer in the *Minnesota Daily Star*, July 14, 1923, page 6. The 3d ward appears to be much better entitled to the designation than the 2d and may have been intended rather than the latter.

[5] The wards are those which (*a*) are below the mean of each city in the percentage of persons 16 and 17 years of age who are attending school, (*b*) are above the city mean in percentage of foreign-born white population, (*c*) are above the city mean in illiteracy. The 11 wards having these characteristics are as follows: St. Paul: 1st, 3d, 5th, 6th, 8th and 9th; Minneapolis: 1st, 3d, 9th, 10th and 11th. It will be observed that these wards in the aggregate gave a higher percentage of their votes to Shipstead in both elections than the "eight labor wards" of Minneapolis named by Mr. Lord.

[6] Numbering 100 in 1920 and 1922.

[7] Numbering 57 in 1920 and 1922.

[8] Numbering 192 in 1920 and 211 in 1922.

[9] In a number of cases, the vote of a village and its adjacent township were not separated. In these cases, the vote was included among that of incorporated places. On the other hand, a number of villages reported by the U. S. Census could not be found in the election reports, and their vote is undoubtedly included with that of the unincorporated area.

of precinct and village boundaries exists in both states. But for this fact the contrast between village and open-country attitudes which is here disclosed would no doubt appear even more striking.

As in Table 10, (page 127) the votes received by Henrik Shipstead for governor of Minnesota in 1920 and for United States senator in 1922 provide indexes of the attitudes which were expressed in the Farmer-Labor Party of that period.

Table 21 exhibits significant differences in these attitudes as between country and village dwellers, and as between city working-class populations and other city dwellers as well. In both elections the farmers were *radical*. In 1920, in a three-cornered contest, half or more of their votes were cast for the radical candidate. On the other hand the small-town voters were highly *conservative*. In the same election, less than one-fifth of their votes were for this candidate. His vote within these "rural" villages, in fact, was pro-portionately less than in any grouping of incorporated places of larger size.

Mr. Shipstead's strongest support came from open-country farming areas and from working-class wards in the cities of St. Paul and Minneapolis. In the case of the latter a sharp difference of attitude between labor and non-labor wards is indicated. In the election of 1922, Shipstead obtained 60.6 per cent of the vote of eight labor wards in Minneapolis. In the remaining wards of the city he received but 32.8 per cent (not shown in the table). If it had been possible to make a segregation of wards in which persons of middle and upper economic status resided equally distinct with the localization of the eight labor wards, there is little doubt that an even sharper economic cleavage would have appeared.

In Wisconsin, the vote cast in the Republican primary of 1920 for John J. Blaine has served as an index of the atti-

tude sometimes termed "La Follette Republicanism." Mr.
Blaine at that time bore the endorsement of the late Robert
M. La Follette, the senior senator from Wisconsin, and also
that of the Nonpartisan League. He was the successful
candidate both in the primary and the general election.

It will be observed from this table that Mr. Blaine received his best support in unincorporated, that is in strictly
farming, areas; in the labor wards of Milwaukee; and in the
cities of from 25,000 to 50,000 population, a number of

TABLE 22 — VOTE OF JOHN J. BLAINE IN WISCONSIN REPUBLICAN PRIMARY,
1920, BY CERTAIN POPULATION UNITS INCLUDING FARMING AND WORKING-
CLASS AREAS [1]

Population Unit	Total vote for Republican Candidates	Vote for Blaine	
		Number	Percentage of total
State..................................	478,263	113,001	29.0
Unincorporated areas.....................	138,667	53,846	38.8
Incorporated places of less than 2500 population..............................	53,654	12,852	24.0
41 incorporated places of 2500 to 5000 population................................	30,143	6,687	22.2
20 incorporated places of 5000 to 10,000 population..............................	25,091	6,698	26.7
12 cities of 10,000 to 25,000 population......	35,083	8,568	24.4
7 cities of 25,000 to 50,000 population.......	44,322	14,978	33.8
Racine (population 58,593)................	9,115	1,344	14.7
Milwaukee............................	42,248	8,028	19.0
5 conservative Milwaukee wards (carried by McCoy, Democrat, in general election) [2]....	12,763	1,355	10.6
10 labor wards in Milwaukee (carried by Coleman, Socialist, in general election) [3]........	13,286	4,386	30.3

[1] Sources: *Wisconsin Blue Book*, 1921, "Election Statistics"; *Fourteenth Census*, Wisconsin, table 13.
[2] The 1st, 3d, 4th, 16th and 18th.
[3] The 7th, 9th, 10th, 11th, 12th, 14th, 20th, 21st, 24th and 25th.

which are highly industrial in character. It is probable that the percentage of votes received by Blaine in the labor wards of Milwaukee would have been higher but for the strength of the Socialist vote in these wards. These results show clearly that farmers and industrial workers tended to throw their votes to the same candidate.[3]

An additional comparison between urban and rural attitudes, based on election returns, was attempted in New York. No light has been thrown by the classifications made for that state upon differences which may exist along economic class lines. Nor has the element of party habit been eliminated in the differentials secured. They merely illustrate the contrast that exists between urban populations and rural with respect to the support given to one of the candidates of an established major party. The gubernatorial vote of 1920 has been selected for analysis. Election returns for that year are available from every city or town in the State.[4] In Table 23 I have segregated the vote polled by Alfred E. Smith, Democratic candidate for governor, in the case of each city of more than 100,000 population, for all other cities combined, for 233 towns containing one election district each and for 168 towns containing three election districts each. In each case the percentage of the total vote received by Smith has been calculated.

It is believed that 233 towns (townships) containing one election district each will contain a population made up preponderantly of farmers. The total vote for governor in 1920 equaled 28.5 per cent of the state's population. If

[3] While this was clearly the case in the Minnesota and Wisconsin elections cited in this chapter, the *general* tendency with regard to a majority of current political issues was elsewhere shown to be opposite in character. That is, farmers and workers *tended* at this period to be in opposition (rather than in agreement) more frequently than their political affiliations would render probable. *Cf. Farmers and Workers in American Politics,* 1924.

[4] *New York Legislative Manual,* 1921.

the ratio of votes cast to population should be the same in these 233 towns, their population would average 982.[5] On the same basis the 168 towns containing three election districts each would average 2,935 inhabitants. The proportion of persons residing in villages within the one-precinct towns cannot be large. The three-precinct towns will contain a considerable proportion of persons who reside in small villages.

TABLE 23 — NUMBER OF VOTES CAST FOR ALFRED E. SMITH, DEMOCRATIC CANDIDATE FOR GOVERNOR OF NEW YORK, 1920, WITH PERCENTAGE OF TOTAL VOTES FOR GOVERNOR RECEIVED BY SMITH, BY VARIOUS POPULATION UNITS

Population Unit	Vote for Smith	Total vote for Governor	Smith vote as a percentage of total for Governor
The State..........................	1,261,812	2,962,645	42.6
New York City.....................	709,604	1,315,658	53.9
"Up-State" (outside New York City) ..	552,208	1,646,987	33.5
All "Up-State" cities...............	320,972	803,038	40.0
Cities of 100,000 or more population:			
Buffalo......................	55,629	135,630	41.0
Rochester....................	33,254	94,755	35.1
Syracuse.....................	23,016	64,102	35.9
Albany.......................	25,096	51,169	49.0
Yonkers......................	14,455	30,959	46.7
All other "Up-State" cities.........	169,522	426,421	39.8
All non-city "Up-State".............	231,236	843,949	27.4
168 towns with 3 election districts each	35,637	140,542	25.4
233 towns with 1 election district each	13,082	65,188	20.1

The above table indicates that the vote for Smith tended to vary directly with the size and urban character of the community. Generally speaking, his vote was relatively larger in the larger cities, smaller in the smaller communities, and

[5] They averaged 280 votes cast to the town.

least in highly rural or farming areas.   The result corresponds with the popular belief that the "up-state" farmers are overwhelmingly Republican and that the working classes in New York City, and to a lesser extent in the smaller cities, are largely Democratic in *state elections.*

An extensive study of votes cast in the presidential election of 1920 in each of the forty-eight states included for each a comparison between the most urban and most rural counties.[6] This led to several conclusions.   In all of the New England states, the Democratic vote was a city vote. For every Democratic voter in the least populous counties of Vermont and Massachusetts there were proportionately more than two in the counties which include Burlington and Boston.   But outside of New England, the larger cities of the country were *more strongly Republican* than the rural counties in their respective states.   Among eleven counties in as many states, each of which contained a city of 400,000 or more population, all but Suffolk County, Massachusetts, polled fewer Democratic votes, relatively, than the counties which were selected as representative of rural sentiment in the same states.

I do not know whether this was the situation in any national election other than that of 1920.   The conclusions seem to belie the general assumption that the south and the northern *cities* are the strongholds of the Democratic party. It may be that there is a general tendency in large cities of the north, as in Greater New York, for the electorate to be Democratic in local politics but Republican in national politics.   Certainly Philadelphia and Chicago would be exceptions even to such a rule.

The problem is interesting because of the further, seemingly antithetical, fact that *Republican strength in the South is*

[6] *Farmers and Workers in American Politics*, pp. 143–148.

rural. In 1920 Harding carried thirty-eight counties in the three southern states of Arkansas, Alabama and Georgia. Of these thirty-one, eighty-two per cent, were wholly rural. This may have represented nothing more than a survival of alignments from Civil War and Reconstruction periods.

If the Republican vote in the rural South does not represent a survival, but rather an entering wedge to the ultimate break-up of the solid Democracy of that region, the fact will tend to discredit an hypothesis advanced by the writer some three years ago which otherwise still seems promising, i.e., it may be that urban communities, admittedly more dynamic and more sensitive to currents of opinion than rural communities, tend to swing more strongly in any direction which public opinion in the nation as a whole is taking.[7] If this be the case, an explanation is found for the greater strength displayed by the Republican ticket of 1920 in the cities than in the rural counties. The nation as a whole expressed in the election of 1920 a strong reaction against the preceding Democratic administration. More facile, more easily swayed by newspaper headlines and the infectious sentiments of the crowd, the cities exhibited this reaction in its most acute form. According to the hypothesis, they would have exhibited equally well a marked shift of public opinion in any other direction. But the hypothesis is still awaiting verification by more extensive analyses of election material.

[7] *Cf.* Chapter XXII.

XIII

Sex, Religion, Nationality, Race, and Other Factors of Political Division

In a review of evidence concerning the use that had been made of the ballot by women in America, Malcolm M. Willey and I reached a conclusion that women tend "to give expression to the peculiar interests and responsibilities of their sex at the polls, although this expression is less marked than is frequently supposed. . . . Although women's attitudes in politics as expressed in their votes are not materially different from those of men, they do incline more strongly to the so-called 'moral' and 'civic' side of issues and react more vigorously against the radical." [1]

These assertions were based on evidence that was scanty in quantity but clear in implication. In a study by Ogburn and Goltra it was shown that women voters in Oregon, in comparison with men, "were more opposed to the eight-hour day for women, to a single tax, to proportional representation, to the abolition of the state senate, to extending certain functions of government, and perhaps to spending public money." [2] On April 1, 1919, the citizens of Chicago

---

[1] "American Women's Ineffective Use of the Vote," *Current History*, July, 1924. The *political* evidences presented here find additional support in the sex differences found by Allport and Hartman in their study of students' attitudes discussed in Chapter VI.

[2] "How Women Vote: A Study of an Election in Portland, Oregon," Ogburn, Wm. F. and Goltra, Inez, *Political Science Quarterly*, Vol. 34, pp. 413–433. The votes of women could not be distinguished from those of men, nor could women be *localized* in certain precincts by the methods of classification employed in the last chapter, and by Ogburn and Peterson in the article there cited. However, the women voters were more numerous proportionately in some precincts than others, and this permitted the use of the method of

passed on the following proposition: "Shall Chicago become antisaloon territory"? The effect would have been to wipe out saloons on May 1 instead of on June 30 of that year in accordance with the state prohibition law. The result was as follows: [3]

	Men	Women	Total
"Yes"	67,707	76,325	144,032
"No"	266,529	124,731	391,260
Total vote	334,236	201,056	535,292

Although the women who voted were almost two to one against ousting the saloons, the men's vote in the same direction was approximately four to one.

Another important collection of data on the matter was assembled by Miss Edith Abbott.[4] It was shown that the women's vote alone in the Chicago primaries of 1915 would have nominated Chief Justice Harry Olson of the Municipal Court for mayor. Judge Olson was the "good government" candidate, supported by various reform organizations. The women gave him a small plurality while the men gave a larger plurality to William Hale Thompson. Two aldermanic candidates of the "gray wolf" type were defeated by the women's votes. In twenty-five of the thirty-five wards in the city the women outdid the men in voting support of the "good government" candidates recommended by the Municipal Voters' League.

The data just cited have come from the two states of Oregon and Illinois. This is due to the unique fact that in Illinois the votes of men and women are separately recorded. The Ogburn-Goltra conclusions for the state of Oregon were

---

partial correlation for inferring their attitudes upon various referendum measures and upon presidential candidates in 1916.

[3] News despatch from Chicago in the *New York Times*, April 2, 1919, p. 1, col. 1. The Times erroneously commented, "In short, the women voted substantially as the men."

[4] *National Municipal Review*, Vol. 4, p. 437.

obtained only by the use of the complex statistical method of partial correlation. Moreover, in the Illinois data entirely and in the Oregon data mainly, the elections involved were state or local.

With respect to the attitude of women toward the presidential candidates in national elections, there are, so far as I have learned, but two bits of evidence available. Ogburn and Goltra found that "quite contrary to popular impression, the women of Portland seem to have voted more generally for Hughes and less generally for Wilson than men did." This refers to the election of 1916.

The second piece of evidence was discovered by Willey and myself. In some respects it seems so striking that it deserves considerable attention from those who are interested in the exact measurement of political phenomena.[5]

In the presidential election of 1920, Illinois was carried by the Republican party with an overwhelming majority. Of the men's votes for Harding and Cox combined, Harding received 71.4 per cent. Of the women voting for the two candidates, 74.6 per cent cast their ballots for Harding. Now the outstanding thing about the support given the Republican candidate by the women is not its proportionately greater extent in the state at large but the constancy with which the percentage of the Harding vote among the women exceeded the percentage of the Harding vote among the men in all parts of the state. The percentage of the combined Harding-Cox vote received by Harding was calculated in the case of each of the 102 counties in Illinois, and the city of Chicago. The percentages received by Harding varied from less than fifty per cent to more than ninety per cent. Yet the cor-

---

[5] This has been reported in a note, "A Sex Cleavage in the Presidential Election of 1920," by Malcolm M. Willey and Stuart A. Rice, *The Journal of the American Statistical Association*, Dec., 1924, pp. 519–520.

responding percentages of the women's votes and the men's votes, when correlated produced the remarkably high coefficient

$$r = .964 \pm .06$$

Class intervals of five per cent were employed in the calculation. Thus in every county in the state, with two exceptions (Union and Green Counties), the proportion of Harding votes among the women represented a slight but constant excess over the proportion of Harding votes among the men.

In the absence of conditions existing in every part of the state of Illinois and peculiar to it alone which might account for the high value of r — and no such conditions are known — it seems legitimate to conclude that there was a general tendency toward sex cleavage in the 1920 election. In other words, it may be inferred that women in general, at least in the northern states, were more strongly Republican than the men. The contrary assumption, that no such cleavage existed in states other than Illinois, necessitates the discovery of a factor or factors operating in all parts of that state and in that state alone to throw more women's votes to Harding. The fact that women are on the "moral" and conservative sides in local elections, combined with the circumstance that Harding of the two candidates was widely believed to be the more conservative and more "dry," together give this statistical conclusion additional weight. If differences between the votes of men and women in national elections are not generally large, then, it may be because in these the radical and "moral" issues are not sharply drawn as they frequently are in local campaigns.

With respect to religion, nationality and race, as factors involved in political cleavage, little quantitative investigation has been carried on, either by the writer or by others. They are introduced as topics here more by way of indicating their importance in a program of political research than for any exhibition of results.

It is probable that religious affiliations and beliefs have played a large part as group-forming influences in the electorate.[6] This is evidenced by the admitted difficulty of nominating a Roman Catholic as a presidential candidate, or for any important elective office in many states of the West and South. No Catholic has ever been president of the United States.[7]

The factor of religious affiliation is closely tied up with that of nationality. The prevailing tacit recognition of the unspoken but pervasive influence of either or both of these factors may be illustrated by a news article in the *New York Times* of October 8, 1922, signed by Ernest Harvier. The correspondent comments upon the nomination of John Burns and John Slattery as Democratic candidates in "the Methodist Belt" of New York state, composed of Columbia, Greene, Schoharie, Sullivan and Ulster counties. The reason for these nominations in this "dry, Wesleyan" area is characterised as "inscrutable" by Mr. Harvier, who adds:

[6] Professor Arthur N. Holcombe, whose book *The Political Parties of Today* more than any other exemplifies the growing tendency toward the use of quantitative methods in politics, says on page 36 of that work: "Religious issues have been kept out of national politics. No successful national politician has ever ventured to promise specially favorable treatment to the adherents of any particular religion in order to bring forward a new party or enhance the popularity of an old one. Although religious animosities have doubtless played some part in the development of the political movements which have been directed from time to time against particular classes of persons, especially against certain classes of alien immigrants, national politicians have been effectually restrained from organizing religious parties such as have existed, and still exist, in some of the principal foreign countries." But the religious factor has nevertheless been continually involved *sub rosa*, as an *underground* influence, and as such has perhaps been more important than if it had constituted a formal basis of party alignments.

[7] *Cf.* statement concerning religious affiliations of the presidents, *World Almanac*, 1927, p. 233.

"Why this year the Democrats of the Methodist Belt, so-called, have made nominations for the two most important local offices least likely to appeal to the sentiments of the great majority of their voters may be explained when the campaign is over. It is difficult to explain it before the campaign has begun." The surprise which is indicated by the correspondent is clearly based upon the (intimated) Irish nationality of the two candidates and the presumption of their Catholic faith.

Perhaps next to party, religion, economic status and the characteristics of urban or rural residence — or perhaps more than these — the practical politician takes into account nationality in his calculations. All of these factors are correlated and the importance of any one depends largely upon the type of issues which are uppermost in the minds of voters. In his study of *Social Cleavages in Texas* [8] W. J. McConnell found that German-Americans were "consistent in voting as a unit in state elections which involve the welfare or national inclinations of the Germans." An instance was in the case of prohibition. Upon this issue Germans in rural communities (as in Wisconsin) tend to unite with voters of the cities. Upon other questions they would stand with other rural dwellers against the cities.[9]

The fixity of political attitudes upon the negro's side of the color line in America has been traditional since the enactment of the Fifteenth Amendment. "Negro voter" has been well nigh synonymous with "Republican." Signs have increased in recent years that the growing strength of the

[8] *Columbia Studies in History, Economics and Public Law*, No. 265, 1925, p. 153 and *passim*.

[9] Another study in which statistical procedure was brought to bear upon the problem of determining political attitudes according to nationality was that by Abram Lipsky, "The Political Mind of Foreign-Born Americans," *Popular Science Monthly*, October 1914. It was held that "an election is a psychological experiment on a large scale."

colored vote in some of the northern cities has been forcing a revision of Democratic attitude toward the colored voters in these cities, with results that may ultimately extend into the solid South.   In the general election of November 2, 1926, the Nineteenth Assembly District of New York County, which includes a large part of the great colored district in Harlem, cast 6,435 votes for Alfred E. Smith, the Democratic candidate for governor, as compared with 4,758 for Ogden L. Mills, the Republican.   The Twenty-First district, which is likewise in large part colored, was carried by Smith with a similar majority.   The Democratic candidate for the Assembly in the latter district was elected by a small margin. The figures indicate that *a large proportion of the negroes voted the Democratic ticket*.[10]   Mr. Walter White, Assistant Secretary of the National Association for the Advancement of Colored People, has asserted in the press that a switch by Negro voters from Republican to Democratic candidates in a number of communities has resulted in the defeat of the former.   The voting habits of colored citizens in the North (where they are enfranchised) together with changes that may be going on with respect to racial cohesion and racial attitudes toward the various parties among these voters, offer a most interesting field for quantitative analysis.

There are numerous other respects in which biological, cultural, or geographical factors are correlated with political attitudes.   Several of these have been traced in North Dakota and Minnesota by George A. Lundberg.[11]   In

[10] By relating individual election districts (the smallest electoral units) to the "sanitary areas" into which New York is divided for census and other purposes, it would be possible to segregate a section of the vote of these two assembly districts which was almost wholly colored, and thereby ascertain its distribution with approximate precision. (*Statistical Sources for Demographic Studies of Greater New York*, 1920. Published by the New York City 1920 Census Committee, Inc., now the Cities Census Committee, Inc.)

[11] "The Demographic and Economic Basis of Political Radicalism and Conservatism," *American Journal of Sociology*, March 1927.

Nebraska, John D. Barnhart found political lines following the distribution of soil areas.[12]

In any particular political situation the various factors that are involved, together with the attitudes to which they are related, are likely to be confused and conflicting. Alignments built upon the basis of one factor are presently crossed by others as new factors rise to importance in the shifting scene. It is then remarked that politics makes strange bedfellows. A recent and somewhat picturesque illustration of a *confused realignment* of political "forces" appeared in the state of Washington following the election of Roland H. Hartley as the Republican governor in 1924. Controversies between the governor and his opponents, the latter including a majority in the Republican legislature, have occupied public attention in the Pacific Northwest since the simultaneous accession of Mr. Hartley to office and the convening of the biennial legislative session in his state in January, 1925. The aspects of these controversies which reached the attention of eastern newspaper readers consisted of "attacks" made by Mr. Hartley upon the administration of the state university and the eventual forced resignation of Dr. Henry Suzzallo, the president of that institution. However, there were other important interests and attitudes involved. At my request, Mr. George P. Stuart of Monroe, Washington, who was actively interested in the campaign undertaken by its alumni association to "protect" the university,[13] prepared the following chart of alignments which had arisen in response to the governor's program:

[12] "Rainfall and the Populist Party in Nebraska, "*American Political Science Review*, Vol. 19, 1925, pp. 527–540.

[13] A recall movement directed against the governor was initiated with the active support of the University alumni association. An insufficient number of signatures upon the recall petitions was obtained to bring the issue to popular vote.

Political Groupings

Governor Hartley's Executive Acts and Self-alleged Policies	Pro-Hartley	Anti-Hartley
A. — Against all land reclamation.	1. Actual "dirt" farmers. 2. Timber owners group.	Land speculators and promoters.
B. — Educational policy.	1. "Reactionaries," opposed to teaching political or social science. 2. The reactionary clergy. 3. Catholic Church.	1. University graduates largely. 2. Teachers in public schools. 3. Educators, modernists, etc.
C. — Good Roads Hampered.	1. Railroad Group. 2. "Reactionaries." 3. Farmers (because most roads have been tourist roads).	1. Chambers of Commerce. 2. Real Estate Promoters. 3. Stage Lines. 4. Labor Groups.
D. — Charity and Penal. (Against charitable institutions and all welfare work).	1. "Reactionaries." 2. "Conservatives." 3. Large tax-paying corporations. 4. Conservative farmers.	1. Welfare workers. 2. Lodge groups. 3. "Progressives."
E. — Against most state inspectional and regulatory services.	1. "Reactionaries." 2. Non-resident and large tax paying groups.	1. Farmers. 2. "Progressives." 3. Labor groups.
F. — Against Industrial Insurance and other Labor Regulations.	1. Loggers (operators). 2. Mill owners. 3. Manufacturers.	1. Labor groups. 2. "Progressives."

The striking things in this chart, apparent to anyone familiar with the preceding political history of the state are, first, the realignments which have occurred; second, the indications that certain groups, in particular the farmers, find themselves pro-Hartley upon some issues and anti-Hartley upon others. As to the first, conservative university graduates, prominent in the business and professional life of the Northwest, have found themselves working side by side in an anti-Hartley agitation with labor leaders at whom they had hitherto looked with distrust and enmity. Labor leaders have been aligned with Chambers of Commerce, their traditional enemies. "Dirt farmers" (who in western Washington have been radical, and who have affiliated with such movements as the Nonpartisan League) have been on the side of Hartley together with conservatives and reactionaries. Summing up the evidence concerning Mr. Hartley's political character, Mr. Stuart remarks "Classify him yourself. After all he seems to classify as a reactionary, although labelled revolutionary and radical."[14]

With respect to all such factors as have been mentioned in this chapter there is unlimited room for research, employing existing reports of election returns and official acts as material, using the basic method of classification, and devising innumerable correlations with other relevant social data. It was by such painstaking and minute studies that the natural sciences were built up.

[14] Some months after making this remark Mr. Stuart has again written me as follows, under date of Nov. 22, 1927: "The longer things go on, the more clear it seems that Hartley has fallen definitely into the reactionary fold, to which he holds with a fair degree of consistency. The Republican majority which has been against him has been the progressive wing, and they still wont play with him. The groups that naturally support a politican of this type have gravitated to his standard, with the exception of the farmers, who accept him in some of his measures and denounce him in others. This has been especially typified by the attitude of the State Grange, which kept its hands off in the recall because they loved him for his stand on irrigation although they were not in sympathy with his educational policy."

XIV

The "Representativeness" of Elected Representatives

Scientists are accustomed to using assumptions or *postulates*, unproven positions which are taken as the basis of a subsequent logical development of argument or proof. *If* such and such assumed conditions are true, *then* such and such conclusions will follow. It is impossible to avoid making assumptions, for no investigator could follow back to their beginnings and prove all of the premises of his work. The important thing is to recognize assumptions for what they are. Once an assumption has been made in the course of a scientific inquiry, however, the proof of the assumption may itself become an object of scientific investigation.

The present chapter is introduced at this point because it exhibits efforts to prove an assumption upon which chapters that follow are based. The studies that have preceded made use for the most part of *popular votes*, or *individual expressions of attitudes*, as the material upon which they worked. But the characteristics of our political system are such that a determination of most political questions is left to *representatives* of the public, elective or appointive, rather than to the direct decision of the voters themselves. The attitudes (or at least the votes) of these representatives are known upon a wide variety of issues. The attitudes of the individual voters upon most questions even when expressed in votes, are anonymous. If the attitudes of elected representatives, then, can be said to reflect the attitudes of those who elect or select them, it will be possible to make inferences concerning the latter from the former. The behavior and opinions of members of a legislative body, for example, are of interest in and of themselves; but they are of added if not greater interest if they can be used for the purpose of inferring something concerning the states of mind of the voters in the electorate.

The problem here set, therefore, is this: in what respects and to what extent are elected representatives *representative* of the voters who elect them? I am not attempting here to deal with the related question, important enough in its place, as to the representativeness of *selected* appointees. Nor am I able to give as yet a satisfactory answer to the problem stated. It is one that has received some recent attention from political scientists.[1] It is possible that the methods I have used in working upon the question may have some usefulness for them. Some *a priori* views upon the general topic of representation in the American political scheme will first of all be discussed. Next I will state the *a priori* position which has served as my own starting point for some of the work discussed in later chapters, followed by an exhibit of two attempts to verify my *a priori* assumptions.

A great deal has been written concerning the theory of representation. I am not prepared to review these theories and arguments systematically. What is said here will be by way of showing (1) that points of view other than my own are traditional in political science, and (2) the relationship of my own version of the problem to these other views.

It appears to me that the problem of representation has been set up in two characteristically different ways which tend to cross each other. Each of these offers contrasted

---

[1] At Round Tables of the National Conferences on the Science of Politics, and otherwise.

viewpoints. The first distinguishes what *ought* to be from what *is*. The second distinguishes the argument that relies upon metaphysical premises (as to what is or ought to be), from the argument that depends upon empirical evidence. Professor John W. Burgess wrote:

"The views of a constituency should always be taken into account as contributing to the make-up of the consciousness of the State, but the will of a constituency has no place in the modern system of legislative representation." [2]

This seems to be a statement of what ought to be, based upon metaphysical premises as to the nature of the state.

Professor Goodnow, in outlining the work of the American Political Science Association, then recently established, said:

"One of the peculiar developments of American political procedure has been the attempt to separate both in organization and action the sovereign state from the government. . . . Is a constitutional convention a representative of the sovereign people and are its enactments absolutely binding upon the courts, are questions which are not as yet answered, and to whose solution the Political Science Association may well be expected to contribute." [3]

Like the statement by Burgess, the words quoted imply a metaphysical state, and a metaphysical problem of representation. The difference appears to be that whereas the first is concerned with the question of *ought*, the second is dealing with the question of what *is* — if one may indeed speak of a metaphysical reality. The questions of Goodnow are potentially susceptible of an empirical answer, while the statement of Burgess could be established only by a prior postulation of ends.

[2] *Political Science and Comparative Constitutional Law*, vol. 2, p. 116 (1913).
[3] "The Work of the American Political Science Association," by Frank J. Goodnow, *Proceedings*, vol. I, 1904, p. 35.

A further stage in the direction of realism is illustrated in the following by Bruncken:

One of the things we have learned during that period (since Bentham) is that elected representatives may be very far from representing the true, deliberate will of their constituents. They may represent a passing phase of popular emotion or delusion. They may stand for nothing but the ambitions, legitimate or otherwise, of individuals. They may be the expression — some would say that they are normally the expression — of special social or economic interest, instead of the commonwealth, and especially of whatever special interest is at any time dominant in the nation.[4]

Mr. Bruncken approaches very close to the viewpoint of the present writer when he continues:

"In every man's nature there is this element of singularity in different proportions: one may assume that in any legislative body there is a greater proportion of it than would be found in an equal number of men taken at random from the outside public. For the very fact that they were elected to representative office shows that a certain element of personal superiority, of leadership, was somehow recognized in them by their constituents, and such superiority implies a degree of singularity. Yet the elements of singularity must not be too great, for people will not accept as leaders men whose characteristics are alien to the masses. It follows, therefore, that notwithstanding the influence of the individual singular ideas, the personnel of representative bodies and the product of their legislative activities mirrors with fair accuracy the present state of public consciousness, and so it remains true, notwithstanding the influence of the personal singularities, that the result of legislative work is, on the whole, determined by popular feeling."

There is here no question of *ought*, but only of what *is*.

---

[4] "Some Neglected Factors in Law-Making" by Ernest Bruncken, *American Political Science Review*, Vol. 8, 1919, p. 222 ff.

Finally the pluralists have come close to putting the value verdict of *ought* upon the realities as portrayed by Mr. Bruncken. Coker explains the position thus:

"The proponents of this idea argue that our present system of representation is based on the fallacious assumption that the common interests of citizens are their community interests, that economic and social needs and opinions vary primarily as we pass from region to region, and that, therefore, the just and logical plan of representation is the territorial system. They maintain that the present system is nonrepresentative and misrepresentative of the interests and views of the people. A territorial region, they hold, is never identified with a particular interest or opinion; each district is the habitation of groups of such various, conflicting economic and social needs and views that no clear mandate for the supposed representative can be fused out of them; so that what is really represented is simply one or few of the stronger among the numerous minority groups.[5]

My own *a priori* position approaches most nearly to that of Mr. Bruncken among the four that have been cited. It is concerned not with what *ought* to be in order to provide the best results in our governmental organization, but with what now *is*. It proceeds not from metaphysical premises as to the nature of the state and of government but from an empirical examination of actual social data. It may be stated as follows:[6]

The legislator is representative, first, because voters tend to select men of their own "kind" to office, even though the similarity in kind may be based in the voter's "identification" of himself with the social, economic, or intellectual

[5] Coker, Francis W. — "The Technique of the Pluralistic State," *American Political Science Review*, Vol. 15, 1921, p. 200.
[6] Reference will be made to the *legislator* because in this book it is this type of representative whose behavior has been studied in reference to the constituency.

attributes of the office-holder. The legislator is representative in a second sense, based upon the first, because he responds to legislative issues on the whole in about the same manner as would his fellow group-members in the constituency. However amenable to "influence" he may be, there is a constant "strain" in the legislator's behavior toward consistency with the *mores* of his various groups. In a sufficiently large number of cases this strain toward consistency with his social heritage is certain to affect any numerical indexes of the legislator's behavior that may be devised. Measurements of group behavior in a legislative body, therefore, may be regarded as indicative of the attitudes of corresponding groups in the electorate — farmer legislators of farmers, Catholic legislators of Catholics, etc.

These are the *a priori* assumptions. There are other respects in which we may be sure that the legislator is *not* representative: in wealth, usually; in ability, perhaps; in legal and political training certainly; and in education and intelligence we may doubtfully hope.[7]

The efforts to support these assumptions (which now become hypotheses) will be given in chronological order.[8]

---

[7] Throughout this chapter I am interested in evidences of representativeness in a *non-rational* sense, i.e., neglecting tendencies by a representative to favor interests within his district from motives that are rational and calculated as to expected effects. The distinction is implied in the following by A. Gordon Dewey ("On Methods in the Study of Politics," *Political Science Quarterly*, vol. 39, p. 222, June 1924). "In regard to votes by representatives from districts, we face a dilemma — rather academic it is true. By assuming strong locality allegiance, we may demonstrate the force of the local interests we have discovered; conversely, by assuming the force of such interests, we may prove the man a 'delegate,' not a 'representative.'"

[8] I wish to acknowledge assistance received from students in gathering the material for these two endeavors; as to the first, from Messrs. F. S. Wilder, R. B. Dwinell, S. G. Chamberlain, C. Blunt, F. B. Brown, B. D. Phillips, and R. W. Emes, at Dartmouth College. For the second, from Miss Marion Schmadel at the University of Pennsylvania, whose rôle has been that of a collaborator.

The first consisted in an attempt to correlate the "progressiveness" of Minnesota legislators with the "progressiveness" of their districts.

In connection with a class of eight students at Dartmouth College, a list of twenty questions was prepared, answers to which were deemed to be indicative of "conservative" or "progressive" attitudes. In part this was an adaptation of a questionnaire employed for a similar purpose with college students by a colleague of that time, President Henry T. Moore.[9] On each question agreement was reached by a number of judges including the class, myself, and several colleagues, as to the answer which would indicate "progressivism" of attitude. No effort was made to determine whether the same answer in each case would have been regarded as progressive in Minnesota, and this may be regarded as a weakness of the procedure. A copy of the questionnaire, which is here exhibited, was sent to each member of the House of Representatives of the state of Minnesota for the session of 1925, at his home address. An addressed and stamped return envelope was enclosed in each with a uniform covering letter.

The legislature of the state of Minnesota was selected for this experiment for several reasons. The state is one in which the issues between "conservatism" and "progressivism" or "radicalism" have been much discussed and between which lines have been closely drawn for a number of years. Moreover, it is the one state in the union known to me in which members of the legislature are elected without political party designation. A further reason of practical importance was that a sufficient number of representatives existed to give hope of statistical utilization of the replies.

[9] *Cf.* President Moore's pioneer and suggestive paper, "Innate Factors in Radicalism and Conservatism," *Journal of Abnormal Psychology and Social Psychology*, vol. 20, pp. 234–244, Oct. 1925.

Lastly, it was possible in most cases to classify popular votes upon a state-wide "progressive" candidacy according to representative districts.[10]

As an index of the density of "progressive" attitudes in each district, the percentage of the senatorial vote received by Magnus Johnson, the Farmer-Labor Party candidate in the general election of 1924 was taken. Thus each district could be rated in "progressiveness" according to its vote for Johnson, while its representative could be similarly rated according to his expression of views upon the questionnaire. The latter rating was purely an arithmetical matter. On each returned sheet the number of "progressive" answers was related as a percentage to the number of questions answered. This constituted the index of the member's progressivism.

Questionnaire sent to members of the Minnesota legislature, together with the answers, "Yes" or "No," which were deemed to be "progressive."

(NOTE: Questionnaires were coded in such a way that they could be related to the corresponding index for the member's district)

Do you in general approve of the following proposals, ideas or conditions? (Please record your answers as YES or NO.)

  1. The policy of isolation of the U. S. from European Affairs?   No.
  2. The restoration of diplomatic and trade relations with the present Russian Government?   Yes.
  3. The proposal to make war a violation of international law?   Yes.
  4. The idea of a federalized international government of the world, preserving, however, local self-government?   Yes.
  5. Government ownership of railroads?   Yes.
  6. Limiting the power of the Supreme Court over legislation?   Yes.
  7. A realignment of political parties upon economic lines, which would bring into existence a Labor Party?   Yes.
  8. Higher taxation than at present (proportionately) upon the wealthy classes?   Yes.
  9. The settlement of governmental questions, so far as possible, by direct vote of the people?   Yes.
 10. The principle of a minimum wage for male workers?   Yes.
 11. The increasing participation of employees in industrial management?   Yes.
 12. Discrimination in favor of immigrants from northern Europe?   No.

[10] The sources used were the Minnesota *Legislative Manual* for 1925, with some auxiliary aids, such as the *Fourteenth Census*.

13. The social intermingling of white and colored young people in schools and colleges? Yes.
14. The right of the state, in the interest of his own health or morals, to prevent an adult from engaging in any occupation? Yes.
15. The prohibition of commercial amusements on Sunday? No.
16. Giving to a child born out of wedlock the same legal status, including the rights of inheritance, as a child born legitimately? Yes.
17. Do you believe that the advantages of trade unionism outweigh its disadvantages? Yes.
18. Are you inclined to be prejudiced against any political candidate who has affiliations with large corporate interests? Yes.
19. Do you believe that poverty is a result primarily of the absence of opportunity, rather than the absence of native ability? Yes.
20. Are you in sympathy with the present-day attacks upon the doctrine of evolution? No.

Of 131 members addressed, 42 returned replies which permitted of rating. The correlation table upon which these ratings, with those of the corresponding districts, were thrown is shown in table 24.

TABLE 24 — CORRELATION TABLE, SHOWING DISTRIBUTION OF INDEXES OF "PROGRESSIVISM" OF 42 MEMBERS OF THE MINNESOTA HOUSE OF REPRESENTATIVES AND THEIR DISTRICTS, 1925.

Rating of District (Johnson vote — per cent)	Rating of legislator ("Progressive" replies as a percentage of all questions answered)								
	25 34	35 44	45 54	55 64	65 74	75 84	85 94	95 +	Total
10–19				1					1
20–29	1	3		1					5
30–39	1	3	1		1				6
40–49	1	2	5	4	1	2	2		17
50–59			1	2		2	3	1	9
60–69	2		1			1			4
Total	5	8	8	8	2	5	5	1	42

When correlated by the usual Pearsonian method we obtained the coefficient

$$r = .327 \pm .093$$

The result is certainly not very significant, but it is suggestive. The *indications* are that attitudes of "progressivism"
among Minnesota legislators tended to vary in accordance
with the density of whatever attitudes among their constituents led to votes for the senatorial candidate of the
Farmer-Labor Party.

The coefficient is perhaps as high as could be reasonably
expected, because it takes no account of the particular group
affiliations of the legislator and his constituents. For example,
it has been shown that sharp differences in attitude toward
a radical candidate existed between farmers and villagers
in the same state a few years earlier (Table 21). Every
legislative district in Minnesota, except those in the cities,
the Mesaba iron ranges in St. Louis County, and perhaps
in some of the timbered regions in the north, contains substantial proportions of *both* villagers and farmers. It would
not be expected, then, as Professor Coker has pointed out
(supra, p. 193), that a legislator could at the same time
reflect the contradictory attitudes of these two electoral
elements. A higher coefficient of correlation might be
expected if the varying progressivism of *village dwellers* in
the legislature could be related to the varying density of
progressivism of the villages in their respective districts;
and so on. This refinement of method would be complex,
but I think it is not impossible of execution. It would tell
more nearly what we really want to know, viz., whether
the social groups to which an individual belongs tend to
impose upon him patterns of attitudes which characterize
these groups, with an indelibility which finds expression in
his legislative behavior. If so, this would be representation,
it seems to me, in a genuine sense.

The social factor selected for attention in a second attack
upon the problem of representativeness was *nationality*.

The probable importance of this factor was pointed out in Chapter XIII. The question is this: do voters tend to select as representatives persons of their own nationality? If so, the nationality of legislators is one respect in which they might be said to have representativeness.

The results so far obtained are again tentative and inconclusive, but suggestive in their direction. The data ulitized consisted of the following: biographies of the members of the State Senate and House of Representatives in Minnesota for the sessions of 1919, 1921, 1923 and 1925, contained in the state's *Legislative Manuals;* biographies of members of both houses of the legislature of Wisconsin for the sessions of 1921 and 1925 contained in the respective numbers of the *Wisconsin Blue Book.* These were selected on the basis of availability; general familiarity with the social and political characteristics of the states named; and an arrangement of legislative districts, generally conforming to county lines, which made it possible to determine the composition of districts according to nationality as recorded for counties in the Fourteenth Census.[11]

By reading the biographies of all members in the sessions named, 107 individuals were found for whom there was definite evidence of birth in a particular foreign land. No account was taken in subsequent calculations of persons of known or obvious foreign descent but of native birth, because this introduced factors of uncertainty that could not be controlled. All doubtful cases were eliminated. Each member was counted but once, regardless of reëlections.[12]

[11] Vol. III, *State Sections for Minnesota and Wisconsin,* Tables 9–13, inclusive, in each.

[12] It could be contended that each member should be included as many times as he was elected to the sessions named. The opinions of the investigators were that a member once elected tends to find means of perpetuating himself in office, so that the fact of original election is the more indicative.

Electoral areas, on the other hand, might be duplicated in the sense that a senator and a representative from corresponding districts, identical in whole or part, might both be included; and in the further sense that more than one legislator of foreign birth might be selected from the same district for the same house during the periods covered, Instead of regarding such duplications as sources of error, it seemed to us proper that districts should be weighted in such ways as these to provide a partial means of overcoming the factor of chance in the determination of a legislator's nationality, a factor for which no formal allowance has been made.[13]

In the case of each foreign-born legislator, the percentage of the general population having his own nationality (foreign born) within his district was ascertained from the Fourteenth Census. This percentage may be called A. Similarly, the percentage of this nationality within the state at large was also determined. This second percentage may be called B. For each such legislator a ratio was then obtained by dividing percentage A by percentage B. That is, the proportion of the given nationality in the district was divided by the proportion of the same nationality within the state. It is evident that if this latter ratio is in excess of 1.0, there are proportionately more persons of the legislator's nationality within his district than within the state at large. A preponderance of ratios in excess of 1.0 would seem to indicate a tendency for nationality to be a factor in representation (if we may neglect *chance*, as making for representation of a numerically strong nationality in a given district.) For convenience, we called the quotient $\dfrac{\text{Percentage A}}{\text{Percentage B}}$, *a ratio of nationality excess.*

[13] This appears to be a serious weakness in the technique employed.

Before a distinction is drawn among the ratios for separate nationalities, the distribution of the entire number as a single series of data may first be examined. Table 25 shows this distribution arranged in sixteen classes from 0.0 to 16.0, having a uniform class interval. It is evident that it can be classed as extremely asymmetrical, being similar to Curve IV in Figure 11, Page 112. All classes above the first in value represent cases in which foreign-born legislators have been elected from districts in which persons of their own nationality were disproportionately numerous as compared with the rest of the state in question.

TABLE 25 — DISTRIBUTION OF 107 "RATIOS OF NATIONALITY EXCESS," WITH CLASS INTERVALS OF EQUAL WIDTH.

Ratio	Frequency
0.0– 0.9	27
1.0– 1.9	37
2.0– 2.9	27
3.0– 3.9	8
4.0– 4.9	2
5.0– 5.9	1
6.0– 6.9	–
7.0– 7.9	1
8.0– 8.9	1
9.0– 9.9	–
10.0–10.9	1
11.0–11.9	–
12.0–12.9	–
13.0–13.9	1
14.0–14.9	–
15.0–15.9	1
	107

But it seems probable that in an attempt to interpret a series of *ratios of nationality excess*, a logarithmic mode of distribution should be employed. To give an illustration, a ratio of 0.10 appears to be as significant in a negative direction as one of 10.0 in a positive direction. In the first case the given nationality is but one-tenth of its "normal quota" (its average distribution in the population of the whole state). In the second it is ten times its "normal." In Table 26 the ratios for all nationalities have been distributed in one series according to what amounts to a logarithmic classification. The frequencies there shown have been plotted upon semi-logarithmic paper in Figure 13.

TABLE 26 — DISTRIBUTION OF 107 "RATIOS OF NATIONALITY EXCESS" AC-
CORDING TO A LOGARITHMIC FORM OF CLASSIFICATION
(NOTE: See text for explanation).

Ratio	Frequency	Ratio	Frequency
.10– .19	1	2.00– 2.19	6
.20– .29	1	2.20– 2.39	11
.30– .39	2	2.40– 2.59	1
.40– .49	4	2.60– 2.79	6
.50– .59	4	2.80– 2.99	3
.60– .69	4	3.0 – 3.4	7
.70– .79	3	3.5 – 3.9	1
.80– .89	5	4.0 – 4.9	2
.90– .99	3	5.0 – 5.9	1
1.00–1.09	5	6.0 – 6.9	–
1.10–1.19	6	7.0 – 7.9	1
1.20–1.29	2	8.0 – 8.9	1
1.30–1.39	4	9.0 – 9.9	–
1.40–1.49	2	10.0 –10.9	1
1.50–1.59	4	11.0 –11.9	–
1.60–1.69	2	12.0 –12.9	–
1.70–1.79	4	13.0 –13.9	1
1.80–1.89	1	14.0 –14.9	–
1.90–1.99	7	15.0 –15.9	1
		Total	107

In Figure 13 each quadrangle above the base line at unity (1.0) indicates one or more districts which have elected persons of foreign birth to the legislature, and in which there is a positively disproportionate part of the population of the same nationality. The vertical distance to which the quadrangle extends above the base line shows geometrically the extent of that disproportion. Similarly, the quadrangles below the line of unity indicate districts in which there was

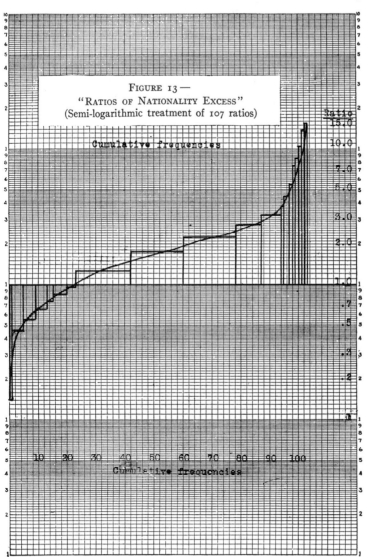

FIGURE 13 —
"RATIOS OF NATIONALITY EXCESS"
(Semi-logarithmic treatment of 107 ratios)

a negatively disproportionate part of the population of the same nationality as the foreign-born legislator. If an arithmetical rather than a geometrical scale had been used, the extent of the disproportion in the first situations would have appeared much greater. The numbers of each as shown on the horizontal scale, however, would have appeared the same.[14] *The figure is sufficient to indicate a well-marked disposition on the part of foreign-born voters to elect men of their own nationality to the legislature.*

When the various nationalities represented among the 107 legislators are separately considered, differences appear. The

TABLE 27 — DISTRIBUTION OF 107 "RATIOS OF NATIONALITY EXCESS," BY NATIONALITIES

Country of Legislators' Nativity	Number of Ratios	Mean Ratio	Median Ratio	Actual Ratio
Norway	28	1.28	1.695	
Sweden	21	2.39	2.26	
Denmark	14	3.45	2.52	
Germany	16	1.44	1.53	
England	9	.92	.80	
Canada *	12	1.70	1.20	
Ireland	2	....	....	4.13 ⎫ .70 ⎬
Switzerland	2	....	....	2.10 ⎫ .48 ⎭
Holland	1	....	....	8.90
Belgium	1	....	....	2.45
Russia	1	....	....	13.43

* Excluding French Canadians.

[14] When the ratios are plotted on double-logarithmic paper, with the ratio values along the X axis, and with frequencies plotted cumulatively on the Y axis, the smooth curve which has been drawn in Figure 13 is reduced to a straight line, cutting the Y axis very nearly at the center of the range, but with the extreme cases at either end atypical.

numbers involved in the case of each are too small to be compared graphically with any degree of profit. Table 27, however, shows the number of legislators of each nationality, and the mean and median ratios for each group of more than two members.

It is difficult to interpret these figures with any assurance. The highest ratios found among the six leading nationalities were in the case of the Danes. The average ratio as regards the Swedes was also high. In the whole state of Minnesota there are nearly seven Swedes for every Dane. Natives of England were elected with *less frequency* from districts in which the English population is larger than its quota, than in districts where the reverse was the situation. This might seem to suggest that the numbers of English were so small that they tended to merge in the general population without providing a basis for political clannishness. But the number of English-born residents in Minnesota is almost equal to that of the Danish-born. It might also be inferred that an Anglo-American prophet has no honor among Anglo-Americans.

But the numbers are really too small for inference, especially as other factors are undetermined. For example, the comparative tendencies of different nationalities toward colonization, or concentration of population in particular districts, has not been investigated. *A priori*, we might anticipate a more equal distribution of the English. Nor have the distributions of the various nationalities with reference to each other been examined. Is there a tendency, for example, for Scandinavians to unite with Scandinavians, regardless of nativity, in opposition to a non-Scandinavian? Or on the other hand, are traditional rivalries between Norwegians and Swedes carried over to northwestern political relationships? Such questions as these (and numerous others) remain concealed in the data.

Instead of supporting or discrediting the hypotheses concerning representativeness, then, the data and the methods presented in this chapter have instead merely given ground for opinion that further work in the general directions here followed might support them. This opinion is itself sustained by "common knowledge" of the mental habits of voters, their prejudices and predilections, and the advantages taken thereof by practical politicians who control the nominating machinery.

To sum up: although in this chapter we have given no clear statistical support to the hypotheses advanced, the methods employed and the tentative results secured seem promising. By further work in the directions indicated it may be possible to obtain more precise knowledge of the respects in which legislators actually represent, and the extent to which they represent, their constituents. Meanwhile, as subsequent chapters will show, it is profitable to proceed with analyses of the voting behavior of legislators based on the twofold *a priori* assumptions, first, that voters prefer and tend to elect to office persons with attitudes in most respects similar to their own; second, that office-holders tend to express in their behavior, in particular in their votes, the attitudes of the groups within the electorate to which they belong.

XV

MEASUREMENT OF GROUP "COHESION" AND "LIKENESS"[1]

Regardless of the validity or falsity of the assumptions (or hypotheses) discussed in the last chapter, the measurement of voting behavior within legislative bodies has a practical value of its own. Once a congress or a legislature is in session the various parties, blocs, and minor groupings that appear therein have a very intimate importance for our public life. The methods of measuring group behavior described and illustrated in this chapter have general application to any group in which questions are decided by *voting*, and in which all individual votes are a matter of knowledge, but in practice their use has so far been largely confined, and will doubtless continue to be largely confined, to legislative bodies in which roll-call votes are taken and made a part of the public record.

Another utilization, which will be mentioned without elaboration, is in the discovery of variations of attitude within small groups that may be experimentally controlled. For example, in one of my graduate classes a series of questions bearing upon personal attitudes were answered anonymously "yes" or "no" by each student. Certain other data concerning sex, place of birth, and occupational environment were at the same time given. It was discovered that agreement was high upon topics related to local uni-

[1] The material in this chapter has been partially taken from two of my previously published discussions: *Farmers and Workers in American Politics*, 1924; and "The Behavior of Legislative Groups: A Method of Measurement," *Political Science Quarterly*, March, 1925.

versity affairs, economics, and political issues generally. Upon matters concerning sex, the family, and moral codes, on the other hand, there was a distinct sex cleavage, the nature and amount of which could be measured.

The first test that any legislative or other group must meet concerns its *cohesion*. Are the members of Group A in their voting behavior more like each other than are the members generally of the more inclusive Group B which includes not only A but non-A individuals as well? For example, are the Republican members in a state senate more alike in their votes than are the members of the senate generally? If so, it may be inferred that they are more like-minded and the Republican group may be called more *cohesive* than the senate as a whole. Similarly it may be asked whether the Republican senators are more or less cohesive than are the Democratic senators. Or take a question still more definite: was the tri-partisan "progressive" or La Follette bloc in the Senate of the Sixty-eighth Congress more or less cohesive than were the various senatorial groups included under each of the formal party designations?

Precision in answering such questions has been obtained by the aid of an *index of cohesion*. This index is based upon the theory of probability.

If roll-call votes were cast according to pure chance, the most probable result in the case of any roll call would be a division in which fifty per cent of the members voted affirmatively and fifty per cent voted negatively. It is evident that the cohesion within the entire body in such a case would be *nil*. Hence a measure of cohesion will be obtained if we determine the degree of departure from the most probable chance distribution of votes, toward complete uniformity of action, i.e., a roll call in which all members vote alike. Referring only to the percentage of affirmative votes for the sake of convenience, it is apparent that zero cohesion (o.o) will be indicated by a roll call in which fifty per cent of the members vote affirmatively. Maximum cohesion (100.0) will be indicated whenever the group is unanimously either for or against a measure; i.e., when it votes either 100 per cent or o per cent in the affirmative. Further, an index of cohesion intermediate between o.o and 100.0 will be determined by the degree to which the percentage of affirmative votes departs from 50.0 in either direction toward o.o or 100.0. For example, when the votes of the group on a given measure are thirty per cent in the affirmative or seventy per cent in the affirmative, the index of cohesion will in both cases be 40.0, for in both there is a 20/50 or forty per cent departure from o.o cohesion toward 100.0 cohesion. When the index of cohesion upon a series of roll calls is to be found, the writer has employed the arithmetical mean of the indexes derived for the various individual roll calls in the series.[2]

Allied to the problem of group cohesion, and likewise requiring measurement, are questions of the extent to which various groups are alike or unlike in their voting responses to political issues. It is useful not alone to the political scientist but to many laymen to know whether farmers and workingmen, when thrown together in a state legislature, tend to be in mutual opposition or in mutual support. If they tend to be in mutual opposition with respect to prohibition and its enforcement (as they do) are they likewise in opposition with regard to labor legislation or political reform? Or, to use the former illustration, was the La Follette bloc in the Sixty-eighth Congress in closer affiliation with the regular

[2] It would be possible to weight the individual measures in any other manner desired, if a basis for the weighting were known.

Republican party or with the regular Democratic party? In either case, how much closer? Answers to such questions based on a "hunch" are unsatisfactory. Measurements are needed.

To place beside the index of cohesion within groups, therefore, I have derived an *index of likeness between groups*.[3] The possible range of this index is likewise from 0.0 to 100.0. If, for example, all Republicans in a legislative session vote affirmatively on a given roll call while all Democrats vote negatively, it is obvious that the behavior of the two groups, so far as it can be expressed by votes, is absolutely dissimilar. One is 100 per cent affirmative, the other 0 per cent affirmative. The arithmetic difference between the percentages of affirmative votes in the two cases is 100.0. This figure thus gives an index of absolute *difference* in voting behavior between the two groups. If, on the other hand, Republicans and Democrats *both* divide at the same time 50–50, or 70–30, or 85–15, the responses of the two groups, as groups, will in each case be the same. It is to be inferred in such cases that the distribution of votes is determined by factors unassociated with party divisions, and Republicans and Democrats may be said to vote *alike* on the issue at hand. The arithmetical difference between the respective percentages of affirmative votes in each such case will be 0.0, and the complement of this figure, 100.0, will be the *index of likeness*. Thus the complement of the arithmetical difference between the percentages voting in the affirmative in each of two

---

[3] Since the index here described was devised and named, I have discovered that Ogburn and Peterson used an index substantially similar but to which no name was given in the article "Political Thought of Social Classes," cited on page 118. I am unable to say whether the idea was unconsciously "borrowed" from them or not, but at any rate they should have the credit for its prior development and use. This acknowledgment has not hitherto been made in my use of the index.

groups gives an index of likeness between them, so far as their voting behavior is concerned. The index of likeness upon a series of roll calls may again be regarded as the arithmetic mean of the indexes derived for the separate roll calls in the series.

The foregoing technique applies to simple and uncomplicated problems of measuring group integration and group relationships. Before proceeding to a more complex situation the simple cases will first be illustrated by measurements of group cohesion and group likeness in the New York State Assembly of 1921. The legislative sessions of New York in that year had particular interest because they displayed the post-war reaction at its maximum. This was the session which enacted the so-called "Lusk" laws, and which disqualified a duly elected Socialist member. The Assembly was overwhelmingly Republican.

It was composed at the outset of 150 members. Eight groups were selected for analysis as a result of preliminary study of the roll calls recorded in the Assembly *Journal*. These were the Assembly as a whole, the Republicans as a whole, the New York City Republicans, the "up-state" Republicans, the Democrats, the Socialists, the Farmers and the Labor members. It so happened that all of the members classified as Farmers or Laborites were also Republicans. Those placed in these categories were members who met certain objective documentary tests concerning occupation and residence. All of the Democrats but two were from New York City. We may classify the members as indicated in the two following tables in order to show the relationships existing between the several groups.

Of 1296 roll calls taken during the session, all but 255 were unanimous. Out of an estimated total of 175,000 votes cast, only 7,595 or four and three tenths per cent were cast in the

TABLE 28 — COMPOSITION OF THE NEW YORK ASSEMBLY, 1921, BY PARTIES
AND TWO SELECTED OCCUPATIONS

Republicans... 119
    Farmers............................. 27
    Laborites............................ 5
    Unclassified.......................... 87
Democrats.. 28
Socialists... 3
Assembly as a whole................................. 150

TABLE 29 — COMPOSITION OF THE NEW YORK ASSEMBLY, 1921, BY PARTIES
AND LOCALITIES

Up-State Members.................................... 88
    Republicans.......................... 86
    Democrats............................ 2
New York City Members............................. 62
    Republicans.......................... 33
    Democrats............................ 26
    Socialists........................... 3
Assembly as a whole................................ 150

negative. The study has been confined, therefore, to roll
calls in which there were six or more opposing votes cast
against the majority action.[4] The results of the study are
presented in Tables 30 and 31.

The number of groups of assemblymen whose votes were
analyzed might have been extended to include categories
based on religious or other lines. Similarly, the roll calls
included in the study, 169 in number, might have been classified into an indefinite number of subordinate categories.
Three sub-classes of measures only are shown in Table 30.

[4] The high degree of like-mindedness indicated by the large proportion
of unanimous roll calls is illusory owing (a) to constitutional specification of
the occasions on which roll calls must be taken in the passage of a measure,
(b) to the legislative device for evading the constitution in this respect known
as the "short roll call." A short roll call is almost invariably indicated when
the recorded number of votes in opposition to the majority action is ten or
less. To be recorded in opposition on a short roll call, the member must rise
in his seat and so request after the presumptive roll has been taken. For a
precedent for disregarding unanimous and near-unanimous roll calls, cf.
A. Lawrence Lowell, as quoted on pages 117-118. But as to the general
question involved, cf. Chapter IX as a whole.

"State issues" include all measures other than those of purely local character. Among seventy-six roll calls affecting single municipalities or counties, fifty-nine were selected which bore upon the affairs of New York City alone. Thus roll calls upon "state issues" and "New York City issues" are referred to in columns 4 and 5, respectively. In column 6 are shown the indexes of cohesion for 8 roll calls affecting the issue of prohibition and its enforcement. The same classification of measures is employed in Table 31.

TABLE 30 — INDEXES OF COHESION WITHIN VARIOUS GROUPS IN THE NEW YORK ASSEMBLY, 1921

1 Group	2 Number in group	3 169 Roll Calls with 6 or more opposing votes	4 94 Roll Calls on "State Issues"	5 59 Roll Calls on New York City Issues	6 8 Roll Calls on Prohibition
Assembly as a whole.......	150	51.4	44.9	......	15.6
Republicans..............	119	74.8	66.0	......	44.9
Up-State Republicans.....	86	87.9	80.7	96.5	89.9
New York City Republicans	33	65.5	63.9	62.1	68.7
Democrats..............	28	77.4	73.0	79.6	100.0
Socialists...............	3	94.0	94.1	......	71.3
Farmers.................	27	91.2	85.6	......	100.0
Laborites...............	5	68.0	59.9	......	12.5

A number of conclusions might be drawn from Tables 30 and 31. Still others might be disclosed if a larger number of the possible comparisons of group likeness were carried through in Table 31. A few of the more significant points indicated in the tables will serve to illustrate the utility of the method:

1. The New York City Republicans, in effect, formed an intermediate party group or bloc between the Up-State Repub-

licans and the Democrats. When all measures are taken together, this bloc of New York City Republicans was more like its Up-State party associates (74.4) than it was like the Democrats (53.0). Yet on such an issue as prohibition, its likeness with the Up-Staters was represented by the index 20.6 as compared with an index of 84.5 between itself and the Democrats. In cohesion, the New York City Republicans were low — 65.5 as compared with 87.9 for the up-state Republicans and 77.4 for the Democrats. This fact is suggestive of a conflict between party loyalty on the one hand, tending toward association with the up-state Republicans, and sec-

TABLE 31 — INDEXES OF LIKENESS BETWEEN VARIOUS GROUPS IN THE NEW YORK ASSEMBLY, 1921

1 *Groups Compared*	*2* *169 Roll Calls with 6 or more opposing votes*	*3* *94 Roll Calls on "State Issues"*	*4* *59 Roll Calls on New York City Issues*	*6* *8 Roll Calls on Prohibition*
Whole Assembly and Farmers..	78.8	76.9	....	58.1
Whole Assembly and Laborites.	86.6	85.4	....	95.1
Whole Assembly and Republicans......................	87.3	88.1	....	85.3
Whole Assembly and Democrats	49.5	53.0	....	41.9
Whole Assembly and Socialists	48.9	....	....	54.6
Republicans and Farmers......	90.4	88.5	....	72.5
Republicans and Laborites.....	88.3	86.4	....	83.8
Farmers and Laborites........	84.8	79.9	....	60.2
Socialists and Laborites.......	52.9	....	....	56.1
New York City Republicans and Up-State Republicans.........	74.4	70.8	75.5	20.6
New York City Republicans and Democrats..................	53.0	60.6	50.9	84.5
Farmers and Democrats.......	....	....	....	0.0
Farmers and Socialists........	36.5	....	....	12.4
Republicans and Democrats....	37.1	....	....	28.0

tional loyalty upon the other, tending toward association with the Democrats, all but two of whom represented New York City districts.

2. The Republican farmers formed a highly cohesive group (91.2) within the relatively cohesive group of up-state Republicans (87.9). It is apparent that the common occupation is a cohesive influence. The cohesion of farmers was exceeded only by that of Socialists (94.0) who were represented a portion of the time by only two members.

3. The laborites showed relatively low cohesion (68.0) although this was probably the result of their division between the up-state and New York City wings of the Republican party. The Republican laborites showed considerably more likeness to the Socialists (52.9) than did the Republican farmers (36.5).

4. The several groups are in the same order with respect to the amount of their cohesion whether all roll calls or only those concerning "state issues" are considered. In each instance, however, the cohesion of the group is less in the case of "state issues." We may infer that local issues, particularly those affecting the city of New York, promote a more uniform response within each group than do issues of more general state-wide significance. It is probable that the long-standing quarrel between the city and the up-state districts tends to produce a more habitual response in each group whenever the issue is presented, whereas "state issues" are more likely to be considered upon their merits and hence produce a more varied response in each group.

5. Up-state Republicans showed almost perfect cohesion (96.5) on the fifty-nine roll calls specifically affecting New York City. They were considerably more united upon these matters than upon any other type of measures segregated, and considerably more united than were the Democrats

(79.6). Hence it may be said that common attitudes regarding the affairs of New York City constituted the outstanding characteristic of the voting behavior of the up-state
Republicans.   The New York City Republicans, on the
contrary, occupied with regard to city issues the same intermediate position as a separate but not very cohesive group
that they occupied upon questions generally.

6. The Assembly was more sharply divided on the issue
of prohibition than on legislative issues as a whole.   There
were eight roll calls taken in which this issue was mainly
involved.   In each case farmers (who were all Republicans)
and Democrats were completely in agreement among themselves, but in *opposite directions*.   That is, the index of
likeness between farmers and Democrats on this type of
issue was 0.0.

The Assembly groups which were segregated for the preceding analysis could be classified with almost the simplicity
of a *dichotomy*.   Except for two up-state Democrats, there
was no overlapping among the several parties and other
divisions in which we were interested.   This is not the case
in the following situation, but the problem may still be set
up in a manner which will preserve simplicity of treatment.
The question concerns the cohesion of the bi-partisan
"progressive" or "La Follette" bloc in the United States
Senate of the Sixty-Eighth Congress, and its "likeness"
to the two regular party groups.   The analysis is based upon
the first fifty-four roll-call divisions.

The formal party affiliations of United States senators are
of record.   Their affiliations or sympathies with conservative,
progressive, or other blocs are not.   On the basis of a variety
of criteria, such as attendance at conferences of "progressives," the following list of thirteen senators in the
Sixty-eighth Congress was segregated.   It is composed of

six Republicans, five Democrats and two Farmer-Laborites: La Follette, Frazier, Brookhart, Norris, Ladd, and Borah, Republicans; Wheeler, Dill, Sheppard, Walsh of Massachusetts, and Ashurst, Democrats; Shipstead and Johnson of Minnesota, Farmer-Laborites. For convenience this group of thirteen senators may be called "radical." Similarly, a larger list of twenty-two senators who may be termed "progressive" was formed by the addition to the first thirteen of nine others with a reputation for progressive leanings, who failed, however, to meet the first criteria of selection. The "progressive" group thus includes the "radical." The various indexes of cohesion that have been derived are shown in Table 32.

TABLE 32 — COHESION OF VARIOUS SENATORIAL GROUPS IN THE SIXTY-EIGHTH CONGRESS

Group	First 54 Roll Calls taken in the Sixty-eighth Congress	47 Roll Calls derived by omitting 7 of comparative unimportance
The Senate as a whole..................	44.2	46.5
Democrats (all so listed)...............	63.6	63.1
Republicans (all so listed)..............	70.0	66.3
"Radical" group of 13..................	66.6	71.0
"Progressive" group of 22..............	62.7	67.2

It is apparent from Table 32 that when all fifty-four roll calls were considered, the "radical" and "progressive" blocs were slightly less cohesive than the Republicans, including under the latter term all who gave this as their party designation in the Congressional Directory. The "radical" bloc, however, was more cohesive than the Democrats. Among fifty-one non-unanimous roll calls, the "radical" bloc was more cohesive than either Republicans or Democrats in the case of eighteen, and more cohesive than (or equally cohesive as) at least one of these parties in the case of twenty roll calls additional, leaving thirteen, twenty-five and five tenths per cent, in which both parties exceeded the "radical" bloc in cohesion.

But among the fifty-four roll calls, some were of greater importance than others. In the last column of Table 32, will be found the indexes of cohesion when seven roll calls upon such matters as the award of individual war pensions and the election of a doorkeeper to the senate were eliminated. In this column it will be discovered that if the more important roll calls alone be considered, both "radical" and "progressive" blocs were more cohesive than either of the parties. It should be remembered that the insurgent tendencies of the progressive and radical senators tend to diminish the cohesion of the formal party organizations. It is probable, though it has not been determined, that the radicals were not so cohesive as the "regulars" in either of the old parties when the latter were taken by themselves. Nor has the index of likeness been used to determine whether the radicals and progressives were more closely aligned to the Republican or the Democratic group. It is a matter of historical knowledge that their affiliations were with the latter.

The investigator's interests will frequently be so directed that his problem cannot be arranged in the comparatively simple form of either of the two preceding illustrations. Neither of these has involved to any degree as variables the factors of party affiliations themselves. Suppose, for example, that one is interested in comparing the legislative behavior of two occupational groups, the membership of either or both of which is to be found in two or more parties.[5] The

---

[5] This was the situation frequently encountered in my attempts to determine the mutual attitudes of farmers and workingmen in state legislatures. *Cf. Farmers and Workers in American Politics*, Chap. VI.

existing political parties, in most cases, provide the major
lines of cleavage within legislative bodies. Party loyalty
usually has a greater influence upon the member's vote than
do factors associated with occupation. If it were not so,
party lines would already have reshaped themselves along
occupational lines. Measurements of cohesion and likeness
will have little significance, consequently, so long as the
party affiliations of farmers and workingmen are variable
factors. For example, the index of cohesion among farmers
in a particular legislative session might be higher than the
index of cohesion among workingmen. If the farmers were
all members of the same political party, while the workingmen were divided between two political parties, the higher
cohesion among the former might safely be attributed in
large part to their common party loyalty. Similarly, the
index of likeness between farmers and workingmen who are
affiliated with the same party will usually be higher than the
index of likeness between farmers of one party and workingmen of another.[6]

[6] Numerous lines of cleavage run through a legislative body. It is quite impossible to take account by classification (the method here adopted) of all of
these simultaneously. Thus if a legislative body were divided into "Protestant,
native-born, Republican farmers," "Protestant, German-born, Republican farmers," etc., the number of classes would far exceed the number of members to
be classified. Since it appears to be the *major* attribute determinative of votes,
party affiliation should be held constant whenever comparisons are made between groups based upon some other attribute, such as occupation. In such a
case we are forced to assume that the apportionment of still other attributes,
such as religion or nationality, is either (a) in some fixed ratio among the various
occupations which remains constant whenever the latter are compared; or,
(b) that these other attributes are wholly unassociated with occupation, so that
their apportionment is a matter of chance whenever occupations are compared.
Thus we might assume (a) that Catholicism as an attribute was present in some
constant high proportion of individual cases whenever working class occupations
were involved; similarly, that protestantism was associated with the occupation
of farming. We would not then be able to say *why* farmers and workingmen dif-
fered in the particulars found, whether because of the influence of their occupations or because of the influence of their religions. We could only venture

At least one practicable means of eliminating the party variable when it is thought to invalidate the result is by the method of classification. Republican farmers may be compared with Republican laborites or with Democratic laborites, but not with a bi-partisan labor group. The indexes of cohesion and of likeness gain significance (when the party variable is held constant in this manner) by comparison with the indexes that would be *probable* on the basis of party affiliations alone. Thus it would be "expected" that the index of likeness between Republican farmers and Democratic laborites would equal the index of likeness between all Republicans and all Democrats if farmers and laborites constituted *random samples* of their respective parties. If in fact the former index is the smaller it is clear that farmers and laborites have a tendency to differ in their votes *relative to their party affiliations,* i.e., more than their party affiliations would call for. Similarly, the cohesion of Group A in Party X relative to the cohesion of X, when compared with the cohesion of Group B in Party Y relative to the cohesion of

---

the opinion that one reason for differences between farmers and workingmen as occupational groups was to be found in their differences with respect to religion. If our comparisons were between religious groups, on the other hand, the corresponding statement might be possible: i.e., one reason for differences between Catholics and Protestants is to be found in their differences of occupation. In the second case we might assume (b) that the attribute of German birth was apportioned with the same frequency among farmers as among workingmen. In this case the apportionment could be regarded as a matter of chance in any particular comparison. Hence the matter of German birth or non-German birth could not (if such an assumption were made) be regarded as one of the explanations for any differences between farmers and workingmen that might be found.

When farmers and workingmen are compared the assumptions involved are more likely to be of the first type than the second. It is likely that the most important cleavage to be found in legislative bodies generally, other than the cleavages of party and occupation, is that between the representatives of urban and rural constituencies. The correlation would be high and constant between the farmer group and the rural group, and between the labor group and the urban group. *Cf.* Chapters XII and XIII.

Y, will indicate whether A or B is the more cohesive relative to party affiliations.

When subordinate groups A and B are both wholly affiliated with Party X, a comparison of their respective indexes of cohesion may be made directly. But it is not so simple to ascertain whether they are tending toward like or unlike voting behavior. At this point precision may be given to the concepts of *swing* and *party wing*, both of which are commonly used in political discussion, and with substantially the same meanings given them here. Do A and B tend to "swing" in the same or in opposing directions within the common Party X? Are they, that is, in the same "wing" or in opposing "wings" of that party?

If the number within the party be large as compared with the numbers in the subordinate groups, the "swing" may be safely determined by comparing the percentage of affirmative votes in the party group as a whole with the respective percentages of affirmative votes in the two subordinate groups. For example, in one roll call on the question of prohibition enforcement in the Pennsylvania House of Representatives of 1919 the Republican group with 175 members voting was 51.4 per cent in the affirmative on a particular presentation of the issue. Of seven Republican farmers, one, or 14.3 per cent, was in the affirmative, while of eight Republican laborites, all or 100 per cent were in the affimative. It will be clear that farmers and labor members, as occupational groups, "swung" to opposing wings of the common Republican party on this particular issue.[7]

The distribution of votes upon this roll call is represented graphically in Figure 14. Each of the dotted squares in the area ABCD represents a Republican member who voted

[7] *Pennsylvania House Journal*, 1919, p. 3352. This was the second roll call upon House Bill No. 1400.

222 QUANTITATIVE METHODS IN POLITICS

"aye." Each of the similar squares in the irregular area CDFE represents a Republican member who voted "no." The area *klnm* represents the labor members, all of whom voted "aye," while the area *pqsr* represents the farmer members, all but one of whom voted "no."

It will be seen that the Republican party group in the House was divided, on this issue into *opposing wings*.[8] If a member of the Republican group were selected at random, without regard to criteria other than his party membership, the chances would have been 51.4 in 100 that he would have belonged to the *affirmative wing*. It is this percentage, 51.4, that constitutes the *probable* or *expected* proportion of affirmative votes within any subordinate group of Republicans, such as Republican farmers or Republican Methodists. By comparing the *actual* with the *expected* division within these intra-party groups, it can be ascertained whether they tend to be found in the same or in opposing wings of the party group. To return to the illustrative analysis of votes in the New York Assembly, it was found there that the farmer and labor groups tended to swing to opposite wings of the common Republican party group in the larger number of roll calls taken.

The exact measurement of the *amount* of swing has presented to me insuperable difficulties. A discussion of these is demanded here, although a reading of the following pages of the chapter should be omitted by those who are without technical interest in the detailed aspects of the method.

The division within the party as a whole will be conditioned by the divisions within each of any subordinate groups into which the party may be segregated. For ex-

---

[8] Whether or not these wings were of permanent character (*i.e.*, were in the nature of *blocs*) does not concern us at this point. Nor are we concerned to learn which of the wings was on the "dry" and which on the "wet" side of the issue.

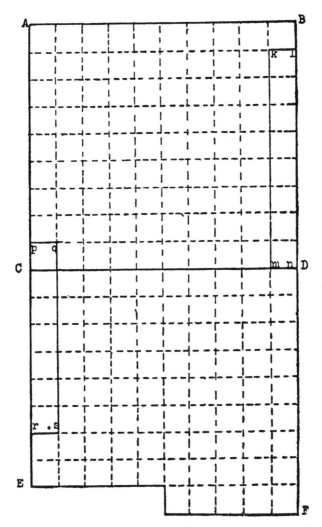

FIGURE 14 — DISTRIBUTION OF REPUBLICAN VOTES IN ONE ROLL CALL IN
PENNSYLVANIA HOUSE OF REPRESENTATIVES, 1919

ample, assume that our interest is with Republican farmers and Republican laborites; then a third group is tacitly understood, namely, Republican non-farmers-non-laborites. The divisions which occur (into "aye" and "no" wings) within these three groups together determine the division within the Republican party group as a whole.

Now the larger the subordinate group, the greater will be its influence in determining the party division. For example, in a group of one hundred Republicans containing fifty farmers and ten laborites, assume that fifty per cent of the farmers vote "aye" on a given roll call. Then twenty-five per cent of all Republicans will vote "aye," even if all non-farmers vote "no." But if fifty per cent of the laborites vote "aye," then only five per cent of the Republicans will vote "aye" if all non-laborites vote "no." It follows that the *mode of division* in the subordinate group (by which is meant the proportions voting "aye" and "no") will have a probability of coinciding with the mode of division in the party group, which will vary directly with the ratio which the subordinate group bears in numbers to the numbers in the party group. Hence, when we compare the votes of a farmer group and a labor group within the same party, we should expect the larger "swing" to occur in the case of that group which was smaller in membership.

This expectation was supported empirically by data gathered in my study of the political relationships of farmers and workers. For convenience further reference on this matter will be to this data. In the case of each of twenty sets of comparisons between farmer and labor sub-groups within the same party group (each set including a considerable number of roll-call votes and the indexes based thereon) there were determined, first, the ratio between the number of farmers and the number of laborites involved; second, the ratio between the "swing" of the labor group and the "swing" of the farmer group. When ranked according to these two sets of ratios, the correlation by grades (see footnote 5, page 160) is found to be

$$r = + .75$$

In other words, the smaller the proportionate number in the sub-group, the greater its "swing."

It appears, moreover, that the tendency for farmers and laborites within the same party to "swing" in opposite directions will increase in inverse ratio to the relative strength of the non-farmer-non-labor group within the party. Thus, if the number of non-farmer-non-laborites shrinks to zero, leaving only farmers and laborites within the party, the "swing" of these groups would necessarily be in opposite directions, unless both divided on the given question in exactly the same proportions. A "swing" by both in the same direction would be an impossibility, for there would be no third group from which the "swing" could occur. When one compares the mode of party division with the modes of division within subsidiary groups of farmers and laborites, one is in effect using the non-farmer-non-labor group as a "frame of reference," with which the votes of farmers and laborites are compared. I have preferred to make measurements with respect to the party as a whole rather than with respect to the non-farmer-non-labor group, because only by so doing could I preserve the mould into which I have attempted to cast data, namely, the "likeness" of farmers and laborites *relative to party*. Republican farmers and laborites contribute to the party attitudes, as has been said, not less than non-farmer-non-labor Republicans.

It might be possible to calculate in *each* case the mathematical probability that farmer and labor members would vote in such a manner that farmer and labor sub-groups would swing in opposing directions from the mode of party division, and then make corrections for this probability. But such calculations would add greatly to the complexity of the work, and I think in most cases would be without corresponding advantage in increased reliability of the results. In the case of the actual farmer-labor material referred to, it was shown that in all probability little effect was present from the disturbing influence here discussed.[9] But this was undoubtedly due to the fact that the farmer and labor groups were relatively small.

The determination of the direction of "swing" involves a comparison of the "mode of division" within the farmer group and the "mode of division" within the labor group with the "mode of division" within the party group as a whole.[10] In practice I have derived the index of likeness between the party and each occupational group in turn. I then derived the index of likeness between the two occupational groups. It is evident that if the farmer and the labor "swings" are in the *same* direction, the "likeness" between them will be greater than the "likeness" between the party and at least one of the occupational groups. If the farmer and the labor swings are in *opposite directions*, the likeness between them will be less than the likeness between the party and at least one of the occupational groups.

It follows that a numerical measure of the tendency toward or against farmer-labor like-mindedness *with reference to party* may be obtained by subtracting one of the

[9] *Op. cit.*, p. 230.

[10] By "mode of division" is meant the proportion of the membership which votes "aye" or "no" on a given roll call. This proportion may be regarded as a mode in the sense that it represents the normal or type division within a group, to which sub-groups, if determined by some method of random selection, would be expected to approximate in the divisions within *them*. In practice, the proportion voting "aye" has been consistently employed to represent the "mode of division."

first two indexes of likeness from the third. The subtrahend in such a subtraction will be the index of likeness between the party and that one of the two occupational groups whose mode of division is most divergent from that of the party. The sign of the remainder will be positive if the "swing" of farmers and laborites is in the same direction, and negative if the "swing" is in the opposite direction.

The numerical result from such an operation, however, will tend to vary as already indicated with the comparative size of the farmer and of the labor groups, and its use, therefore is not suggested. In view of all the considerations here given, it seems as yet to be impracticable to attempt the derivation of *amounts* by which sub-groups within a larger group tend to swing toward or away from each other on particular roll calls or groups of roll calls. Disparity of numbers in the two sub-groups would alone make this inadmissible. Instead, it seems preferable to accept as definitive in any set of comparisons merely the *number of instances* in which the *direction* of swing was in a common direction as compared with the instances in which the directions were opposed. Moreover, the concept of swing in any form is of doubtful value unless the subordinate groups together make up a relatively small proportion of the membership of the larger common group.

XVI

The Identification of Blocs in Small Political Bodies [1]

For the use of the twin measuring devices described in the last chapter and called an *index of cohesion* and an *index of likeness between groups,* two conditions only are in practice required:

(1) The votes of individuals must be recorded. This requirement is met in certain stages of the work of most legislative and administrative bodies, although by no means in all, even of American legislatures. (2) Supplementary information must be available, permitting the classification of the membership into the desired sub-groups. In the case of the members of a state senate, for example, it is usually possible to learn from documentary sources the party affiliations, the occupations, and the types of communities in which the members reside. It is sometimes possible to determine various social and economic characteristics of the legislative districts from which the members are elected. Using any of these factors as criteria, the membership may be classified, the cohesion of any class of two or more members determined, and the likeness between any two of these calculated.

In this method, the existence of a group made up of certain predetermined individual members must be postulated before the tests of cohesion and likeness can be applied. The

---

[1] Reprinted, except for minor changes, from *The American Political Science Review,* Vol. XXI, No. 3, August 1927, with the kind permission of the editors. *Cf.* my own comments upon this chapter on page 4.

methods cited will not serve to determine automatically the effective groupings that actually exist within the body. Nor will the presence of a non-cöoperative member who lowers the cohesion of the group necessarily be observed. For example, having guessed or postulated in advance the presence of alignments within a state senate based upon party, occupation, rural or urban habitat, or the economic interests of constituents, and having tested the cohesion of each alignment, we might still fail to discover the most cohesive groupings, because of the lack of an objective empirical method for ascertaining the latter. The present chapter deals with an attempted solution of this problem.

The difficulty of the solution resides in the enormous number of possible combinations among the members of even a small legislative body. This number increases geometrically at a very rapid rate with the growth of the body. The number of combinations of n things taken r at a time is represented by the formula in footnote 20, page 146.

For example, the number of combinations between members taken two, three, and four at a time, respectively, in a legislative body of 400 members (i.e., the number of possible blocs composed of two, three, and four members) would be expressed as follows:

$$C_{400 \cdot 2} = \frac{400 \times 399}{1 \times 2} = 79,800$$

$$C_{400 \cdot 3} = \frac{400 \times 399 \times 398}{1 \times 2 \times 3} = 10,586,800$$

$$C_{400 \cdot 4} = \frac{400 \times 399 \times 398 \times 397}{1 \times 2 \times 3 \times 4} = 1,050,739,900$$

The number of combinations for each value of r will increase steadily (though at a decreasing rate) until $r = 200$. The total number of possible combinations of members within the total body (the number of possible blocs of two or more members) would be the sum of all values of C for all values of r.

I have not succeeded in devising a practical objective method for the determination of groupings in a legislative body of these proportions. Certain results have been obtained, however, by employing the principles embodied in the above formula in bodies of small size. To exemplify the method of analysis I selected the New Jersey senate in 1914, including all non-unanimous roll calls (forty-eight in number) recorded in the Senate Journal from February 9 to March 15 inclusive. This period followed the initial sessions devoted to organization.

The senate was composed of twenty-one members — ten Republicans and eleven Democrats. Following is a rough classification of the forty-eight roll calls by subject matter as indicated by their titles: local government and improvements, 14; courts and judicial procedure, 7; taxation, 4; amendments to constitution, 4; medical practice, 3; electoral procedure, 3; senate rules and procedure, 2; social welfare, 2; game law, 2; property law, 2; miscellaneous, 5. However, no attempt was made in the analysis to distinguish between types of measures.

The immediate objectives with reference to the data may be stated as follows: (1) Can it be determined by reference alone to the votes of these senators among which of the possible combinations or blocs among them the highest cohesion is exhibited? (2) Having determined the combinations or blocs of highest cohesion, is it then possible to discover the common factors to which likeness of voting behavior is related?

A degree of precision sufficient for the purpose of this study has never before been given to the term "bloc." The term will here be defined as any combination of two or more individuals within a larger group, and not including all members of the latter, between every pair of whom there is a ratio of agreement in voting behavior equal to or greater than an assigned figure. By requiring every pair of individuals within a bloc to present an assigned minimum of agreement, it will be possible to base the determination of blocs of larger size upon a prior comparison of agreements between pairs of individuals. Thus among the twenty-one members of the New Jersey senate, there are 2,118,006 possible blocs composed of from three to eighteen members each. There are, however, but 210 possible combinations among pairs of these twenty-one senators. If two senators fall below a prescribed minimum of agreement between themselves they obviously cannot, in compliance with the definition, together enter into a combination or bloc of larger size.

The first step, then, is to ascertain the extent of agreement exhibited in their votes between each of the 210 pairs of senators. It should be noted that the actual agreement shown by roll-call votes in the aggregate is greater than appears in the data, for the reason that unanimous roll calls are excluded from consideration. The number of these is much greater than that in which differences appear. The effect of their inclusion would merely be to increase the agreement shown between all pairs of members, without substantially altering the comparative or relative agreements exhibited.[2]

[2] The relative agreement would be altered slightly because of the fact that not all members vote on every roll call. It is not, however, possible to say that the revised indexes would be more indicative of the real relationships among the members than are those obtained by omitting the unanimous votes; for less than the total are usually recorded as voting in both cases. This is a factor for which it has been impossible to make allowance in any of the writer's analyses of data of this kind. The attempt to take it into consideration amounts to the inquiry in the case of every absentee: how would he have voted had he been present?

For convenience in tabulation, each senator was assigned a number according to alphabetical position from one to twenty-one. The possible combinations of these numbers, two at a time, were then arranged in systematic order in vertical columns, and opposite each were checked the agreements and disagreements which appeared from the Journal record. The total number of agreements and disagreements between pairs was 5,802. For each pair of senators the agreements and disagreements were totaled in a fourth column, representing the number of times when both answered to the same roll call. The percentage of agreements between each pair was then set down in a fifth column.

From inspection of these percentages in the last column, it was possible immediately to count up the number in which the agreement equalled or exceeded any given ratio from 0 to 100. By referring to the party affiliations of the individuals concerned the comparative strength of the party influence was apparent. The distribution of percentages of agreement between fellow members of both parties and between members of opposing parties is shown in Table 33.

This table is of particular interest for two reasons. First, it shows the range of agreement that may occur even among members of the same party. For example, one pair of Republicans was in agreement on but little more than half of the roll calls voted upon, while another pair was in agreement on almost all of them. This is in spite of the fact that the two parties were very evenly divided, and party discipline was in consequence likely to be high. Second, it shows that certain pairs of members of opposite party were in agreement in a higher proportion of the votes which both at the same time cast than were other pairs taken from the same party. Thus, one pair composed of a Republican and a Democratic senator were in agreement a number of times proportionately equalling or exceeding the number of agreements among sixty pairs composed in each case of members of the same party. On the other hand, if all pairs in which the agreement equals or exceeds 80 per cent be segregated there will be forty-one, composed in each case of fellow party members; and if all in which the agreement falls below 55 per cent be segregated there will be 61, composed in each case of members of the opposite party. It is clear that if combinations or blocs of two members each having a relatively high percentage of agreement be segregated, there will be a high probability that both members of the combination

TABLE 33 — DISTRIBUTION OF PERCENTAGES OF AGREEMENT BETWEEN PAIRS OF MEMBERS, NEW JERSEY SENATE, 48 ROLL CALLS, SESSION OF 1914

Percentage of Agreement	Numbers of			
	Pairs of Republicans	Pairs of Democrats	Pairs of Opposite Party	Total Pairs
15–19	....	....	1	1
20–24	....	....	—	—
25–29	....	....	—	—
30–34	....	....	3	3
35–39	....	....	7	7
40–44	....	....	13	13
45–49	....	....	13	13
50–54	....	....	24	24
55–59	1	....	18	19
60–64	2	6	18	26
65–69	4	6	7	17
70–74	5	14	4	23
75–79	9	13	1	23
80–84	10	4	....	14
85–89	8	8	....	16
90–94	5	4	....	9
95–100	1	1	....	2
Total	45	56	109	210

have the same party affiliation. Other common characteristics can be determined by a direct comparison in each case of available biographical material.

In common speech, however, it is unusual to speak of a bloc of two members. To ascertain the existence of blocs having more than two members, it is necessary to specify (1) the minimum number to which consideration will be given as a bloc, among whom (2) there is a designated minimum of agreement between each pair of members. The selection of these minima must be purely arbitrary, inasmuch as we are dealing in both instances with continuous variables. However, due consideration will be given in practice to the amount of labor involved. This will be decreased by the selection of relatively high minima in both cases.

With reference to the present data, then, it was asked: among what combinations of four or more members each is there to be found 80 per cent or more agreement? Employing, as before, the numbers by which members are designated, there was set down upon a work sheet the paired combinations of each member with every other in which the required amount of agreement had been found. As previously noted, there were forty-one of these combinations, but each will appear twice if the suggested technique is employed. If any number did not enter at least three pairs of such combinations, it could be immediately discarded. Thus member eight showed 80 per cent or more agreement with members four and fifteen only. It is obvious that member eight could not appear in any bloc of four or more members. In this manner, members two, eight, and eleven were at once eliminated, together with all combinations into which they entered.

The elimination of other possible combinations may be illustrated by member four, who was paired in 80 per cent or more agreement with members six, eight, thirteen, fifteen, seventeen, and twenty-one. These seven members contain thirty-five possible combinations of four members each, twenty-one combinations of five members, and seven of six members each. But member eight has already been eliminated, as noted in the preceding paragraph. By inspection it is seen that member twenty-one cannot enter the combination, because his own combinations of 80 per cent or more agreement are with members three, four, six, and ten, only two of which are in the first collection of pairs. There now remain members four, six, thirteen, fifteen, seventeen. By inspecting the combination of required high agreement between each of these and the other four, it is quickly seen that combinations are missing between certain pairs. Therefore the five together cannot present the required bloc character. But bloc combinations of four each still appear to be possible. It is convenient, therefore, to set down the five possible combinations of four among these five and consider each in turn, as follows:

(1) 4 13 15 17
(2) 4 6 15 17
(3) 4 6 13 17
(4) 4 6 13 15
(5) 6 13 15 17

But (1), (2) and (4) are now quickly seen to be eliminated because members fifteen and seventeen lack the necessary agreement, and (3) and (5) fail similarly because of low agreement between members six and thirteen.

In similar fashion, the possible combinations hinging around each member in turn have been considered. Those meeting the minima which were set up are as follows:

Bloc A: Members 1, 5, 7, 18.
Bloc B: "   3, 6, 16, 17, 21.
Bloc C: "   9, 12, 14, 20.

It is interesting to note that in the present case none of these overlap.[3] Blocs A and C are composed entirely of Democrats, and Bloc B of Republicans.

In determining bipartisan groupings, a similar process was employed, although in this case it seemed desirable to take formal recognition of the existence of party affiliations. The question was framed thus: what bipartisan combinations exist, composed of two or more members of each party, showing 80 per cent or more agreement between each pair of members of the same party and 60 per cent or more agreement between each pair of members of opposite party? The following groupings of this character were discovered:

	Rep.			*Dem.*			
Bloc D	3	6	17	12	20		
" E	3	6	16	9	12	20	
" F		3	16	11	14		
" G		3	16	9	12	14	20
" H		3	17	11	14		
" I		3	17	12	14	20	
" J		3	21	11	14		
" K		3	21	5	14		
" L		3	21	12	14		
" M		6	17	12	20		

It appears that the first of the general questions propounded above with reference to the inquiry (page 230) has now been answered in the affirmative: by reference to the votes alone (so far as method has been concerned) all possible groupings or blocs of specified minimum number of members (four) and having a specified amount of agreement between all pairs of members (80 per cent) have been segregated. These

[3] Bloc B, composed of five members, might be resolved into its five possible combinations of four members each, although this would serve no practical advantage.

combinations have been designated Blocs A, B, and C. In addition, by recognition of party affiliations as a major factor in group alignment, Blocs D to M have been segregated on a bipartisan basis, with a reduced amount of required agreement (60 per cent) among pairs of members of opposing party affiliation. By employing the same methods, the possible combinations of any given minimum number of members and of any high minimum agreement between pairs could be ascertained.

Turning to the second question concerning discoverable common factors among the members of the blocs segregated, we are handicapped by the absence of complete biographical data concerning the senators involved. That which is available for each consists of a short sketch appearing in the Legislative Manual, and presumably written by the member himself with an eye to political potentialities. Nevertheless, certain interesting suggestions appear. Thus five of the twenty-one members, namely, twenty, fifteen, three, six, and twenty-one, refer to their membership in Masonic orders. Of these, the last three are members of Bloc B, and Republicans. Member twenty, a Democrat, appears in five bipartisan blocs with one or more of these three. Member fifteen, a Republican, is below average in agreement with one, about average with another, and high in agreement with the remaining two. Again, four members, namely, one, five, seven, and eleven, appear to be of Irish birth or ancestry. Of these, the first three are among the four members of Bloc A. Member eleven, like one, five, and seven, is a Democrat, but is average or below in agreement with these other three. The five counties of least population in the state were represented by members nine, twelve, twenty, eighteen, and ten. The first three, Democrats, were among the four members of Bloc C, while the fourth member of this bloc was from a county which was by no means large. Two members, Democrats in Bloc A, refer to their interest in social reform, while only two other members make statements that seem intended to give similar impressions. From clues such as these it may be inferred that wider information concerning the member's social background and personality would point strongly to some of the reasons for the high agreements that were found.

In conclusion, a technique has been devised for the determination of effective blocs or groupings within small legislative or other bodies, according to the principle that each pair of members in such a grouping must have a specified amount of agreement between them. The determination may be made by consideration alone of the votes cast on roll calls. Application of the technique is not practicable in bodies exceeding twenty-five or thirty in membership, because of the inordinate amount of labor which the tabulation and computation would involve.[4]

[4] I am indebted to Professor H. R. Kemp, of the University of Toronto, for the suggestion that the possible range of application might be extended by the use of electric sorting machinery. Thus a punch card might be prepared for each roll call or division of the house, the assigned number of each member being punched in one of three columns, e.g., "Aye," "No," or "Not Voting." The combinations of agreement by pairs could then be determined mechanically by the tabulating machine. The technique of "inspection" could not profitably be dispensed with from this point onward, however. Moreover, the rapidity with which the cards could be punched would depend upon the arrangement of the "yes" and "no" votes in the legislative journal. Experiment would be necessary to determine how much labor could be saved by the mechanical sorting and tabulating process.

XVII

GROWTH AND DECLINE OF POLITICAL ATTENTION

All of the studies described in preceding chapters have had one characteristic in common; they have made no allowance for changes over periods of *time*.[1] They have discussed variation and change, but in terms of space or according to classification by attributes only. It has been asked, how do attitudes change as one passes from one county to another, or from one social group to another, or as some social attribute or some natural factor in the environment appears more or less prominently among individuals or groups.

A shift of interest will now occur. Instead of being a constant in the studies which follow, time will become a variable, in some cases the *independent* and in others the *dependent* variable. Contrariwise, the factors of space and of attribute will in the main be regarded as constant. In other words, the studies in this book are conforming in plan of presentation to the major distinction usually drawn by statisticians between time series on the one hand and those upon the other which are static from a temporal standpoint.

One of the most common political observations has to do with the changes constantly taking place in public attention. Analogous changes in attitude will be taken up in later chapters. While attitude is no doubt in part characterized by its comparative intensity (a function of attention) as well as by its quality or direction, a practical distinction between

[1] An exception was Chapter XI, where the time factor entered as a variable. Chapter XI was placed in Part IV rather than in Part VI, because of its logical relationship to Chapter X.

the two is usually drawn. Thus, a majority of Americans probably maintain approximately the same attitudes toward the alleged revolutionary propaganda of communists that they held in 1920, but to no small degree their attention is no longer given to alarums upon the subject. On the other hand, public attention to European affairs has seemed to remain high, although attitudes have in many respects changed, especially toward our late enemies in the World War.

Some of the most obvious and outstanding sources of data concerning public attention are the newspapers and other periodicals, the stage and motion-picture screen, sermons, lectures, attendance at athletic and sporting events, sales of commodities having specific reference to given activities (swimming suits, or golf clubs, for example) and street-corner conversations. Many others could be named. The number of inquiries making use of these materials, in view of their volume and importance, has been very limited. A few may be mentioned. Some years ago President Henry T. Moore recorded the subject matter of conversations casually overheard among pedestrians on Broadway in New York. These were classified according to the number and sex of the participants, and some interesting conclusions were reached therefrom concerning sex differences.[2] Newspapers have reported data showing the growing public attention to such sports as football, baseball and boxing contests, using gate receipts or admissions as indexes. A great quantity of data has accumulated concerning the production and sale of commodities. From these, implications of an economic character have been drawn, but sociologists have been slow to extract their meanings concerning changing folkways, mores, and ephemeral interests.

[2] "Further Data Concerning Sex Differences," *The Journal of Abnormal Psychology and Social Psychology*, 17: 210–214, July–September, 1922.

Perhaps the most significant and consistent efforts of this kind have been directed toward the study of newspaper content. For many years Professor Alvan A. Tenney has been enlisting the interest of students in his sociology seminars at Columbia University in this problem. His persisting faith in its importance has inspired a recent pioneer attempt to work out a technique of newspaper analysis by Professor Malcolm M. Willey.[3] Similar efforts by other investigators to classify and measure the subject matter of motion-picture films have made some progress but have not, so far as I am aware, led as yet to definitive results.

Within a field more precisely political, much attention has been given of late to *non-voting* — surely an index of public attention to the process of political government itself. The outstanding work upon the subject up to the present is that of Merriam, Gosnell and Arneson.[4] These authors, however, were interested not primarily in the *trend* but rather in the causes which led citizens to refrain from voting and in possibilities of its stimulation.

A few years ago Professor Malcolm M. Willey and I sought to arrive at an estimate of the numbers and proportions of eligible voters who had failed to vote in the presidential elections of 1880, 1900, and 1920. These years were selected because of their coincidence with the decennial census enumeration. Our immediate object was to gain some accurate notion of the numbers of eligible women who go to the polls since the adoption of suffrage, and to compare them

[3] *The Country Newspaper*, North Carolina Press, 1926.
[4] *Non-Voting: Causes and Methods of Control*. By Charles E. Merriam and Harold F. Gosnell, University of Chicago Press. " An Experiment in the Stimulation of Voting," by H. F. Gosnell, *American Political Science Review*, 20: 869–874, 1926. *Getting Out the Vote — An Experiment in the Stimulation of Voting*. By H. F. Gosnell, University of Chicago Press, 1927. "Non-Voting in a Typical Ohio Community," by Ben A. Arneson, *American Political Science Review*, 19: 816–825, Nov., 1925.

in this respect with the men.[5]   Apart from the single state of Illinois, this must be wholly a matter of estimate.   We proceeded as follows:

Twenty-one northern states, not territories in 1880 and not granting suffrage to women in 1880 or 1900, were selected for the basis of estimate.   This gave us the main essentials of comparability for the three given years.   Among other difficulties removed was that which would be faced if the negro vote were included.

After various computations, it was decided to take no account of those persons rendered ineligible for the franchise by incarceration in asylums or prisons, or through inability to meet state or local residence requirements.   The aggregate of these is large.   The latter class of persons especially has perhaps been growing relative to population as a result of the presumptive increase in mobility of the population, stricter suffrage requirements, and possible decline in the urban practice of "colonization."   The seasonal and casual workers, who seldom remain in one locality a sufficient length of time to gain a residence, have been estimated to number as high as several millions.   In the absence of sufficient bases for a reasonable estimate, however, it was felt that less error would be introduced if no deductions were made for the causes named.   This has the misleading effect of making it appear that the ratios of voters to persons qualified were lower than they were in reality.   It has the advantage, on the other hand, of allowing the assumption that the error was a constant one in all three years, so that the trend of change will be unaffected.

In determining the number of presumptive eligibles for 1880 we faced the difficulty that at that time aliens were

[5] "American Women's Ineffective Use of the Vote," *Current History,* July 1924.

generally allowed to vote under certain conditions of residence and otherwise. The proportion of foreign-born who were thus eligible, however, could not be determined from the census data. That is, our presumptive total of eligible male voters in 1880 was composed of three parts: (1) native, white, twenty-one years and over, the number of which was given in the census; (2) colored, twenty-one years and over, also given; (3) foreign-born, twenty-one years and over (given in the census) but having certain other requirements of status, the number meeting which was not given.

In 1900 the situation as well as the census categories had changed. The foreign-born white population was now so subdivided as to distinguish those who were naturalized and those who had first naturalization papers. In five of the twenty-one states the latter were legally eligible to vote. In these five states the foreign-born males, twenty-one and over, naturalized and with first papers, were added to the native white and colored population of similar sex and age to constitute the total eligibles. In the remaining states the naturalized only were included in the summation. For each state the percentage of foreign-born whites of appropriate age and sex whose eligibility to vote had been thus determined was also calculated.

These latter percentages were then applied in each state to the 1880 totals of foreign-born males twenty-one years and over (not strictly comparable with the foreign-born white males of the 1900 determination) to secure a series of state estimates for the third part of the summation required for that year.

The corresponding figures for 1920 involved less unreliability and calculation. For each state they consisted of an aggregate of the numbers of men and women twenty-one years and over; native white of native, foreign and mixed parentage; negro; and naturalized foreign-born white.

The estimates of eligible voters for each year were then made up of the respective sums of the individual state estimates. This gave us the estimate in Table 34 for the twenty-one states. This table shows that the proportion of actual to eligible male voters dropped from 87.2 per cent in 1880 to 82.2 per cent in 1900.[6]

TABLE 34 — ESTIMATED NUMBERS OF ELIGIBLE VOTERS AND ACTUAL VOTES
CAST IN 21 NORTHERN STATES, 1880, 1900 AND 1920
(See text, page 244, for certain deductions not made)

Estimated Eligibles				Actual Vote Cast	Per cent of Eligible Vote Cast
Year	Men	Women	Total		
1880	7,329,000		7,329,000	6,394,000	87.2
1900	11,703,000		11,703,000	9,618,000	82.2
1920	16,605,000	16,296,000	32,900,000	18,528,000	56.3

But the question which we hoped to answer was still unsolved. To what extent did the new women voters contribute to the striking decline (to 56.3 per cent) in 1920? Was the drop, in other words, due to an acceleration of the rate of decrease in the votes of men, and to what extent, or was it due to failure on the part of the women to vote in numbers equal to the men?

No reliable answers to these questions can be given. The most rational assumption to make would seem to be that the proportion of men voting declined between 1900 and 1920 at the same rate as in the preceding twenty years, i.e., 5.7 per cent. This would reduce the proportion in 1920 to 77.5 per cent. The number of male voters would then have been 12,869,000 and the number of female voters 5,659,000 or 34.7 per cent of their eligible number. In Illinois, however, the

[6] Bearing in mind that both percentages as well as that for 1920 should really be higher. See page 244.

proportion of actual to eligible women voters was in the same year 46.5 per cent. The actual proportion of eligible women in the North and West who in 1920 took advantage of their political equality, was probably somewhere between these two figures, i.e., between 34.7 and 46.5 per cent. The first figure is probably too low, other evidence indicating that the male vote has declined at an accelerated rate. The second is probably too high because the tendency to vote is more marked in Illinois than elsewhere, and because limited suffrage was given women in that state at a relatively early date, probably resulting among them in some development of the voting habit.

It may be needless to say that my colleague and I felt considerable skepticism concerning the accuracy of the facile estimates of the amount and tendencies of non-voting which were so prevalent at about the time of the general election of 1924.

Another modest investigation seems to me to have interest because it suggests that public attention to political innovations may conform to a curve of growth and decline which resembles the bell-shaped curve of the normal frequency distribution. The hypothesis was suggested by a study of the operation of the initiative and referendum in the states of Washington and Oregon, some data from which have been cited above in Chapter XI.

In Figure 15 this seeming tendency is illustrated, first, by the number of magazine articles on the initiative and referendum listed in the *Readers' Guide* for each year from 1900 to 1922; second, by the numbers of states adopting these governmental instruments during the same years.[7] From 1923 to 1926 inclusive three additional references are recorded in the *Readers' Guide*, one of them referring to the

[7] As listed in the Encyclopedia Americana.

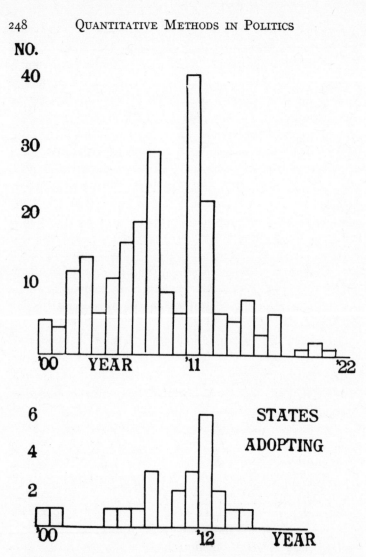

FIGURE 15 — MAGAZINE ARTICLES ON INITIATIVE AND REFERENDUM LISTED IN "READERS' GUIDE," 1900–1922 INCLUSIVE, WITH NUMBER OF STATES ADOPTING INITIATIVE AND REFERENDUM LEGISLATIVE DEVICES IN THE SAME YEARS

occasion for which my own paper was prepared. In the year 1926, however, the forgotten referendum issue acquired a new or special direction of attention, and in that year five articles are noted concerning referendums on *prohibition*.

From Figure 15 and the data upon which it is based it may be inferred that there was both an increasing development of attention to the subject and an increasing tendency to adopt the principle from 1900 to the year 1911 or 1912. A correlation between the two would be expected, and it is apparent. In the latter years, we may suppose the initiative and referendum "movement" to have been at its height. Following these years a decline in the "movement" is similarly evident — a decline even sharper than the earlier rise.

In Figure 16 I have shown the number of initiative and referendum measures voted upon in Washington and in Oregon for each biennium.[8] Oregon, a pioneer in direct legislation, utilized the "I and R" in a manner that followed closely the cycle of public interest observable in Figure 15. A total of 214 or more measures were voted upon within the period shown. Washington, after an initial period of active experimentation with its new device, fell in with the general decline of public interest in the subject. One took up the movement at the beginning of its *growth*, the other at the beginning of its *decline*.[9] This seems to explain why as compared with its next door neighbor to the south, Washington has made so little use of these direct legislative devices.

[8] Compiled from list of measures given in the Oregon *Blue Book*, 1921–1922, pp. 179 ff, for that state. For Washington, I have combined the complete list of measures from 1914 to 1921 enumerated in the Session Laws of 1921, with the measures shown in the 1922 Report of the Election Division, Department of State, voted upon in 1922. The Washington list excludes constitutional amendments proposed to the voters by the state legislature, although these are included in the official "Pamphlet" regarding measures that is prepared by the Secretary of State.

[9] Unfortunately, the data with which to bring these charts up to date has been unavailable.

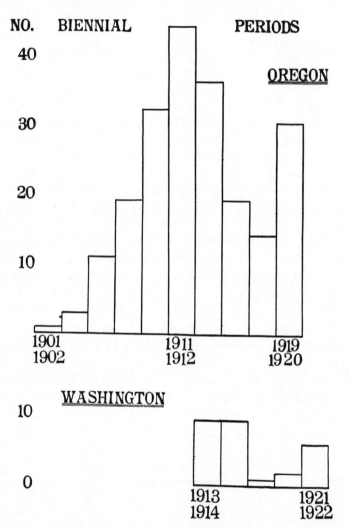

FIGURE 16 — INITIATIVE AND REFERENDUM MEASURES VOTED UPON IN
OREGON AND WASHINGTON, 1901–1922

XVIII

CHANGES OF ATTITUDE ATTRIBUTABLE TO DEFINED STIMULI

The measurements to be discussed in this chapter are similar in type to those involved in *experimentation* in natural science. Into a group over which some degree of experimental control exists, a new factor, presumably affecting specific modes of attitude among the group members in some direct manner, is introduced. This factor is defined and so far as possible controlled. Other factors are assumed to remain constant. The problem is to secure, through appropriate indices, a measure of direction or intensity of attitudes concerning the topic involved prior to the introduction of the new factor, and again after its introduction. The factor that is introduced is known, in psychological terminology, as a *stimulus*.

Because of the degree of control exercised by the teacher, the school or college classroom offers an exceptional opportunity for experimentation of this kind. An offsetting disadvantage of the classroom for political experimentation is its atypicality. Pupils of the public schools cannot mirror adult political attitudes with nicety, however good a sample they may be of the general intellectual levels of the population. College students who have attained maturity, on the other hand, are undoubtedly atypical with respect to information and opinion, and perhaps with respect to intelligence.[1] The advantages of the classroom for working out the

[1] Compare by the present writer, "The Distribution of Intelligence Among College Students," *The Journal of Educational Psychology*, Feb. 1925.

technique of experimentation, however, are supplemented by the direct advantage which it has for research concerning the effects of the educational process. In the colleges at least the latter subject of research has immediate importance for the study of politics.

Possibilities of measuring the effects, if any, of their teaching in changed student attitudes (not merely in the acquisition of information and the formal acceptance of the views of instructors and text-book writers) are available to teachers of social science in almost every course. They are so obvious that surprise must be felt at the exceedingly limited utilization made of them. A recent study of this kind made by Professor Donald R. Young[2] in connection with a sociology course on race problems stands out as almost a unique investigation of its kind. By securing from his students un-thought classifications of attitude toward races and nationalities other than their own at the beginning and the end of the term, Dr. Young discovered that surprisingly little change in attitude had occurred. The formal *intellectual apprehension* that had been gained with respect to race differences and prejudices, on the other hand, was all that an instructor would normally expect.

The stimuli to which the students were subjected in this experiment of Young's were varied and spread over half of an academic year. In this respect it resembles somewhat the experiment that will be described in the next chapter. An opportunity for measuring the immediate short-time changes resulting from an outstanding social stimulus was given to the writer and his colleague, Professor Malcolm M. Willey, by the visit of the late William J. Bryan to Dartmouth College

[2] "Some Effects of a Course in American Race Problems on the Race Prejudices of 450 Undergraduates at the University of Pennsylvania," *Journal of Abnormal and Social Psychology*, Vol. XXII, October–December, 1927, pp. 235–242.

on December 8, 1923. While the subject of Mr. Bryan's address, "Science vs. Evolution," was not explicitly political, a similar or improved technique of analyzing its effect could be applied to almost any political address. The situation measured possessed added interest because it involved two sets of stimuli operating in direct opposition. Dartmouth was at the time the one college in this country in which all students were required to take in their freshman year a full semester course in evolution. Mr. Bryan's well-known and implacable opposition to the hypothesis, therefore, ran squarely counter to class-room stimuli to which each of his student hearers had been subjected.

No visitor in recent years had been awaited with more expectancy. For a week before his arrival the college paper, *The Dartmouth*, had been framing the issue; and when Mr. Bryan actually appeared every available inch in the college auditorium had been taken. For a week after he had gone, the problems which he had raised were the chief topics of conversation whenever Dartmouth men came together. The endeavor of Professor Willey and myself to *measure* the changes of attitude taking place as a result of this situation were supplemented by qualitative statements of these changes, and of the attitudes both "before and after." This seems to be very often a necessary supplement to the quantitative approach.

One obvious criticism of our measurements, as described below, is that the student's appraisal of his own attitude toward evolution before listening to Mr. Bryan was made subsequent thereto. That is, he was asked at the same time to ascertain his present attitudes introspectively and his attitudes a few hours earlier retrospectively. The necessity of this procedure arose from lack of foresight on the part of the investigators themselves. We did not plan our experiment, in other words, until it was already under way, and evidences were about us of changes in attitude that were taking place.

A further comment pertains to the matter of constants and variables. The important variables introduced in the situation were the address of Mr. Bryan itself, the attendant publicity before and after his address, incidental personal contacts with him by individuals, class-room comments by instructors, and vigorous interstimulation between and among the students themselves. Of these the first and the last were probably of greater importance. The point to note is that our measurements pertain to the effects of a *group of related variables* and not to a single factor. On the other hand, there were no variables which were not the result of Mr. Bryan's visit. In this respect a single variable was isolated from its surrounding constants as effectively, perhaps, as is ever possible in the case of a new point of view thrown into the discussion process.[3]

At the first meeting of our classes following Mr. Bryan's lecture, we submitted to our students the following questionnaire, the introduction of which is intended to be a fair statement of the generally accepted principles of the evolutionary point of view:

"With reference to the doctrine that man evolved from lower animal forms in harmony with general principles of organic evolution:

1. I *reject* the doctrine completely.

[3] The remainder of the chapter is reprinted, with minor changes, from a portion of an article by Professor Willey and myself, "William Jennings Bryan as a Social Force," *The Journal of Social Forces*, March 1924. It is used here with the kind authorization of the editor and of my collaborator. The same material was used in somewhat more popular form in the *New York Times*, Sunday, Jan. 13, 1924, under the title "Dartmouth Charts Mr. Bryan's Arguments." The latter article was reprinted in *Mental Hygiene*, Jan. 1924.

2. While I do not *reject* it completely I do not believe that the evidence favors it.

3. I am undecided whether to reject or to accept it.

4. While I do not *accept* it completely I believe the evidence favors it.

5. I *accept* the doctrine completely."

Those students who heard Mr. Bryan were then asked to indicate which of these statements coincided most nearly with their own beliefs both before and after hearing Mr. Bryan. No class-room discussion was permitted until after the questionnaires had been returned.

Among the students to whom this questionnaire was submitted and all of whom had heard Mr. Bryan, were 39 members of the freshman class, none of whom at the time had taken the compulsory course in evolution. The remainder, numbering 136, were sophomores, juniors and seniors. While the number of cases, a little less than ten per cent of the entire student body, is not large it may fairly be regarded as an adequate sample of the relatively homogenous college enrollment.

The net results of Mr. Bryan's visit upon the minds of members of the three upper classes may be summarized in the table 35.

Thus before hearing Mr. Bryan, 70 of the men in the above table accepted without reservation the doctrine of organic evolution (Proposition 5). After hearing him this number had been reduced to 59. Before the lecture only two of these men rejected the doctrine completely; after, four men rejected it completely, etc. The column of Net Change shows that a net number of 8 men who were previously on the side of evolution were drawn to a position of doubt; and 7 others were drawn over to the side of non-acceptance.

Some facts of interest are observed when the above table

TABLE 35 — NET EFFECT OF MR. BRYAN IN CHANGING BELIEFS AMONG
SOPHOMORES, JUNIORS AND SENIORS

Belief *	Before hearing Mr. Bryan		After hearing Mr. Bryan		Net change in numbers
	Number	Per cent	Number	Per cent	
5	70	51.6	59	43.4	− 11
4	52	38.2	48	35.7	− 4
3	7	5.2	15	11.0	+ 8
2	5	3.7	10	7.3	+ 5
1	2	1.5	4	2.9	+ 2
Total	136	100.0	136	100.0	

* Refers to the five statements in the questionnaire.

is compared with the similar returns obtained from the members of the freshman class, who, it should be remembered, had not at the time taken the course in evolution. The freshman table is as follows:

TABLE 36 — NET EFFECT OF MR. BRYAN IN CHANGING BELIEFS AMONG
FRESHMEN

Belief *	Before hearing Mr. Bryan		After hearing Mr. Bryan		Net change in numbers
	Number	Per cent	Number	Per cent	
5	5	12.8	4	10.2	− 1
4	16	40.9	14	35.9	− 2
3	7	17.9	10	25.	+ 3
2	6	15.4	6	15.4	0
1	5	12.8	5	12.8	0
Total	39	100.0	39	100.0	

* Refers to the five statements in the questionnaire.

Before hearing Mr. Bryan, 5 members of the freshman group accepted without reservation the doctrine of organic evolution. This number represents 12.8 per cent of the entire freshman group as compared with 51.6 per cent holding similar views in the upper-class group. Similarly, 5 members of the freshman group, 12.8 per cent, rejected the doctrine of evolution without qualifications before hearing Mr. Bryan, as compared with 2 members in the upper-class group, or 1.5 per cent. After hearing Mr. Bryan the number of freshmen accepting the doctrine completely had been reduced from 5 to 4, or to 10.2 per cent, the number rejecting the doctrine completely remained as before, etc.

Here attention may be called to the first result of the inquiry. Partly, it may be presumed, as a result of greater maturity, but in greater part due to their familiarity with the principles of evolution acquired in the compulsory course the percentage of students accepting the doctrine without qualifications was four times greater in the sample representing the upper classes than in the freshman group. Conversely, the percentage of freshmen rejecting the doctrine completely was between eight and nine times as great as the percentage of upper classmen. Moreover, the proportion of freshmen who, while not rejecting the doctrine of evolution completely (before hearing Mr. Bryan) nevertheless believed that what evidence they had did not favor it was four times greater than in the corresponding group representing the upper classmen. Also, as might be expected, the freshman group neither accepting nor rejecting the doctrine was over three times as large proportionately as the corresponding group representing the other classes.

Here, then, is one index of the change of ideas brought about as a result of the impingement of the scientific point of view upon the student mind. As an indication of the change of ideas brought about by the opposing force represented by Mr. Bryan, however, the above tables do not present a wholly comprehensive summary. The extent of the change becomes clear only when a study is made of the shifts of opinion of the individual men, rather than the net results.

In table 37 we compared the actual number of shifts of opinion indicated in our returns with the number of shifts which theoretically might have occurred within the limited number of categories represented in the questionnaire. For example (within the group of upperclassmen shown in Table 35) any of the 70 students who accepted Proposition 5 (complete acceptance of evolution) theoretically might have shifted to a qualified belief in evolution, to indecision, to qualified rejection or to total rejection. In any of these cases, the shift would have been *away from* the evolutionist beliefs. He could not in any case (within the categories laid down) have shifted to greater adherence to the doctrine, for the formulation of the question itself would prevent. Similarly, two men who were completely opposed to evolution might become more favorably disposed to it, but could not reject it any more completely. Obviously, the men in opinion classes 2, 3 and 4

TABLE 37 — COMPARISON OF ACTUAL WITH POSSIBLE SHIFTS IN OPINIONS —
BY NUMBER AND PER CENT OF MEN INVOLVED

Direction of shift	Possible changes — Number	Actual changes — Number	Per cent, Actual of Possible
Upperclassmen			
Toward evolution................	66	5	7.6
Away from evolution............	134	32	24.0
Either direction.................	136	37	27.9
Freshmen			
Toward evolution................	34	4	11.8
Away from evolution............	34	7	20.5
Either direction.................	39	11	28.2

might shift in either direction.   It will be clear that ratios between the numbers of actual shifts and the numbers which are theoretically possible will provide a significant measure of the tendencies to change.

This table gives us our second conclusion. The views of more than one-quarter of Mr. Bryan's hearers were changed substantially as a result of his discussion. Among the larger of the two groups represented, nearly one-quarter of the men who were not already complete disbelievers in evolutionary doctrine were influenced in the direction which Mr. Bryan intended.

This does not mean, however, that these men were actually converted to Mr. Bryan's views. Some of them (whose views before hearing Bryan were represented by Proposition 2) were already disbelievers in evolution and were merely strengthened in their disbelief (and hence shifted to a belief in Proposition 1). Likewise, other men who accepted evolution completely before hearing him afterward changed so that their positions coincided with Proposition 4, which is still upon the side of evolution. A complete analysis of the figures makes it necessary to determine how many of the students represented in the samples shifted from acceptance of the doctrine in greater or less degree to a position of uncertainty and how many to a position of rejection in greater or less degree; how many from the position of uncertainty to positions of rejection and acceptance; and how many from positions of rejection to positions of acceptance or uncertainty. This is shown in the following table.

Thus, 8.8 per cent of the upperclassmen shifted their position from complete or partial acceptance to a position of uncertainty, etc. From this table it is again clear that the shift in opinion is in the direction of Bryan doctrine, although reversals of opinion are relatively few.

TABLE 38 — NUMBER OF CONVERSIONS TO AND FROM ACCEPTANCE, UNCERTAINTY AND REJECTION, WITH PERCENTAGES OF ENTIRE NUMBER IN EACH SAMPLE SO CONVERTED

	Upperclassmen		Freshmen	
	No.	Pct.	No.	Pct.
Acceptance to uncertainty...............	12	8.8	6	15.4
Acceptance to rejection.................	4	2.9	0	0.0
Uncertainty to rejection................	3	2.2	1	2.5
Uncertainty to acceptance..............	1	0.7	2	5.1
Rejection to acceptance................	0	0.0	1	2.5
Rejection to uncertainty...............	0	0.0	0	0.0
Unconverted (in any category)..........	116	85.4	29	74.5
Total..............................	136	100.0	39	100.0

A third conclusion which was derived from our analysis, therefore, was that Mr. Bryan's appearance on the Dartmouth campus served not so much to create converts as to arouse an attitude of skepticism or caution toward the deductions of the classroom. Whether or not this effect was transitory or permanent is of course not made evident.

It is obvious that the changes cited above have been arrived at in a manner almost mechanical, and in no way show what occurred in the minds of the students. Interesting as are these tables it is equally clear that their value would be enhanced if they were supplemented by data of a qualitative nature. In the attempt to get at the mental processes involved, the students were requested to append to each questionnaire an anonymous statement giving the writer's impressions of Mr. Bryan and his arguments. We now turn to a general appraisal of these replies:

The first conclusion to be drawn from this qualitative data is that many of the students who were unqualified adherents to the doctrine of evolution before hearing Mr. Bryan were reënforced in their convictions, even though our questionnaire did not permit them to express a quantitative change of opinion in the direction of increased intensity of belief. Thus, in several instances men who recorded themselves as accepting Proposition 5 before, attempted to indicate still greater conviction afterward by recording their beliefs as 5 + or 6, even though this was not permissible within the framework of the questionnaire. Moreover, such comments as the following indicate inclination of the same kind [4]:

The more he talks the better for evolutionary doctrine.

When analyzed (his) statements were so obviously untrue or senseless that they resulted against rather than for his point.

It seems to me that Bryan would throw most students (who are) on the fence to the side of evolution with his old-fashioned ideas of hard-boiled religion, for that is the way I interpreted *his* religion.

Bryan only strengthened my firm belief in evolution.

It is a great satisfaction to know from personal observation that the great opponent of creative evolution is only a garrulous old man.

There were a few indications of shifts in the opposite direction by men whose opinions had not undergone any formal change according to our classification.

The second conclusion to be drawn from this qualitative data is that there was almost general agreement upon the excellence of Mr. Bryan's oratory. Even the most convinced evolutionists among his hearers were frank to express their admiration in this regard. But a third conclusion represents an antithesis to this; there was likewise almost general

---

[4] All of the citations are presented with a conscious effort to represent fairly the various points of view which were disclosed. But we took particular pains to represent adequately all opinions favorable to Mr. Bryan's views. The qualitative material which appears below is, if anything, weighted in that direction.

agreement, even among those who held to his point of view, that Mr. Bryan's argument against evolution did not constitute an example of what to them seemed rational thinking.

These conclusions were illustrated by the following citations. The first are from the comments of upperclassmen who both before and after hearing Mr. Bryan were unqualified adherents to the views which he attacked:

Bryan is a silver-tongued orator and held the audience not so much by the stating of facts as by ability, taught by long experience, to keep the audience in the proper frame of mind.

Mr. Bryan is a wonderful orator. He got himself out of many a hole through the use of his wit, humor and evasion.

In my opinion, Bryan is a wonderful orator; he has the power to please an audience and arouse their emotions, but these two things do not make him a scientist.

With regard to his argument, we set in opposition to these citations the comments of freshmen (presumably the least mature of the two groups of students) who, before hearing Bryan, were unqualified *disbelievers* in evolution:

I was very disappointed in Mr. Bryan; although he gave his speech very well his argument, examples and references were not good or sound.

I admire the way he upheld the old sound home teachings about religion. The world needs a little more religion in its makeup. However, I do not think he proved anything except his ability to talk.

Throughout the comments, in fact, the evidence showed that the students almost without exception were able to discriminate between Mr. Bryan's oratorical ability and the logic that he employed. They did not allow his skill in the former to becloud their capacity to think upon the subject in hand. This conclusion may seem inconsistent with the facts, previously pointed out, that many of Mr. Bryan's listeners were changed in their beliefs after hearing him. No more can be done than to point out that where this inconsistency existed, it was usually recognized by the students themselves. Thus:

Bryan is without doubt a great orator and it was his oratory rather than his evidence against evolution that somewhat swayed my opinion.

I do not think that he proved anything. He made me, however, undecided as to the true origin of man.

All of his arguments, I thought, were poor, as they did neither break down the ideas of evolution nor build something better in its place. He did, though, make me undecided.

Now, coming back to the previous point, the following citations give additional evidence of the student's ability to distinguish oratory from reason.

He was very clever to bring in ridicule all through the talk, but I think he rather evaded the issue. . . . In short Bryan did not prove any facts for religion nor did he disprove any of the *facts* of evolution. He was very interesting but hardly instructive.

His speech, which was well delivered, was poor in itself and outside of its emotional appeal very unconvincing. No one would worry about the so-called danger to religion a minute if he had read the speech in a book and not heard Bryan deliver it.

He seemed to me to obscure the real and essential points under a cloud of ridicule and raillery that no doubt pleased the audience but in no way changed our opinions.

Bryan was extremely unfair in his whole argument. In the first place he gave the college to understand that his topic was "Science *vs.* Evolution." He knew that he could not get an audience if he had announced that he was to give only the theological arguments against evolution, so he stated that he would combat it from the standpoint of science.

He really proved nothing. Whenever a point arose which tended toward a decisive argument for his opponents he dodged it completely.

His arguments were weak and poorly founded. He seemed to be ridiculing evolution, not arguing against it; or probably he considers this a good way of arguing against it.

Bryan said: "Why base your philosophy of life on a theory you can't prove?" Great Cæsar! Is there anything more impossible of proof than the Bible itself and the whole story it tells, both in the old and new testaments?

Vituperation and wit are poor and surely non-convincing substitutions for criticism and argument.

He indulged too much in sarcasm and used wit rather than reason to "get across" to his audience.

Instead of trying to bring up the most salient points of conflict between the fundamentalist and evolutionist points of view, he resorted for the most part to ridicule and sarcasm, at which he is master, but which proves *nothing*.

He does not seem able to get right down to hard cold facts. He is forever wandering about giving little examples that the people think are very good at the time . . . (but which later one realizes) are rather weak.

All of these quotations in one way or another seem to indicate that the students possess intellectual honesty to a considerable degree, a fact that is further made evident in the following quotations:

He said that a belief in evolution made one agnostic. Even if this were true, its teaching should not be forbidden. How about the search for truth and freedom of speech?

He claimed to have an argument between religion and evolution. Can there be an argument between intelligence and emotion, between fact and feeling?

His whole argument seems to be, "Evolution is wrong because it tends to undermine our faith in God," which after all is no argument at all. It is like saying "Evolution is wrong because it is wrong."

He said that evolution tends to destroy one's belief in a God, especially in a personal God, and that is true; nevertheless, that is a pretty weak argument that evolution is wrong. I had rather laugh at the Bible and believe in evolution than accept unquestioningly a piece of fiction as the truth! How can we accept a thing as true if it will not bear scientific investigation? We have got our minds to think with. Why not try to use them once in a while instead of following a fool like Bryan who says his heart tells him that God is there. He'd better have his heart examined.

Some inkling as to the causes which led more than one-quarter of the men to change their opinions after hearing Mr. Bryan is disclosed in the following citations, which have been prefaced with numerals referring to the propositions in the questionnaire, thus indicating the change which occurred.

(5-4) Although Bryan failed to win me over to his side completely he caused me to reconsider the whole matter and it is through this reconsideration that I intend to draw my final conclusion.

(5-4) He did succeed in showing me that the theory (of evolution) was not absolutely proven, and that there are many loopholes in it, but he did not succeed in making me give up the theory.

(5-4) He opened up a new door of thought on this subject which I haven't fathomed yet.

(5-4) He did leave me with the impression that evolution had not as yet been proven as fact, but that it is the result of logical reasoning and experimentation.

(5-4) He did not state facts and therefore I do not believe that he proved anything. However, by his sincerity and masterful oratory he brought back to me the feeling that religion holds a very important place in life and is essential to harmony and human welfare. It is this fact which makes me doubt whether evolution is correct in every detail or not.

(5-4) His argument concerning the missing link in the origin of species seemed to me a very strong one.

(5-3) I was impressed by the way he emphasized the fact that it (evolution) was a guess.

(4-5) Under the stimulus of Bryan I really looked into the theory of evolution and was more firmly convinced that it is correct.

(4-5) His feeble attempt convinced me more than ever that evolution was indisputable.

(4-3) He clearly showed that the "facts" of evolution were based merely on resemblances.

(4-2) Bryan's argument cast enough suspicion on the evidence supporting evolution, to make me feel that it was no harder to believe in the miracles of Christ than it was to believe that man was descended from lower life.

(4-2) Bryan convinced me that there was something more to the evolution of man than the mere Darwinian theory.

In view of Mr. Bryan's statement that the chief cause of the antagonism between fundamentalism and evolution lies in the fact that the acceptance of evolutionist doctrines almost inevitably undermines the Christian faith, it is interesting to read some of the comments of the students upon this point. They are by no means in agreement. The following statements are made by some of those who with Bryan hold to the irreconcilability of the two doctrines:

(5-5) I have lost a great deal of the inborn faith at college and I lost some of it in evolution. If this is a menace, why not "put the label" on the course as Bryan suggested, give everyone the facts at the start, and part of Darwin's life. Then teach the course. We will be prepared.

(5-4) I do believe, as he does, that the theories of evolution are degrading to religion. It has expelled a good many of my former beliefs from my mind.

(5-3) One thing which he said was true — evolution has killed any spiritual God that I used to believe in.

(4-4) He had one good argument and that was that evolution in most cases is ruining the students' religion and ultimately lowering their morality. . . . A person should have some sort of religion and this fact must be met in some way.

(3-4) I remain or am confirmed in my agnostic beliefs.

(4-4) When he says that evolution undermines religion, I agree with him completely. And no greater catastrophe could happen to our nation. But Mr. Bryan is not openminded enough to take into consideration that the facts point to the acceptance of the theory of evolution no matter how distasteful they may appear.

As against this point of view may be cited an even larger number of cases in which the entire compatibility of a belief in evolution with a religious belief is stoutly maintained:

(5-5) My experience has been that before I took evolution I was an agnostic. Evolution brought my religion back. To me it is a most Christian doctrine and in no way incompatible with religion. It made religion real to me — a scientific reality at the basis of everything.

(5-5) He did say one thing that I agree with, and that is, we should come nearer to God and believe in Him more fully. But the question with me is, which form of belief, Bryan's or the evolutionists', leads us nearer to God? I believe the latter by all means, if it is taught in the right way.

(5-5) Bryan believes that man cannot believe in God and evolution. He believes in God as a static influence and that the world is making no improvement. This does not agree with my point of view that God is a constructive influence and that evolution tells of the improvement of both men and animals.

(5-5) He does not seem to realize the fact that evolution stops at a certain point and that evolutionists call from then on upon some force — "and whether we call it God or anything else — what's the difference?"

(5-5) The fact that so many ministers accept the doctrine contradicts Bryan's doctrine that evolution is destroying Christianity.

(5-5) He proved that some professors who believe in evolution were agnostics but that does not prove that the average person who accepts the general theory would become an agnostic. Might not the professors become agnostic because of their scientific attitudes in general and not just through evolution?

(5-5) His major premise seemed to be — evolution destroys Christianity and Christianity is necessary in this world. I believe that this is false. Evolution may destroy the creeds and dogmatic codes of the old religion but out of it will grow a rational religion based on fact and intelligence and reason and love of humanity. This religion will be a much better one than the old, narrow, bigoted one of the past.

(4-5) I believe he is absolutely wrong in saying that acceptance of the doctrine of evolution destroys the Christian principles of morals and liberty. It makes my faith in the heavenly power stronger.

(2-2) It seems to me that evolution augments the facts given in the Bible. It teaches that the world was created in six periods of time, not stating how long. Evolution tells us how it was done.

The data which have been summarized, in both quantitative and qualitative aspects, present a fair picture of the results of Mr. Bryan's appeal, regarded as a social stimulus, upon a relatively small, self-contained, homogeneous and critical student body. The results of the same stimulus upon another group, other factors remaining constant, would have varied according to the prevailing psychological patterns within the latter. In most instances, perhaps, the ideas and attitudes of Mr. Bryan's hearers would have been such as to give him a greater measure of success in redirecting attitudes to correspond more nearly with his own.

It must be conceded that the ultimate effects of even a

single conversion of attitude from one position to another are beyond calculation. Lord Alfred Tennyson expressed something like a theory of the *conservation of personal influence* in the lines

> "Our echoes roll from soul to soul
> And grow forever and forever."

It is part of Christian doctrine and evangelical rationalization that unlimited expenditure of effort is justified for the "salvation" of a single "soul"; that is, for the accomplishment of a (presumptive) fundamental change in certain patterns of attitude. The underlying idea seems to be similar, at least in part, to that of the poet; every convert is a point of origin for a new geometrical series of changing attitudes.

Efforts at conversions of attitude in economics and politics, however, usually have a more direct and immediate goal. "We want to persuade you to buy our product, or to vote for our candidate, *now*. The future can take care of itself. Tell your neighbor, of course, but comply with our suggestions yourself first." This being the case, the measurement of immediate results from business advertising or from political campaigning acquires practical importance. Much work is being done with reference to the first, but comparatively little with regard to the second. Controlled experimental studies which would endeavor to determine the comparative effectiveness of differing types of appeal to voters; or which would endeavor to obtain some estimate, for example, of the cost *per vote immediately secured* of a campaign address, might have real bearing upon the organization of the election process.

XIX

ATTITUDE RESULTANTS OF UNDEFINED AND CON-
FLICTING STIMULI [1]

Prodigious efforts are devoted in modern society to changing the attitudes and opinions of individuals. Innumerable
organizations and unattached but single-minded zealots are
striving continually to "convert" people to one or another
religious, economic, aesthetic, moralistic, philosophical or
political point of view. In the political field, the scramble of
contending groups to secure converts culminates every four
years in the grand clamor of a presidential election.

Efforts to measure the effects of the social-psychological
forces released by the various parties in their campaigns,
either in the net aggregate or in their minutiae, are seldom
made. The utility that such measurements might have was
pointed out at the end of the last chapter. It is true that
when the ballots are counted, the result appears in a certain
numerical form. One party or candidate *wins by so many
votes*. But no one has more than a guess concerning the
degree to which the outcome is due to the antecedent campaign or to any of the specific campaign devices. The
winning party may even have lost votes steadily during, and
as a result of, its attempts at persuasion. In other words,
the final election figures give no indication of the previous
changes in attitude that have occurred. The experiment consists in an undefined, unmeasured social situation, into which

[1] The greater part of this chapter has been reprinted from my article
"Differential Changes of Political Preference Under Campaign Stimulation,"
The Journal of Abnormal and Social Psychology, Vol. XXI, No. 3, October–
December, 1926. The editors' kind permission is here acknowledged.

are introduced a conflicting variety of partially defined but largely unmeasured stimuli, and from which emerges a measured and partially defined resultant.

The central problem for the political scientist in this virgin field of experimentation is to classify, define, and measure changes in attitudes among a variety of types of persons, in relation to varied stimuli. It is clear that the problem is very complex. Experimentation may proceed in a variety of ways. One was illustrated in the preceding chapter by the endeavor to measure the effects in the minds of students of an address by William Jennings Bryan. Students of method in rhetoric and argumentation are attempting to arrive at more general results by employing as variables stimuli which are both more narrowly defined and more effectively controlled. For example, they attempt to measure the effectiveness of various types of argumentative appeal upon selected audiences.[2] Another conceivable type of experimentation might be carried out with the coöperation of the opposing political managers concerned, under conditions such that no favoritism toward either side would result. That is, certain precincts of known and equivalent political characteristics might be placed during a campaign and election under controlled conditions, so far as overt campaign efforts were concerned. A comparison of the effectiveness of various methods for influencing the voter might thereby be possible. Again, the studies of Moore (page 195), of Allport and Hartman (page 82) and of Sturges[3] bear upon one or another aspect of the same central problem.

[2] Cf. "The Relative Effectiveness of the Condensed and Extended Motive Appeal," by George Rowland Collins, Quarterly Journal of Speech Education Vol. 10 (1924), p. 221, together with comments upon the same by William E. Utterback, ibid, p. 385 ff.

[3] Supra, p. 71. I am indebted to Professor Sturges for the privilege of examining some of his unpublished studies on "the dynamics of attitude."

With respect to the degree of experimental control that is present in experiments designed to measure changes of attitude resulting from stimuli, the study which is to be described in the present chapter may be related to several of those which have been mentioned along a scale, as follows:

Upper extreme: relatively high control
1. Effectiveness of types of argumentative appeal upon audiences: Studies of Collins and Utterback, cited *supra* in footnote 2.
    2. Measurement of effects of Bryan's address at Dartmouth College by Willey and myself, described in preceding chapter.
        3. The study to be described in the present chapter.
            4. *A priori* inferences drawn by political workers or observers, from observation, from election returns, etc.
                Lower extreme: relative absence of control

The occasion of the measurements here reported upon was the presidential campaign of 1924, the subjects being students of sociology in the three upper classes at Dartmouth College. The original aim of the experiment was two-fold; first, to determine the form of the distribution of generalized attitudes toward political and social change; second, to discover whether there was a relationship between the position occupied upon the scale of attitudes and the tendency during the campaign to change preferences among the concrete alternatives represented by the three major presidential candidates. The method employed was that of two successive "ballots" or questionnaires. In consequence, the study has as an outstanding defect the circumstance that the individual ratings upon the scale of attitudes were determined by a subjective appraisal of himself by each subject.

Some more objective process of rating, such as that employed by Moore in the paper cited (page 195) would have been preferable but was precluded by the circumstances under which the study was made.[4]

The opinions of the subjects were first obtained, in a uniform manner, on October 7 and 8, and again on November 3 and 4. The responses made on the latter dates were presumably those, with approximate correctness, that might have been registered at the election on November 4. Two days were necessary to complete the questionnaire in both cases because of the fact that the recitation periods of the classes involved fell upon alternate days. Thus twenty-seven days elapsed between the two tests in the case of the larger number of students.[5]

The period between the two tests contained the greater number of political stimuli to which the students were exposed. In addition to the political columns carried in newspapers and magazines of general circulation, there were campus campaign rallies for various candidates; articles in the daily student paper written by members of the faculty on behalf of Coolidge, Davis and La Follette; a non-partisan political forum; a straw ballot in which all students and members of the faculty were asked to participate; and the innumerable "leagues"[6] and secondary discussions which resulted from the more general campaign efforts. Thus it was possible to measure only the combined result of all of these and other stimuli, rather than the effects of any individual stimulus. The earlier and later questionnaires

[4] The writer was given the assistance of five colleagues in the Department of Sociology, in connection with their regular class work, and he wishes here to express his appreciation for their aid.

[5] There were exceptions in some cases.

[6] The "league" is a campus institution, consisting of a small fortuitously gathered and informally organized forum, in which the participants discuss any and all subjects.

will be referred to in each case as the October and the November ballot, respectively.

Upon the October ballot, the student was requested to draw the following eight-point scale, which, it was explained, purported to represent the distribution of political opinion from extreme radicalism at one end to extreme reaction at the other.[7] Upon this scale he was requested to indicate by

	X			
Radicalism	Liberalism	Conservatism	Reactionaryism

an X his own general political attitude, as closely as it could be estimated. Thus, if he were a liberal conservative in his own estimation, he would place an X within the Conservative sector, but within that half of the latter adjacent to the Liberal sector. If he were a radical liberal, he would place an X at the point indicated in the above diagram. The eight steps on the scale were assumed to be equi-distant. Below the diagram, each student was asked to write in alphabetical order the names of the three leading candidates for president and to note opposite these his first, second and third choice. Each student was asked to *identify* his paper, whether by name, initials, or some other symbol that he would remember.

Upon the November ballot, the same identifying symbol was repeated. The generalized political attitude, being regarded as a constant, was not again requested, but the student was asked once more for his *present* first, second and third choices with respect to Coolidge, Davis and La Follette.

[7] This involved the assumptions, which are by no means established, that generalized political attitudes exist and can be determined by the person holding them. It seems probable that there is at least a positive correlation between the conservatism or radicalism of an individual's attitudes upon each of a number of specific matters of political controversy. *Cf. Radicalism, Conservatism and Scientific Method*, by A. B. Wolfe, whose terminology was here employed.

A number of the subjects were present on one of the two dates only. Hence the ballots received were of differing degrees of utility. Those which could be matched together for the two dates numbered 340. However, 406 October ballots could be distributed according to the opinion scale, while 443 October participants and 385 November participants expressed preferences regarding candidates. Some of the tabulations and inferences drawn therefrom follow:

1. The distribution along the scale of opinion of the October ballots was as follows:

Extreme radical................................	2
Liberal radical................................	6
Radical liberal................................	47
Conservative liberal............................	199
Liberal conservative...........................	136
Reactionary conservative.......................	13
Conservative reactionary.......................	2
Extreme reactionary...........................	1
Total....................................	406

The distribution, while suggesting the normal type, is skewed to the left. This might be expected among those whose youth is presumed to be a factor making for radicalism. Moreover, Dartmouth is liberal. On the other hand, many students were undoubtedly influenced by the connotations of the terms employed. The word "liberal" is highly respected on the Dartmouth campus, and it is probable that many students who awarded themselves this designation would not merit it by any objective test. The term "reactionary" carries an opprobrium that would preclude most reactionaries from recognizing themselves by that name. It is likely that those who claimed the title did so as an expression of humor, for two of the three in that category cast first choice votes for La Follette. The same element of unreliability may apply to the class "reactionary conservative."

2. Nevertheless, it is apparent that a significant relationship existed between the student's estimate of his generalized political opinion and his expression of political preference. The percentages in the main opinion classes who expressed a first choice for La Follette on the October ballot were as follows:

Radicals (both classes).....................	100.0
Radical liberals............................	48.3
Conservative liberals.......................	15.5
Liberal conservatives.......................	0.8
Reactionary conservatives..................	0.0

In the same classes, those who expressed a first preference for Davis constituted percentages as follows:

Radicals (both classes).....................	0.0
Radical liberals............................	20.7
Conservative liberals.......................	28.2
Liberal conservatives.......................	19.5
Reactionary conservatives..................	46.1

For Coolidge, the first choice votes, in percentages, stood:

Radicals (both classes).....................	0.0
Radical liberals............................	31.0
Conservative liberals.......................	55.2
Liberal conservatives.......................	79.7
Reactionary conservatives..................	53.8

If the small and unreliable class of reactionary conservatives be omitted, it is seen that La Follette obtained decreasing support from left to right along the scale, that the Coolidge support increased in the same direction, and that the Davis vote was strongest in the central group of conservative liberals.[8]

3. With respect to the changes occurring between the test dates, the *drift* was clearly to Coolidge, and most strongly

[8] It is possible that some subjects determined upon their rating on the scale *in the light of* their conscious presidential preference, in which case the apparent relationships here disclosed would be spurious. The order of procedure followed in the experiment, however, was designed so far as possible to prevent such an association of ideas.

away from La Follette. Table 39 gives the percentages of the total received by each of the candidates at both dates, both for first choice and for first and second choice combined:

TABLE 39 — CHANGES IN PRESIDENTIAL CHOICE AMONG 340 STUDENTS IN DARTMOUTH COLLEGE DURING 27 DAYS PRIOR TO THE ELECTION OF 1924

	Percentage of first choice votes		Percentage of first and second choice votes combined	
	Oct.	Nov.	Oct.	Nov.
Coolidge	57.0	60.8	38.5	39.3
Davis	25.0	22.1	40.3	41.5
La Follette	18.0	17.2	21.2	19.3
Total	100.0	100.0	100.0	100.0

While Davis and La Follette both lost strength as first choice candidates, Davis gained as second preference.

4. Davis was evidently a good compromise candidate, for in first and second choice votes combined, he possessed a plurality. Moreover, he received a majority of the second choice votes of the supporters of both Coolidge and La Follette. Thus, second choice support was distributed as follows:

Coolidge supporters, for second choice gave

Davis.............. (Oct.) 77.9% (Nov.) 82.5%
La Follette......... (Oct.) 22.2% (Nov.) 17.5%

Davis supporters, for second choice gave

Coolidge........... (Oct.) 53.1% (Nov.) 51.7%
La Follette......... (Oct.) 46.9% (Nov.) 48.2%

La Follette supporters, for second choice gave

Coolidge........... (Oct.) 37.5% (Nov.) 37.9%
Davis.............. (Oct.) 62.5% (Nov.) 62.1%

Coolidge supporters were less likely to favor La Follette for second choice than were La Follette supporters to favor Coolidge. It may be inferred from this that both extremes regarded Davis as essentially conservative. Hence he was generally favored above La Follette by the Coolidge men, but was not correspondingly favored above Coolidge by the La

Follette men. The swing away from La Follette for second choice among the Coolidge adherents increased during the period of the experiment. There was a slight disposition, on the other hand, for Davis men to transfer second choice support from Coolidge to La Follette.

5. The net changes of preference disclosed by the above comparisons were not large. Nor was the gross change as large as might have been expected. Among 340 students, 44 only or 12.9 per cent changed in their first preferences. An additional 34, or 9.9 per cent changed in their second but not in their first preferences. Hence 264 or 77.2 per cent remained unchanged in first, second and third choice.

6. It may next be asked whether the tendency to change varied with the position of the student upon the attitude scale. That such was the case is indicated by Table 40, in which the number of changes within each of the four larger attitude classes is given as a percentage of the total in each class.

TABLE 40 — PERCENTAGE OF PRESIDENTIAL PREFERENCES CHANGED AND UNCHANGED, ACCORDING TO POSITION UPON OPINION SCALE

| | Per cent of total | | |
	Unchanged	Changed in first preference	Changed in second preference only
Radical liberals	65.6	24.1	10.3
Conservative liberals	76.6	11.7	11.7
Liberal conservatives	80.5	7.6	11.9
Reactionary conservatives	84.6	7.7	7.7

It is clear that stability of preference varied directly with increasing conservatism. The latter term, it must be remembered, is based upon the subjects' own appraisals. The impossibility of extending the conclusion beyond the immediate election situation should also be pointed out. In this particular situation the conservative was likewise the standpatter. This result is contrary to the hypothesis with which the writer began,[9] and is likewise opposed by Moore's findings,[10] the difference in result being even more apparent in Table 41. This relates the number of changes to the first preference on the October ballot.

TABLE 41 — PERCENTAGE OF PRESIDENTIAL PREFERENCES CHANGED AND UNCHANGED, ACCORDING TO FIRST PREFERENCE ON FIRST BALLOT

	Per cent of total		
	Unchanged	*Changed in first preference*	*Changed in second preference only*
Oct. Coolidge supporters	83.4	6.9	9.8
Oct. Davis supporters	70.6	21.2	8.2
Oct. La Follette supporters	64.0	22.0	14.0

La Follette's supporters did not "stick," as did those of Davis, nor did the latter's adherents remain as loyal as did those of Coolidge.

There are undoubtedly many other classifications within the electorate that would prove significant with reference to changes of political opinion during a period of campaign stimulation. Moore (*op. cit.*) in showing the association between various innate personality factors on the one side and radicalism and conservatism upon the other, used an approach that was essentially *static*, in the sense that variations in time following differential stimuli were not considered.[11] It would be interesting to employ his personality criteria to a determination of comparative changes of attitude in response to what might be called a *time series* of stimuli.

[9] *Cf.* pp. 86–89.

[10] *Supra*, p. 195: "Eighty-eight per cent of the radicals offered as much or more resistance to majority influence as did the average conservative, while only 14.3 per cent of the conservatives offered as much or more resistance than the average radical."

[11] An exception to this was his measurement of susceptibility to majority influence, referred to in the preceding footnote, in which the original list of judgments was repeated at the end of an hour during which the majority judgments of a list of one thousand college students elsewhere were presented.

XX

Time Series: Party Turnover in New Jersey, 1877–1924 [1]

The invention and improvement of precise statistical methods for analyzing time series has been one of the more important developments of recent years for the whole domain of social science. The use of these methods has been almost confined, however, to the special field of economics. There they have come to be of invaluable aid in charting those myriad fluctuations of business activity in which practical men are interested. In particular they have been used for discovering the relationship, or correlation, between pairs of series each of which varies over a period of time. As illustrations might be mentioned such studies as those between the production and the prices of various agricultural commodities, or between the prices of stocks and bonds.

So far as I know, the studies which follow in this chapter and in chapters XXI and XXII represent the first attempts that have been made to apply these methods to political data. The subjects with which they deal are perhaps relatively unimportant in themselves. (This has been true also of the subject-matter of other studies described in this volume.) They have significance because they tend to show that the same *types* of variation which have become familiar in economics are to be found also in politics and,

---

[1] Some results of this study were included in "Some Applications of Statistical Method to Political Research," (see note 3 page 101). The supporting data upon which the results rested, however, were not included. Use in this chapter of material from the paper, as in Chapters VIII and XXI, is with the kind permission of the editors.

hence, that the same general methods of analysis are applicable. This has hitherto been an *a priori* assumption only.

Variations over time in economic data are usually credited to one or another of four types of factors. There are, first, those factors whose combined influence operates with a degree of constancy, or a degree of constant change, over a relatively long period of years. The effects of these factors, when isolated, give rise to what is termed "secular trend." There are, next, those which result in cycles of several years' duration, giving rise, when isolated and plotted, to a more or less wave-like curve about the line of trend. Third, there are frequently seasonal influences, causing a somewhat rhythmic pulse within the yearly period. Lastly, there are fortuitous factors like the World War, unassociated with the trend, the cycle, or with seasonality. The methods of correlation may reveal certain regularities of relationship in the seasonal or the cyclical variations of two time series; but it is first necessary to segregate the effects upon the data of the four types of influences just named. The determination of any one of the four may be an important end in itself.

It cannot be taken for granted that all of these types of causes will be found in whatever series of political data may be constructed. On the other hand, it is possible that causes of variation may be found in politics with which the economic statistician is unacquainted. As a matter of fact both of these situations have been encountered in the present studies. It is obvious that political science has few, if any, indices of a sort from which seasonality of political attitudes could be determined, if it exists, although seasonal indexes with respect to political administration should not be difficult to obtain. Thus the monthly financial and administrative "load" placed upon the Street Cleaning Department of New York City could be easily reduced to index numbers.

But the type of "politics" which has occupied attention throughout the present book is not directly concerned with questions of public administration, or any of the bookkeeping aspects of government. I have been dealing, rather, with available evidences concerning those factors or "forces" that give rise to political activity and that determine its forms and its direction. From the standpoint of this interest, it is apparent that while political attitudes may or may not show seasonal fluctuations, any device such as monthly elections to determine the matter would quickly defeat its own ends!

As a practical matter, then, indexes of seasonality in politics, corresponding to the monthly reports of sales now obtained by the Federal Reserve Board from a variety of retail and wholesale industries, must be dispensed with. Even data from which annual indexes of attitude may be derived are none too frequently found in election reports and similar documents. We are left then, with trends, cycles (derived at best from annual data), and irregular fluctuations to investigate. But in at least one instance, as will presently appear, account has had to be taken of another type of recurrent factor as to which the categories of economic variation would give no hint. Further investigation of political time series may disclose more of such instances.

For experimental purposes, I have developed a number of series of data, each of which may be regarded as providing a reflection in some degree of political attitudes. Several of these have been based upon the vote for assembly candidates in New Jersey, from 1877 to 1924 inclusive. This is a state in which annual elections are held, in which assembly candidates have usually run for office under the banner of a recognized party, and in which the county or district vote for the individual party designees has been officially recorded in the state Legislative Manual during the period named.

The immediate aim of the study, in terms of subject-matter rather than of method, was to ascertain the existence and character of *cycles of party turnover*. It is a well observed fact that voters seem to turn at intervals from one party to another. The question was, do these turnovers conform to a cyclical rhythm, analogous to that with which the public has become acquainted in the case of business?

For each year, aggregating the vote for individual candidates in the twenty-one counties, I have computed on several bases the percentages of the votes which were cast for Republican candidates, for Democratic candidates, and for minor party candidates. The fact that these percentages refer to the aggregate vote for a number of candidates tends to neutralize the effect of personal popularity or unpopularity in the case of individuals. The result is a truer indication of the party vote in each year than would be, say, the vote for governor, president, or congressmen. It was felt that the changing percentages of Republican votes, with reference to the combined Republican and Democratic votes, let us say, would be some indication of what is sometimes called the pendulum of political opinion. The changing percentages of the minor party votes, with reference to the total of all parties, would give some index of the growth or subsidence of dissent from both of the major party organizations.

The original data that was compiled is published here in Tables 42 and 43 in considerable detail.[2] Their possibilities for political research extend beyond the use that I have been able to make of them. No attention at all has been paid by myself, for example, to variations with respect to the minor parties, to which I have just referred.

[2] In some issues of the New Jersey *Legislative Manual*, the required data is given in summary form. More frequently it was necessary to compile it laboriously from the detailed tables of votes for the individual candidates. Travel to several New Jersey cities was necessary to complete the data.

TABLE 42 [3] — AGGREGATES OF VOTES CAST FOR INDIVIDUAL ASSEMBLY CANDIDATES OF VARIOUS PARTIES, NEW JERSEY, 1877–1924

Year	Republican	Democratic	Greenback	Prohibition	Socialist Labor	Indep. Dem'i.	Indep. Rep'n.	Peoples	Labor	Independant	Miscel.
1877	85,453	95,712	2,222	783						2,337	
1878	89,291	83,513	18,247	844		417	349				645
1879	77,504	78,913	2,558	575		1,644	1,686				779
1880	120,125	122,222	3,159	213							1,486
1881	89,175	89,186	2,101	1,336		946				2,128	1,539
1882	94,664	102,470	3,195	2,302					380		2,166
1883	94,781	105,520	1,814	2,746			1,082				268
1884	128,896	128,407		5,158							2,836
1885	84,446	91,183	716	9,241		3,016					
1886	107,398	111,225		17,715		1,613			2,770		
1887	107,026	104,407		12,622					8,964		
1888	138,132	150,608		6,710						922	
1889	125,893	132,358		7,107		2,364					
1890	111,291	125,128		4,938							
1891	98,534	113,084		7,585					335		
1892	160,932	162,427		7,920	465			302			
1893	152,319	128,490		8,518	2,018			161		1,329	1,329
1894	162,136	115,415	*Socialist*	7,550	5,309			2,675			919
1895	161,966	134,277		6,992	3,938			1,466			
1896	217,357	136,241		5,836	3,834	3,521					
1897	131,777	122,916		8,043	4,360			153			1,539
1898	164,793	156,338		6,975	5,018			83			
1899	151,228	126,478	967	7,063	3,824						1,930
1900	219,391	165,908	4,221	7,144	1,692						
1901	187,997	160,478	3,119	5,593	1,658						
1902	184,392	163,446	4,835	6,017	2,332			321	655		152
1903	169,374	140,793	4,972	6,575	1,937						
1904	240,963	168,306	9,445	6,914	2,469			1,532			
1905	211,431	153,168	7,501	4,766	1,755						340
1906	170,248	168,816	7,431	4,174	1,484		*Progressive*		1,970	612	9,729
1907	197,433	181,807	6,720	4,805	1,104				83		233
1908	252,758	191,172	4,770	10,437	677				28	1,505	2,452
1909	210,659	169,157	6,246	4,998	921	1,163					269
1910	199,046	213,516	10,400	5,386	1,606		139		970		2,383
1911	157,081	160,184	15,762	7,141	1,142				1,613		1,997
1912	92,707	163,969	15,701	6,010	1,205		89,679				
1913	130,005	148,897	16,814	5,705	1,021		48,894				
1914	173,960	154,549	16,152	8,989	837		21,236				437
1915	185,081	150,576	11,513	11,847	292		6,903				6,649
1916	240,601	175,588	15,867	10,147	429						
1917	173,461	138,752	29,460	12,061	1,740						14,554
1918	167,596	145,838	12,935	4,091	104				3,762		1,424
1919	208,589	177,662	16,340	3,293	311						13,605
1920	556,356	278,081	17,677	1,708	680						998
1921	326,053	259,550	9,061		345						6,847
1922	394,974	380,984	7,231		662						5,031
1923	373,914	338,750	4,319		197					1,564	6,079
1924	606,140	345,650	9,697		165		8,706				5,326

1878: Temperance Party vote included under Prohibition.
1879:   Do.
1881: Miscellaneous entry is for Anti-Monopoly Party. Temperance Party vote included under Prohibition.
1883: Miscellaneous includes National Party 150, and not stated, 118.
1884: Miscellaneous includes National Party 1709, and not stated, 1127.
1894: Beginning with this year, members are elected at large from counties. Prior to this they had been elected from districts. The vote used has been that of the average of the nominees of each party in each county where more than one has been nominated.
1899: Social-Democratic and Indep. Socialist vote recorded under Socialist.
1902: Workingmen's Party recorded under Labor.
1904: People's Democratic recorded under Peoples.
1905: In Ocean County, the Independent Republican vote having been included in the Democratic Party column, the Assembly vote was eliminated from the totals, and the votes for Sheriff on the respective tickets were substituted.
1906: In Cape May County, 1723 votes in the Democratic column include votes cast for Democratic, Prohibition and Roosevelt Republican candidates. In Morris County, 4,948 votes recorded as Democratic include also votes for Independent Democracy candidates.
1906, 1907, 1908: Union Labor votes recorded as Labor.
1908: Miscellaneous represents Local Option League votes.
1910: Progressive entry is designated Progressive Republican.
1912: Hudson County cast 19,764 votes for candidates designated as Progressive (Roosevelt) and Republican. These are included in the Progressive column.
1913: Progressive candidates in Burlington county (3,603 votes) carried endorsement of the National Prohibition Party.
1917: Miscellaneous represents 14,554 votes for Independent Clean Government candidates in Hudson County, which appear to be normally Republican.
1918: Miscellaneous includes Single Tax, 1298, and National 126.
1919: Miscellaneous includes Single Tax, 3,417; Personal Liberty Progressive, 1,542; Independent Constitutional Liberty, 1,096; Independent Citizen candidate, 738; Soldiers, Sailors and Marines, 1,544; Veterans Citizen Labor, 5,269.
1920: Miscellaneous includes Single Tax, 396; Non-Partisan League, 465; Enforcement of Volstead Act, 147.
1921: Miscellaneous includes Labor and Non-Partisan, 5,798; Single Tax, 1,049.

[3] Many perplexing problems of classification are concealed in the figures given in this table. When there has been no legislative candidate of a recognized major party in a given district, the vote of this party for state senator, or for some other representative office has frequently been supplied. By no means all of the special steps taken can be indicated, but the following notes should accompany entries for the years named:

1922: Miscellaneous includes Single Tax, 4,131; American Labor, 900.

1923: In Camden County, Republicans and Democrats entered a coalition against a Non-Partisan League organization. The coalition cast 26,317 votes to 23,064 for the Non-Partisan League. The total vote was distributed, 32,690 to the Republican column and 16,691 to the Democratic column, on the assumption based upon a trend line established for years preceding and following, that 66.2 per cent of the combined Republican and Democratic vote was "normally" Republican for that year.

1924: In several cases the same candidates were endorsed by both major parties. The entire vote, in these instances, was eliminated, since percentages, rather than totals, are the matter of major interest in the present study. Miscellaneous includes: Clean Government, 4,659; Workers', 535; Commonwealth Land, 84; Anti-Tobacco, 48. La Follette-Wheeler Progressive and Socialist-Progressive votes have both been included under Progressive.

TABLE 43 [4] TOTALS OF VOTES CAST FOR INDIVIDUAL ASSEMBLY CANDIDATES, NEW JERSEY, 1877–1924, TOGETHER WITH CERTAIN SUB-TOTALS AND PERCENTAGES BASED THEREON

(This may be regarded as a continuation of Table 42, upon the data of which it is based. That is, the total here shown in Column II, summarizes the individual entries in the various columns of Table 42).

Yr.	Total Vote	Total Republican & Democratic Vote	Percentage of total vote			Percentage of total Republican and Democratic vote	
			Repub.	Dem.	Minor	Repub.	Dem.
I	II	III	IV	V	VI	VII	VIII
1877	186,507	181,165	45.8	51.3	2.9	47.2	52.8
1878	193,306	172,804	46.2	43.2	10.6	51.7	48.3
1879	163,659	156,417	47.4	48.2	4.4	49.6	50.45
1880	247,205	242,347	48.6	49.4	2.0	49.6	50.4
1881	186,411	178,361	47.8	47.8	4.3	50.0	50.0
1882	205,177	197,134	46.1	49.9	4.0	48.0	52.0
1883	206,211	200,301	46.0	51.2	2.8	47.3	52.7
1884	265,297	257,303	48.6	48.4	3.0	50.1	49.9
1885	188,767	175,629	44.7	48.3	7.0	48.1	51.9
1886	240,721	218,623	44.6	46.2	9.2	49.1	50.9
1887	233,019	211,433	44.7	46.3	9.0	50.6	49.4
1888	296,372	288,740	46.6	50.8	2.6	47.8	52.2
1889	267,722	258,251	47.0	49.4	3.6	48.7	51.3
1890	241,385	236,719	46.1	51.8	2.1	47.1	52.9
1891	219,538	211,618	44.9	51.5	3.6	46.6	53.4
1892	332,046	323,359	48.5	48.9	2.6	49.8	50.2
1893	294,164	280,809	51.8	43.7	4.5	54.2	45.8

TABLE 43 (Continued)

Yr.	Total Vote	Total Republican & Democratic Vote	Percentage of total vote			Percentage of total Republican and Democratic vote	
			Repub.	Dem.	Minor	Repub.	Dem.
I	II	III	IV	V	VI	VII	VIII
1894	294,004	277,551	55.1	39.3	5.6	58.4	41.6
1895	308,639	296,243	52.5	43.5	4.0	54.7	45.3
1896	366,789	353,598	59.3	37.1	3.6	61.5	38.5
1897	268,788	254,693	49.0	45.7	5.2	51.7	48.3
1898	333,207	321,131	49.5	46.9	3.6	51.3	48.7
1899	291,490	277,706	51.9	43.4	4.7	54.5	45.5
1900	398,356	385,299	55.1	41.6	3.3	56.9	43.1
1901	358,845	348,475	52.4	44.7	2.9	53.9	46.1
1902	362,150	347,838	50.9	45.1	4.0	53.0	47.0
1903	323,651	310,167	52.3	43.5	4.2	54.6	45.4
1904	429,629	409,269	56.1	39.2	4.7	58.9	41.1
1905	378,961	364,599	55.8	40.4	3.8	58.0	42.0
1906	364,464	339,064	46.7	46.3	7.0	50.2	49.8
1907	392,185	379,240	50.3	46.4	3.3	52.1	47.9
1908	463,799	443,930	55.0	41.2	3.8	56.9	43.1
1909	393,413	379,816	53.5	43.0	3.5	55.5	44.5
1910	433,446	412,562	45.9	49.3	4.8	48.2	51.8
1911	344,920	317,265	45.5	46.4	8.1	49.5	50.5
1912	369,286	346,370 *	49.4 *	44.4	6.2	52.7 *	47.3 *
1913	351,336	327,796 *	50.9 *	42.4	6.7	54.6 *	45.4 *
1914	376,160	349,745 *	51.9 *	41.1	7.0	55.8 *	44.2 *
1915	372,861	335,657 *	51.5 *	40.4	8.1	55.1	44.9
1916	442,632	416,189	54.4	39.7	5.9	57.8	42.2
1917	370,028	312,213	46.9	37.5	15.6	55.6	44.4
1918	335,750	313,434	49.9	43.4	6.7	53.5	46.5
1919	419,800	386,251	49.7	42.3	8.0	54.0	46.0
1920	855,510	874,437	65.0	32.5	2.5	66.7	33.3
1921	601,856	585,603	54.2	43.1	2.7	55.7	44.3
1922	788,882	775,958	50.1	48.3	1.6	50.9	49.1
1923	724,823	712,664	51.6	46.7	1.7	52.5	47.5
1924	975,684	951,790	62.1	35.4	2.5	63.7	36.3

* Republican and Progressive votes are added and counted as Republican.

[4] The same procedures and interpretations noted in Table 42 apply to the present data throughout. The procedure in the years 1912–1915 in including the Progressive Party vote with the Republican is questionable. For those who might wish to eliminate the Progressive vote from columns III, IV, VII and VIII for those years, the following figures and percentages are offered:
1912: Tot. Rep. and Dem., 256,676; Percentage Rep. of Grand Total, 25.1;
    Percentage Rep. of Tot. Rep. & Dem. 36.1; Percentage Dem. of
    same 63.9.

Only one of the series presented in Tables 42 and 43 in fact, has received careful analysis. This is the *percentage Republican of the total vote*, shown in column IV of Table 43. A methodological problem was presented here by the consistent increase of the Republican vote, both absolutely and relatively, in the quadrennial presidential elections.[5] So pronounced was the phenomenon that it was felt necessary to make a correction for it. This was accomplished by the calculation of an *index of quadrennial variation*, similar to the index employed by Professor Warren M. Persons in making correction for seasonal factors when determining cycles and trends.[6] The recurring years of each quadrennium beginning with the year of the presidential election were designated as P_0, P_1, P_2, and P_3 respectively. Thus 1880, 1884, 1888, etc. were all designated P_0; 1881, 1885, etc. were designated P_1, and so on. Link relatives were obtained by expressing the datum of the series for each of these years as a percentage of the figure for the preceding year. For example, the datum for 1880 (P_0) divided by the datum for 1879 (P_3) gives a link relative for 1880 and is one of 12 such relatives for P_0. Average link relatives for P_0, P_1, P_2, and P_3, separately, were then secured, the median, arithmetical

---

1913: Tot. Rep. and Dem., 278,902; Percentage Rep. of Grand Total, 37.0; Percentage Rep. of Tot. Rep. & Dem., 46.6; Percentage Dem. of same, 53.4.

1914: In same order, 328,509; 46.2; 53.0; 47.0.

The title of the table is misleading in that, since 1894, candidates were elected at large by counties. The totals in the table, then, are totals of *county averages* for the separate parties since that date.

[5] This phenomenon has led in both New Jersey and New York to efforts by Republicans to take advantage of it by adjusting the time of state elections to correspond with the national election. *Cf.* editorial, "Scrambled Elections," *New York World*, Oct. 12, 1927. In both states, constitutional amendments looking in this direction were defeated in 1927.

[6] *Review of Economic Statistics*, January, 1919, pp. 18–31. See also Mills, Frederic C., *Statistical Methods*, Chapter VIII.

mean and geometric mean all being obtained. The former appeared to be the most representative average and was employed, as by Persons. Chain relatives with P_0 as 100.0 were then calculated and corrected. The corrected chain relatives were then converted in such a manner that the average of P_0, P_1, P_2 and P_3 equalled 100.0 (rather than $P_0 = 100.0$). The figures thus obtained gave the *indexes of quadrennial variation required.* The steps taken are summarized in Table 44.

TABLE 44 — STEPS TAKEN IN CALCULATION OF INDICES OF QUADRENNIAL
VARIATION

(Consult text concerning data and symbols)

	$\dfrac{P_0}{P_3}$	$\dfrac{P_1}{P_0}$	$\dfrac{P_2}{P_1}$	$\dfrac{P_3}{P_2}$
Number of relatives.....	12	11	12	12
Median link relative...	107.5	97	99	100.0

Year	Link Relative (Median)	Chain Relative	Corrected Chain Relative	Index of Quadrennial Variation
P_0	107.5	100.0	100.0	104.
P_1	97.	97.	96.	100.
P_2	99.	96.	95.	99.
P_3	100.0	96.	94.	98.
P_0		103.	96.	(av.) 100.0

The necessity of calculating similar indexes for the triennial election of a governor was considered as a possibility, but rejected when it was found that substantially little error appeared to result from this cause.

Various linear and parabolic trend lines were fitted,[7] both to this entire series and to particular segments as well. For the entire period of forty-eight years, the following equations were obtained, the origin in each case being in the center

[7] *Cf.* Mills, *op. cit.*, Chap. VII.

of the series with x deviations representing one half-year each:

Linear:

$$y = 50.4125 + .0851\, x$$

2d Deg. Parabolic:

$$y = 50.787 + .0851\, x - .00049\, x^2$$

3d Deg. Parabolic:

$$y = 50.787 + .0851\, x - .00049\, x^2 + .00036\, x^3$$

The difference among these is not large, and it appeared on the whole that a straight line was to be preferred as representing the secular trend of the series. Ordinates to represent the "normal" for each year were obtained from the above "Linear" formula, and multiplied by the appropriate index of quadrennial variation. The products were deducted from the corresponding annual item in the original series (column IV of Table 43) and the remainder (positive or negative) converted to a percentage of the normal of the trend. These percentage deviations were then used for the calculation of a *standard deviation*, or σ; and *cycle figures*, consisting of deviations in terms of decimal parts of the standard deviation, were finally obtained. These are given in Table 45.

When correlated with cycles of business indexes developed by Ogburn and Thomas,[8] without lead or lag, the coefficient of correlation (r) for the period 1877–1920 equals −.247. This is the highest correlation coefficient that has been obtained in a very few efforts to relate the series to other business and social data.

The reader will be well justified, has he reached this point, in asking what it is all about. A brief answer will be given. I have been trying to discover if there were cycles in the

---

[8] "The Influence of the Business Cycle on Certain Social Conditions," by Wm. F. Ogburn and Dorothy Thomas, *Journal of the American Statistical Association*, 1922, pp. 324–340.

TABLE 45 — CYCLE FIGURES, SHOWING DEVIATIONS IN TERMS OF THE STAND-
ARD DEVIATION, FOR THE SERIES MADE UP OF THE PERCENTAGES REPUB-
LICAN OF THE TOTAL VOTE FOR INDIVIDUAL ASSEMBLY CANDIDATES, NEW
JERSEY, 1877–1924

Cycle		Cycle		Cycle	
Year	Figure	Year	Figure	Year	Figure
1877	− .199	1893	+ .828	1909	+ .491
1878	+ .031	1894	+ 1.963	1910	− 1.656
1879	+ .199	1895	+ 1.242	1911	− 1.656
1880	− .061	1896	+ 2.362	1912	− 1.488
1881	+ .429	1897	− .245	1913	− .475
1882	− .230	1898	.000	1914	− .077
1883	− .153	1899	+ .844	1915	− .092
1884	− .291	1900	+ .844	1916	− .230
1885	− .982	1901	+ .583	1917	− 1.825
1886	− .920	1902	+ .230	1918	− .844
1887	− .767	1903	+ .752	1919	− .798
1888	− 1.150	1904	+ .920	1920	+ 2.607
1889	− .460	1905	+ 1.380	1921	+ .092
1890	− .644	1906	− 1.242	1922	− .966
1891	− .920	1907	− .061	1923	− .455
1892	− .767	1908	+ .368	1924	+ 1.549

tendency of voters in New Jersey, over a period of forty-
eight years, to turn their favor toward, and then again away
from, the Republican Party. (Other series in Table 43
could be used for answering similar questions concerning the
Democratic Party, or minor parties.)   It was necessary,
first, to isolate and eliminate the secular *trend*, which shows
an annual increase of favor toward the Republicans amounting to .0851 per cent of the total vote per year (Linear
equation on p. 290). It was also necessary to eliminate the
tendency for the Republicans to poll a higher proportion of
the votes in presidential election years. Having "corrected"
for these influences, we obtain the figures given in Table 45,

which represent the cyclical tendency referred to. These are
shown, together with the similar indexes of business obtained
by Ogburn and Thomas in Figure 17. It is apparent that

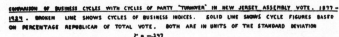

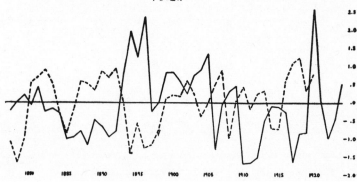

FIGURE 17 — COMPARISON OF BUSINESS CYCLES WITH CYCLES OF PARTY
"TURNOVER" IN NEW JERSEY ASSEMBLY VOTE, 1877–1924

cycles are present, although they do not seem to occur so
frequently as the business cycles. On the whole, there is a
slight tendency for voters to *turn toward the Republican
Party* (indicated by the solid line rising above the base line)
when business conditions are bad (indicated by the dotted
line falling below the base line).

If I may venture an interpretation of a matter which is
by no means clear, it would appear from this analysis that
cycles of party turnover in New Jersey are to be attributed to
some factor or factors of changing attitude which are *not*
closely related to changes in business prosperity. The evidence for this is found largely in the fact that the cycles
appear to be of dissimilar duration or period in the two
curves. Hence any adjustment of one to the other by means

of *lead* or *lag* places portions of the two curves in opposition at the same time that other portions are in corresponding phase. But it must be remembered that a single series from a single state is the basis of this opinion. The data given in the tables of this chapter have by no means been "worked" adequately. One reason for giving the raw figures in such detail has been the hope that other students might utilize them for further calculations, and thus be spared the tedious and extensive labor which has gone into the original compilations presented.

XXI

Time Series: Age and Service of Congressmen, 1790–1924.

The germ of the idea upon which the inquiries in this chapter were based was obtained from Professor Alvan A. Tenney in his graduate seminar at Columbia University, a number of years ago. Professor Tenny suggested that increasing age was probably a factor making for comparative conservatism of attitudes. If, then, some measures of relative age levels in different legislative bodies were secured, they might be found to correlate with the types of legislation, whether radical or conservative in tendency, that these bodies produced. With this idea in my mind it was subsequently noted that the leaders in the new Free State government of Ireland were predominantly young men, a fact which, in view of their revolutionary attitudes, seemed to support the hypothesis. Later on, having become interested in the statistical analysis of political time series, I found a dual interest in choosing for experimental inquiry data concerning the ages of Representatives in the first sixty-eight sessions of the American Congress. Closely allied to the question of age was that of the length of service.

As compared with many economic data, and even as compared with the series given in the preceding chapter, the ages and duration of service of congressmen have little bearing upon short-time fluctuations of political attitude. We have to be content with *biennial* indexes presented by the congressional elections. To offset this inherent defect is the fact that determinations may cover a span beginning with the First Congress in 1789.[1]

Four major series were constructed, concerning the two matters of interest that have been mentioned. These are given in detail in Table 46. They consisted of (1) the median age of all members of the United States House of Representatives from the First to the Sixty-eighth Congress inclusive; (2) the median age of the members serving their first term in each of these Congresses; (3) the percentage of members in each session serving a first term; and (4) the average experience of the members of the House in each Congress. Other series could be constructed from the variability among the members' age or experience during the several sessions. Such series, however, have not been constructed. They would involve calculations with the original detailed entries on the work sheets in the writer's possession.

Issues of the *Congressional Directory* provided the necessary data for recent sessions. For the period prior to the Sixty-Second Congress, they were taken from the ten or twelve thousand individual biographies contained in the *Biographical Congressional Directory*.[2]

The technique of compilation may be a matter of some interest, inasmuch as the arrangement of biographies in the latter source is alphabetical, without reference to the dates of service. It includes the biographies of United States Senators, Delegates to Congress and members of the Congress under the Articles of Confederation as well as Representatives. Frequently the same individual served in more than one of these bodies. To secure the required data,

---

[1] The series might have been projected backward in some cases by including corresponding data for delegates to congress under the Articles of Confederation.

[2] Sixty-First Congress, 2d Session, Senate Doc. 654.

TABLE 46 — ORIGINAL SUMMARY DATA CONCERNING AGE AND LENGTH OF
SERVICE OF AMERICAN CONGRESSMEN, FIRST TO SIXTY-EIGHTH CONGRESSES
INCLUSIVE, 1790–1924.

Congress Session	Year of beginning term	Median age in years and decimal fractions at start of term		Percent. First-term Members	Average number of terms served prior to present session
		All members	1st term members		
I	II	III	IV	V	VI
1	1789	43.69	43.69	100.0	0.0
2	1791	40.93	40.14	46.5	0.54
3	1793	42.00	40.73	56.5	0.64
4	1795	40.25	39.07	38.9	1.00
5	1797	40.45	39.09	43.1	1.03
6	1799	43.45	43.09	36.0	1.23
7	1801	42.38	37.20	42.5	1.25
8	1803	44.34	40.35	46.9	1.14
9	1805	42.30	39.63	36.9	1.36
10	1807	43.88	42.53	36.2	1.54
11	1809	44.60	43.57	35.9	1.71
12	1811	42.51	39.53	38.5	1.83
13	1813	43.25	41.47	52.6	1.31
14	1815	42.19	36.79	42.9	1.48
15	1817	40.26	38.47	59.2	.93
16	1819	41.78	41.93	40.8	1.15
17	1821	41.57	37.48	45.2	1.23
18	1823	41.10	39.21	43.2	1.29
19	1825	41.38	39.90	39.4	1.42
20	1827	42.02	39.39	33.2	1.68
21	1829	42.87	40.51	41.0	1.55
22	1831	43.19	40.66	38.0	1.59
23	1833	43.06	41.04	53.7	1.15
24	1835	42.42	38.25	40.0	1.23
25	1837	41.04	39.45	48.6	1.13
26	1839	41.45	38.44	46.3	1.17
27	1841	42.06	39.74	37.7	1.30
28	1843	40.73	38.67	66.7	.76
29	1845	41.07	38.74	49.0	.90
30	1847	41.12	41.08	50.4	1.00
31	1849	41.26	40.50	53.1	.92
32	1851	41.49	40.53	53.3	.84
33	1853	41.65	41.35	60.5	.69
34	1855	42.75	42.06	57.5	.81
35	1857	42.17	41.14	46.2	1.04
36	1859	41.95	40.96	45.1	1.02
37	1861	43.37	42.29	53.9	.83
38	1863	44.40	44.10	58.1	.75
39	1865	46.31	44.12	44.3	1.00

Table 46 (*Continued*)

Congress Session	Year of beginning term	Median age in years and decimal fractions at start of term		Percent. First-term Members	Average number of terms served prior to present session
		All members	1st term members		
I	II	III	IV	V	VI
40	1867	45.99	43.91	46.0	1.12
41	1869	44.64	41.71	49.2	1.04
42	1871	45.41	44.54	46.5	1.11
43	1873	46.54	45.06	52.0	1.07
44	1875	46.69	45.09	58.0	.92
45	1877	47.76	45.44	46.6	1.11
46	1879	48.09	45.35	42.3	1.21
47	1881	48.33	45.26	31.8	1.56
48	1883	47.27	44.80	51.5	1.22
49	1885	48.13	44.90	38.0	1.41
50	1887	47.45	46.47	35.6	1.54
51	1889	47.80	43.40	38.1	1.61
52	1891	48.37	48.15	43.8	1.44
53	1893	48.09	45.48	38.1	1.65
54	1895	47.90	45.04	48.6	1.25
55	1897	46.86	44.56	37.9	1.59
56	1899	47.10	43.27	30.1	1.79
57	1901	47.72	44.17	24.4	2.11
58	1903	47.36	43.04	31.3	2.10
59	1905	47.87	44.35	21.0	2.48
60	1907	48.71	43.29	22.5	2.61
61	1909	49.63	45.60	19.9	2.84
62	1911	49.40	47.38	30.5	2.62
63	1913	47.93	44.35	34.4	2.14
64	1915	48.60	43.85	27.2	2.44
65	1917	49.24	45.58	16.0	2.83
66	1919	49.62	46.53	22.7	2.74
67	1921	50.53	45.69	23.6	2.69
68	1923	51.04	47.35	27.1	2.57

therefore, involved careful preparation and methodical procedure.

Sheets of paper were numbered at the upper right-hand corner of each from 1 to 68, representing the several sessions of Congress. As any one of these became filled with entries it was replaced by another in the same numerical order. Beginning with the letter A, the biographies were read in turn. The birth date of each representative was mentally noted, together with the serial numbers of the Congressional sessions in which he served. On the sheets corresponding to each of the latter, the birth date was entered in abbreviated fashion. For example, August 29, 1857, would have been entered as 8/29/57. The number of terms served by the member, inclusive of the session on which the posting was entered, was also noted. Having completed these entries [3] those for each session were classified by years of birth, first for all members, and second for first-term members. Having located the median birth-year, in both cases, further classification determined the *birth date of the median-born member.* This was then converted into the *age of this member at the time of beginning* his term of service, months and days being expressed in each case as a decimal fraction of a year. These median ages are those which appear in columns III and IV of Table 46.

The percentage of first-term members was obtained easily by relating the number of individuals in the first series to the number in the second on a second collection of work sheets. In calculating average experience, a fractional part of a term served by interim appointment or election or a term ended by death or retirement before completion was counted in each case as a full term. The determination of this average required another set of entries, which in practice were made upon the second set of work sheets mentioned above. On each session sheet were placed the series of numbers 0, 1, 2, 3, . . . *n.* That is, the series extended as far as was required. A first-term member was tallied opposite 0; a second-term member opposite 1, and so on. The latter entry indicated, for example, one member who had served one previous term

[3] To read the biographies and post the entries required the equivalent of several weeks of full-time work.

as a representative. After all postings had been made, the total number of terms previously served by all members was obtained, and this figure divided by the number of members to give the average. It will be seen that first-term members counted as o in this process and reduced the average accordingly. As a member's terms increased, however, he contributed proportionately each year to raising the average.

To none of the four series that have been described was it found feasible to fit curves covering the entire period of one hundred and thirty-six years. Good fits in most cases have been obtained, however, by breaking the series into shorter segments. The lines connecting the original plottings, together with fitted curves and their equations, are shown for several of the series in Figures 18 to 21, inclusive.

It is apparent that down to the Civil War period there

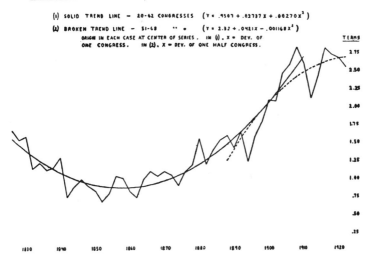

FIGURE 18 — AVERAGE EXPERIENCE OF UNITED STATES REPRESENTATIVES —
20–68 CONGRESSES

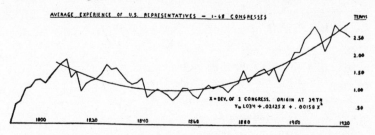

FIGURE 19 — AVERAGE EXPERIENCE OF UNITED STATES REPRESENTATIVES — 1–68 CONGRESSES — WITH PARABOLIC TREND LINE FITTED FOR CONGRESSES 10–68 INCLUSIVE

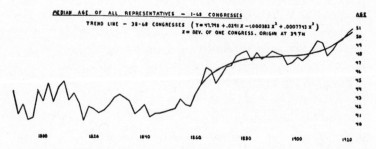

FIGURE 20 — MEDIAN AGE OF ALL REPRESENTATIVES — 1–68 CONGRESSES

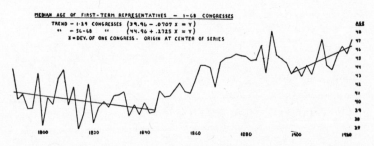

FIGURE 21 — MEDIAN AGE OF FIRST-TERM REPRESENTATIVES — 1–68 CON-GRESSES

were trends in the direction of electing younger men to Congress and retaining members there for shorter periods of time. From the Civil War period onward the age of first-term members has increased, reaching especially high averages with the men elected in 1890, 1910, and 1922. With this change came about a tendency to leave congressmen in office for longer periods of service. As would be expected, there has resulted a greatly increased average age of all members. As to the causes of these changes, the lengthening expectation of life is perhaps an important factor, but one for which no statistical allowance has been made. The opinion may be hazarded that another factor has been a gradual departure from the Jacksonian type of democratic sentiment which prevailed during the time when the curves were trending downward. As to the results of these changes, no statistical statement can be made. The hypothesis which inspired the study has received no discredit, however, and on the contrary may seem to have obtained some support. Not only increasing average age, but increasing average tenure of office as well would seem, *a priori*, to be influences making for conservatism in legislation. Whether or not conservatism has actually shown corresponding growth is still a matter of opinion concerning attitudes which are vaguely defined.

The presence of cycles about the several lines of trend is as marked as the trends themselves. What meaning they may have, I shall not venture to guess. Efforts to correlate them with cycles in other social series have as yet been insufficient to ascertain their absolute or comparative periods. Nor have their amplitudes been studied. A single significant relationship has been discovered. For the variable "average experience," I have fitted a parabolic trend line, concave downward, for the sessions from the Fifty-first to the Sixty-eighth inclusive, that is, from the elections of 1889 to 1923. This appears as the dotted line in Figure 18. With the biennial deviations about this line, I have correlated figures representing the *mean* of the business cycle figures used by Ogburn and Thomas for the *corresponding year and the year preceding*.[4] This has given a positive coefficient of correlation, without lead or lag, of .449, suggesting some degree of relationship between business prosperity and the state of mind in the electorate which results in the reëlection of experienced congressional incumbents.

It is with regret that I am unable to say more concerning these data. As with the data in the preceding chapter, these offer numerous opportunities for further "working." Perhaps I may be permitted to hope that additional utilization of them may be made by other investigators.

[4] See note (8), page 290.

XXII

Social Contact and the Amplitude of Electoral Swing

This chapter deals with still another hypothesis and with one effort to verify it. The hypothesis was developed out of reflection concerning the tremendous "landslide" for Warren G. Harding in the presidential election of 1920. The Harding majority was great in absolute number of votes beyond all precedent. But it was also larger relatively than in any election since the Civil War. Table 47 gives some measure of the "turnover" between presidential elections in the voting strength of the two major parties since 1856.

Numerous explanations have been advanced for the Democratic debacle in 1920 and the still more pitiful showing of that party in 1924. (Davis received 28.8 per cent of all votes cast for president in the latter year.) It occurred to me that more fundamental causes than were suggested by factors in the immediate political situation might be operating to account in part for the striking reversals of attitude that were indicated by the Republican landslide.

Increasingly throughout the past century the people in this country have been placed in closer contact with each other, and hence more certainly subjected to whatever currents of opinion or emotion might arise in any part of the group. In part this fact results from urbanization and the process of settlement that has been "filling up" the nation. In greater part it results from the universal "education" and the mechanical developments that are utilizing and contributing thereto — agencies of transportation and communication,

303

TABLE 47 — ARITHMETICAL DIFFERENCES IN PERCENTAGES OF TOTAL VOTE
POLLED AT SUCCESSIVE PRESIDENTIAL ELECTIONS BY REPUBLICAN AND DEMO-
CRATIC PARTIES[1]

Presidential Elections Compared	Change in Percentage of vote polled by Republican Party	Change in Percentage of vote polled by Democratic Party
1856–1860	6.8	2.2[2]
1860–1864	15.2	2.6[2]
1864–1868	2.4	2.4
1868–1872	2.7	3.3
1872–1876	8.1	6.2
1876–1880	1.0	2.0
1880–1884	.1	.6
1884–1888	.4	.1
1888–1892	5.2	3.0
1892–1896	8.3	.6
1896–1900	.8	.4
1900–1904	4.7	7.9
1904–1908	4.8	5.4
1908–1912	1.0[3]	1.1
1912–1916	1.0[3]	7.3
1916–1920	14.2	15.0
1920–1924	6.5[4]	5.5[4]

[1] A portion of this table appeared in my *Farmers and Workers in American Politics*. It is calculated from figures given in *Smull's Legislative Handbook* (Pennsylvania) 1921–1922, pp. 270 ff. and *The World Almanac*, 1927, pp. 817 and 865–867. It should be noted that if there were but two parties in the field at each election, the corresponding figures in the two columns would necessarily be equal. The discrepancies between them arise from the existence of minor parties which cut in more heavily on the vote, now of one of the major parties and now of the other. For example, in 1880 the total vote for President was distributed in percentages as follows: Garfield, Republican, 48.3%; Hancock, Democrat, 48.2%; Weaver, Greenback, 3.3%; scattering, 0.1%; total, 100%. In 1884 the distribution was: Blaine, Republican, 48.2%; Cleveland, Democrat, 48.8%; Butler, Greenback, 1.3%; St. Johns, Prohibition, 1.5%; scattering, 0.1%; total, 100%. Hence the party changes in percentage of votes cast was as follows: Republican, 48.3%–48.2%, or 0.1%; Democratic, 48.8%–48.2%, or 0.6%; minor candidates, 3.4%–2.9%, or 0.5%.

[2] The votes for Breckinridge and for Douglas in 1860 are combined.

[3] The votes for Roosevelt and Taft in 1912 are combined.

newspapers, moving pictures, radio, etc.[5] It would seem reasonable to suppose therefore (and this is the hypothesis) that a mass tendency by the electorate to favor one candidate rather than others would *carry its influence farther* in more recent than in earlier times. To adapt a statistical term, the *amplitude* of electoral swing might have been expected to increase steadily during the past century. The question is, did it do so [6]?

Some of the data already assembled, especially in Chapter XX, may bear upon the hypothesis. Mr. Walter E. MacDonald of the University of Pennsylvania has worked out some new time series which were designed to throw light upon it. For this purpose he has compared the returns for candidates in elections for governor of New York since 1801, New Jersey since 1844, Pennsylvania since 1790 and Ohio since 1803. In the case of each election he has ascertained the vote received by the successful candidate and his nearest competitor, together with the percentage of the total vote polled for each. The original data as derived from various official sources are given in full in Tables 48 to 51, inclusive.

These several tables have been devised, not to show variations in popular favor toward particular parties, as in Chapter XX, but rather to show variations in the "swing" toward the winning candidate of whatever party. This may be referred to as the "landslide tendency." Thus the votes

---

[4] The La Follette vote in 1924 was not combined with that of either Coolidge or Davis (as was the Roosevelt vote with that of Taft in 1924). Hence the changes in the vote for both the Republican and Democratic candidates represent reductions in their respective percentages of the total in 1924 as compared with 1920.

[5] *Cf.* the discussions by LeBon and others of the *psychological crowd* and its behavior. Something of the same idea is involved here.

[6] This question was implied in a study by F. Stuart Chapin, "The Variability of the Popular Vote at Presidential Elections," *The American Journal of Sociology*, Vol. 18 (1912–13), pp. 222 ff.

TABLE 48 — VOTES FOR TWO LEADING CANDIDATES AT ALL ELECTIONS FOR
GOVERNOR IN THE STATE OF NEW YORK, 1801–1924, SHOWING VARIATIONS
IN "LANDSLIDE TENDENCY"

Year	Leading candidate Number of Votes	Party[7]	Second Candidate: Number of Votes	Balance[3]	Grand Total[3]	Decimal fractions of total vote — Leading Candidate	Second Candidate	Dif. bet. VII & VIII
I	II	III	IV	V	VI	VII	VIII	IX
1801	24,808	D.R.	20,843	......	45,651	.543	.457	.086
1804	30,829	D.R.	22,139	......	52,968	.582	.418	.164
1807	35,074	D.R.	30,989	......	66,063	.531	.469	.062
1810	43,094	D.R.	36,484	......	79,578	.542	.458	.084
1813	43,324	D.R.	39,718	......	83,042	.522	.478	.044
1816	45,412	D.R.	38,647	......	84,059	.540	.459	.081
1817	43,310	D.R.	1,417	......	44,727	.968	.032	.936
1820	47,447	D.R.	45,990	......	93,437	.519	.503	.016
1822	128,493	D.R.	2,910	......	131,403	.978	.022	.756
1824	103,452	D.R.	87,093	......	190,545	.543	.457	.086
1826	99,785	D.R.	96,135	......	195,920	.509	.491	.018
1828	136,794	D.	106,444	33,345	276,583	.495	.385	.110
1830	128,842	D.	120,361	2,332	251,535	.512	.479	.033
1832	166,410	D.	156,672	......	323,082	.515	.485	.030
1834	181,900	D.	169,008	......	350,908	.518	.482	.036
1836	166,122	D.	136,648	3,496	306,266	.542	.446	.096
1838	192,882	W.	182,461	......	375,343	.514	.486	.028
1840	222,011	W.	216,726	2,662	441,399	.503	.491	.012
1842	208,072	D.	186,091	7,263	401,426	.518	.464	.054
1844	241,090	D.	231,057	......	472,147	.511	.489	.022
1846	198,878	W.	187,306	......	386,184	.515	.485	.030
1848	218,776	W.	122,811	118,404	459,991	.476	.267	.209
1850	214,614	W.	214,352	......	428,966	.500	.500	.000
1852	264,121	D.	241,625	19,661	525,407	.503	.460	.043
1854	156,804	W.	156,495	122,282	435,581	.360	.359	.001
1856	264,400	R.	198,616	130,870	593,886	.445	.334	.111
1858	247,953	R.	230,513	60,880	539,346	.460	.427	.033
1860	358,272	R.	294,812	19,841	672,925	.532	.482	.050
1862	306,649	D.	295,897	......	602,546	.508	.492	.016
1864	369,557	R.	361,264	......	730,821	.506	.494	.012
1866	366,315	R.	352,526	......	718,841	.510	.490	.020
1868	439,301	D.	411,355	......	850,656	.516	.494	.022
1870	399,532	D.	366,436	......	765,968	.522	.478	.044
1872	445,801	R.	392,350	......	838,151	.532	.468	.064

TABLE 48—(Continued)

Year	Leading candidate		Second Candidate: Number of votes	Balance [8]	Grand Total [8]	Decimal fractions of total vote		
	Number of votes	Party[7]				Leading Candidate	Second Candidate	Dif. bet. VII & VIII
I	II	III	IV	V	VI	VII	VIII	IX
1874	416,391	D.	366,074	......	872,465	.532	.468	.064
1876	519,831	D.	489,371	......	1,009,202	.513	.483	.030
1879	418,567	R.	375,790	77,566	901,544	.467	.416	.051
1882	535,318	D.	342,464	25,783	915,539	.585	.374	.211
1885	501,465	D.	490,331	30,867	1,026,239	.489	.478	.011
1888	650,464	D.	631,293	30,215	1,317,263	.494	.479	.015
1891	582,893	D.	534,956	30,353	1,165,085	.500	.459	.041
1894	673,818	R.	517,710	23,525	1,275,671	.528	.406	.122
1896	787,516	R.	574,524	26,698	1,434,046	.549	.401	.148
1898	661,707	R.	643,921	23,860	1,359,190	.488	.473	.015
1900	804,859	R.	693,733	22,704	1,556,520	.523	.445	.078
1902	665,150	R.	655,398	23,400	1,389,799	.478	.471	.007
1904	813,264	R.	732,704	36,259	1,625,907	.500	.451	.049
1906	749,002	R.	673,268	21,751	1,492,219	.501	.451	.050
1908	804,651	R.	735,189	43,212	1,653,856	.492	.450	.042
1910	689,700	D.	622,299	48,470	1,445,249	.477	.430	.047
1912	649,559	D.	444,105	56,917	1,611,672	.403	.276	.127
1914	686,701	R.	412,253	45,586	1,486,875	.462	.277	.185
1916	835,820	R.	686,862	52,560	1,715,768	.487	.400	.087
1918	1,009,936	D.	956,034	121,705	2,192,970	.460	.436	.024
1920	1,335,878	R.	1,261,812	159,804	2,962,645	.451	.426	.025
1922	1,397,670	D.	1,011,725	99,944	2,521,391	.554	.401	.153
1924	1,627,111	D.	1,518,550	99,178	3,244,839	.501	.468	.033

recorded in column II of each table are those which the
winning candidate received at each election, while the corresponding figure in column IV is in each case the vote of
the second highest competitor. The equivalent proportions

[7] The following symbols are employed: D.R. — Democratic-Republican.
D. — Democrat. W. — Whig. R. — Republican.

[8] "Balance" may represent remainder of all votes or only votes for the
third candidate. The manner of arrangement of the data in the original
source documents governed here. Grand total includes all votes.

TABLE 49 — VOTES FOR TWO LEADING CANDIDATES AT ALL ELECTIONS FOR GOVERNOR IN THE STATE OF NEW JERSEY, 1844–1922, SHOWING VARIATIONS IN "LANDSLIDE TENDENCY"

Year	Leading candidate		Second Candidate		Balance [9]	Grand Total [9]	Decimal fractions of total vote		
	Number of Votes	Party	Number of votes	Party			Leading Candidate	Second Candidate	Dif. bet. VII & VIII
I	II	III	IV	IV A	V	VI	VII	VIII	IX
1844	37,949	W.	36,591	D.	76	74,616	.509	.490	.019
1847	34,765	D.	32,166	W.	342	67,273	.517	.478	.039
1850	39,723	D.	34,054	W.	.....	73,777	.538	.462	.076
1853	38,312	D.	34,530	W.	.....	72,842	.526	.474	.052
1856	50,903	.R.	48,246	D.	.....	99,149	.513	.487	.026
1859	53,315	R.	51,714	D.	.....	105,029	.508	.492	.016
1862	61,307	D.	46,710	R.	.....	108,017	.568	.432	.136
1865	67,525	R.	64,736	D.	.....	132,261	.511	.489	.022
1868	83,619	D.	79,072	R.	.....	162,691	.514	.486	.028
1871	82,362	D.	76,383	R.	.....	158,745	.519	.481	.038
1874	97,283	D.	84,050	R.	.....	181,333	.536	.464	.052
1877	97,837	D.	85,094	R.	6,508	189,439	.516	.449	.067
1880	121,666	D.	121,015	R.	2,954	245,635	.495	.493	.002
1883	103,856	D.	97,047	R.	7,113	208,016	.499	.467	.032
1886	109,939	D.	101,919	R.	19,808	231,666	.464	.440	.024
1889	138,245	D.	123,992	R.	6,853	269,090	.514	.461	.053
1892	167,257	D.	159,362	R.	9,982	336,601	.497	.473	.024
1895	162,900	R.	136,000	D.	12,709	311,609	.523	.436	.087
1898	164,051	R.	158,552	D.	12,842	335,445	.489	.473	.016
1901	183,814	R.	166,681	D.	10,772	361,267	.509	.461	.048
1904	231,363	R.	179,719	D.	21,356	432,438	.535	.416	.119
1907	194,313	R.	186,300	D.	13,671	394,284	.493	.473	.020
1910	233,682	D.	184,626	R.	14,984	433,292	.539	.426	.113
1913	173,148	D.	140,298	R.	61,871	375,317	.461	.374	.087
1916	247,343	R.	177,696	D.	21,107	446,146	.554	.398	.056
1919	217,486	D.	202,976	R.	21,592	442,054	.492	.459	.033
1922	427,206	D.	383,312	R.	8,101	818,619	.522	.468	.054

W.—Whig.   D.—Democrat.   R.—Republican.

[9] See note to Table 48.

of the total vote for these two candidates are shown by decimal fractions in columns VII and VIII, while the *spread* between these (i.e., the arithmetical differences between the fractions in columns VII and VIII) appear in column IX. These last figures (column IX) then may serve as indexes of the "landslide tendency." If the vote between the two leading candidates is evenly divided the index will be 0.000. If a single candidate should receive all of the votes it will be 1.000. The hypothesis calls for an upward trend in the indexes shown in column IX.

In determining the secular trend of landslide tendency, account was taken of the likelihood that special factors were in operation in each of the four states to produce variations in column IX. If the four series were combined into one, these special factors would to some degree cancel out. A single combined series was therefore sought. In obtaining it another difficulty was immediately encountered — one which is more likely to appear in political time series than in the case of analogous observations from the field of economics, i.e., the time intervals between the points plotted do not follow a regular sequence for any one of the individual series. The terms of service and the dates of election of governors have changed in each of the states. The X plottings (the dates of election) do not correspond as between pairs of series, nor can they be made to do so by any arrangement of lead or lag in one or another.

As a rough and ready device for overcoming this difficulty, Mr. MacDonald followed this suggestion: each of the state series represented by column IX in tables 48–51 was plotted as precisely as possible upon uniform coördinate paper, vertical distance indicating the magnitude of the "landslide tendency" or swing (the values in column IX) and uniform horizontal distances standing for intervals of one year.

TABLE 50 — VOTES FOR TWO LEADING CANDIDATES AT ALL ELECTIONS FOR GOVERNOR IN THE STATE OF PENNSYLVANIA, 1790–1922, SHOWING VARIATIONS IN "LANDSLIDE TENDENCY"

Year	Leading candidate		Second Candidate		Balance[10]	Grand Total[10]	Decimal fractions of total vote		
	Number of votes	Party	Number of votes	Party			Leading Candidate	Second Candidate	Dif. bet. VII & VIII
I	II	III	IV	IV A	V	VI	VII	VIII	IX
1790	27,725	D.	2,802	F.	......	30,527	.908	.091	.817
1793	18,590	D.	10,706	F.	......	29,296	.634	.365	.269
1796	30,020	D.	1,011	F.	......	31,031	.967	.032	.935
1799	38,036	D.	32,641	F.	......	70,677	.538	.462	.076
1802	47,879	D.	9,499	F.	7,632	57,472	.833	.165	.668
1805	43,644	I.D.	38,438	D.	395	82,082	.531	.468	.063
1808	67,975	D.	39,575	F.	4,014	111,564	.609	.354	.255
1811	52,319	D.	3,609	F.	1,675	57,603	.908	.062	.846
1814	51,099	D.	29,566	F.	928	81,593	.626	.362	.264
1817	66,331	D.	59,272	F.	11	125,614	.528	.471	.057
1820	67,905	F.	66,300	D.	21	134,226	.506	.494	.012
1823	89,928	D.	64,211	F.	8	154,147	.583	.417	.166
1826	72,710	D.	1,175	F.	1,174	75,059	.969	.016	.953
1829	78,219	D.	61,776	A.M.	12	140,007	.559	.441	.118
1832	91,335	D.	38,165	A.M.	......	129,500	.705	.295	.410
1835	94,023	A.M.	65,804	I.D.	40,586	200,413	.469	.328	.141
1838	127,825	D.	122,321	A.M.	......	250,146	.511	.489	.022
1841	136,504	D.	113,473	W.	786	250,763	.544	.453	.091
1844	160,322	D.	156,040	W.	2,566	318,928	.503	.478	.025
1847	146,081	D.	128,148	W.	13,114	287,343	.508	.446	.062
1848	168,522	W.	168,225	D.	72	336,819	.500	.499	.001
1851	186,489	D.	178,034	W.	1,917	366,440	.509	.486	.023
1854	203,822	W.A.	166,991	D.	2,227	373,040	.546	.448	.098
1857	188,846	D.	146,139	F.S.	28,180	363,165	.520	.402	.118
1860	262,346	R.	230,230	D.	......	492,576	.533	.467	.066
1863	269,506	R.	254,171	D.	2	523,679	.515	.485	.030
1866	307,274	R.	290,096	D.	......	597,370	.514	.486	.028
1869	290,552	R.	285,956	D.	......	576,508	.504	.496	.008
1872	353,287	R.	317,760	D.	1,250	672,297	.525	.473	.052
1875	304,175	R.	292,145	D.	13,244	609,564	.499	.479	.020
1878	319,567	R.	297,060	D.	85,411	702,038	.455	.423	.032
1882	355,791	D.	315,589	R.	72,423	743,803	.478	.424	.054
1886	412,285	R.	369,634	D.	37,293	819,212	.503	.451	.052
1890	464,209	D.	447,655	R.	16,332	928,196	.500	.482	.018
1894	574,801	R.	333,404	D.	44,812	953,017	.603	.350	.253

TABLE 50 —(*Continued*)

Year	Leading candidate			Second Candidate		Balance[10]	Grand Total[10]	Decimal fractions of total vote		
	Number of votes	Party	Number of votes	Party				Leading Candidate	Second Candidate	Dif. bet. VII & VIII
I	II	III	IV	IV A	V	VI	VII	VIII	IX
1898	476,206	R.	358,300	D.	137,236	971,742	.490	.369	.121
1902	593,328	R.	450,978	D.	50,465	1,094,771	.542	.412	.130
1906	506,418	R.	458,054	D.	42,105	1,006,577	.503	.455	.048
1910	415,614	R.	382,127	K.	200,707	998,448	.416	.383	.033
1914	588,705	R.	453,880	D.	68,667	1,111,252	.530	.408	.122
1918	552,537	R.	305,315	D.	47,183	905,035	.611	.337	.274
1922	831,696	R.	581,625	D.	51,351	1,464,672	.568	.397	.171

D.—Democrat.   R.—Republican.   F.—Federalist.
I. D.—Independent Democrat   A. M.—Anti-Mason.   W.—Whig.
W. A.—Whig and American.   F. S.—Free Soil.   K.—Keystone.

Straight lines were drawn between the points plotted for each series. *Annual* figures for interims between election years were then interpolated by reading off values from the vertical scale where the lines crossed the corresponding perpendiculars from the horizontal (time) scale.

As to the theoretical validity of this process there is more than doubt. It involves an assumption that changes in attitude by an electorate which lead to an increased or lessened "swing" to the winning candidate are evenly distributed over the intervening period between elections.[11]

[10] See note to Table 48.

[11] The influence of party loyalty, moreover, is wholly disregarded in this assumption. Thus, the party elected triumphantly to power at one election might be rejected with equal enthusiasm at the next, and hence leave the items in Column IX unchanged for the two election years. Party shifts of this kind are undisclosed by the indexes employed.

TABLE 51 — VOTES FOR TWO LEADING CANDIDATES AT ALL ELECTIONS FOR GOVERNOR IN THE STATE OF OHIO, 1803–1924, SHOWING VARIATIONS IN "LANDSLIDE TENDENCY"

| Year | Leading candidate | | Second Candidate: Number of Votes | Balance[12] | Grand Total[12] | Decimal fractions of total vote | | |
	Number of Votes	Party				Leading Candidate	Second Candidate	Dif. bet. VII & VIII
I	II	III	IV	VI	VII	VII	VIII	IX
1803	4,564	D.	......	......	4,565	1.00	....	1.00
1805	4,788	D.	......	......	4,788	1.00	....	1.00
1807	5,550	D.	4,757	......	10,307	.538	.462	.076
1808	7,293	D.	5,601	3,397	16,291	.447	.344	.103
1810	9,924	D.	7,731	......	17,655	.562	.438	.124
1812	11,859	D.	7,903	......	19,762	.600	.400	.200
1814	15,879	D.	6,171	......	22,050	.720	.280	.440
1816	22,931	D.	6,295	1,607	30,833	.744	.204	.540
1818	30,194	D.	8,075	......	38,269	.789	.211	.578
1820	34,836	D.	9,426	4,348	48,860	.713	.193	.520
1822	26,059	D.	22,889	11,060	60,008	.434	.381	.053
1824	39,526	D.	37,108	......	76,634	.516	.484	.032
1826	71,475	F.	4,765	4,192	84,733	.844	.056	.788
1828	53,971	F.	51,951	......	106,034	.509	.490	.019
1830	49,668	F.	49,186	......	99,080	.501	.496	.005
1832	71,251	D.	63,185	......	134,469	.530	.470	.060
1834	70,738	D.	67,414	......	138,190	.512	.488	.024
1836	92,204	W.	86,158	......	178,562	.516	.483	.033
1838	107,884	D.	102,146	......	210,037	.514	.486	.028
1840	145,442	W.	129,312	......	274,762	.529	.471	.058
1842	119,774	D.	117,902	1,534	242,850	.493	.485	.008
1844	146,333	W.	145,062	8,898	300,304	.487	.483	.004
1846	118,869	W.	116,484	10,797	246,196	.483	.473	.010
1848	148,756	W.	148,445	......	297,943	.499	.498	.001
1850	133,093	D.	121,105	13,747	267,945	.497	.452	.045
1851	145,654	D.	199,548	16,918	282,182	.516	.424	.092
1853	147,663	D.	85,857	50,346	283,866	.520	.302	.218
1855	146,770	R.	131,019	24,276	302,065	.486	.434	.052
1857	160,568	R.	159,065	10,272	329,905	.487	.482	.005
1859	184,557	R.	171,226	......	355,783	.519	.481	.038
1861	206,997	R.	151,774	......	358,880	.577	.423	.154
1863	288,826	R.	187,728	......	476,554	.606	.394	.212
1865	223,642	R.	193,797	......	417,799	.535	.464	.071
1867	243,605	R.	240,622	......	484,227	.503	.497	.006
1869	236,082	R.	228,576	679	465,337	.507	.491	.015

TABLE 51—(*Continued*)

Year	Leading candidate		Second Candidate: Number of Votes	Balance[12]	Grand Total[12]	Decimal fractions of total vote		
	Number of Votes	Party				Leading Candidate	Second Candidate	Dif. bet. VII & VIII
I	II	III	IV	V	VI	VII	VIII	IX
1871	238,273	R.	218,105	4,068	460,446	.517	.474	.043
1873	214,654	D.	213,837	10,278	448,878	.478	.476	.002
1875	297,817	R.	292,273	2,593	592,700	.502	.493	.009
1877	271,625	D.	249,105	16,912	554,967	.489	.449	.040
1879	336,261	R.	319,132	9,072	669,157	.503	.477	.026
1881	312,735	R.	288,462	16,597	624,226	.501	.462	.039
1883	459,693	D.	347,164	8,362	721,310	.499	.481	.018
1885	359,281	R.	341,830	24,081	733,967	.490	.466	.024
1887	356,534	R.	333,205	29,700	746,970	.477	.446	.031
1889	379,423	D.	368,551	26,504	775,721	.489	.475	.014
1891	386,739	R.	365,228	23,472	795,631	.486	.459	.027
1893	433,342	R.	352,347	22,406	835,604	.519	.422	.097
1895	427,141	R.	334,519	52,675	846,996	.504	.395	.109
1897	429,915	R.	401,750	7,555	864,022	.498	.465	.033
1899	417,199	R.	368,176	106,721	920,872	.453	.400	.053
1901	436,092	R.	368,525	9,878	840,147	.519	.439	.080
1903	475,560	R.	361,748	13,502	877,203	.542	.412	.130
1905	473,264	D.	430,617	17,795	961,505	.492	.488	.044
1908	552,569	D.	533,197	28,573	1,123,198	.491	.475	.016
1910	477,077	D.	376,700	60,637	932,262	.512	.404	.108
1912	439,323	D.	272,500	87,709	1,036,731	.424	.263	.161
1914	523,074	R.	493,804	60,904	1,129,223	.463	.437	.026
1916	568,218	D.	561,602	39,908	1,174,057	.484	.478	.006
1918	486,403	D.	474,459	......	960,862	.506	.494	.012
1920	1,039,835	R.	918,962	42,889	2,003,183	.514	.458	.056
1922	821,948	D.	803,300	......	1,625,799	.506	.494	.012
1924	1,064,981	D.	888,139	11,776	1,973,364	.540	.450	.090

D.—Democrat.   R.—Republican.   F.—Federalist.   W.—Whig.

There is *a priori* evidence to the contrary. Thus the party which is in control of the presidency has come to expect reversals or lessened majorities in the mid-term congressional elections, but nevertheless anticipates a return to popular

[12] *Cf.* note to Table 48, which applies here.

favor at the next presidential poll. The curve which would express this expectation between any two presidential years would seem more likely to be parabolic in appearance, concave upward, than linear. Nor is the justification for interpolation apparent on any basis. If it is to be resorted to, on the other hand, no other assumption seems warranted than that which was made by Mr. MacDonald.

Having obtained actual or interpolated values for each year in the four state series (corresponding to column IX) the next step was to combine these four. Two methods suggested themselves. One was to obtain a mean of the four items for each year; the other to obtain a mean of the two median items. The latter had in its favor the fact that special disturbing influences in the separate states would, likely, be eliminated. In the end, however, the means of the four series of items were chosen for further analysis.

The presence of cycles, but without a clearly indicated trend prior to the Civil War, was manifest. From 1867 or 1868 to 1921, however, an upward trend and five completed cycles seemed to be apparent. These are shown in Figure 22, together with a trend line *drawn by inspection* to fit the series of means from 1868–1921 inclusive. Fictitious accuracy would have resulted from a trend line fitted by mathematical means.[13] The "normal" appears to have risen from something like .03 in 1868 to nearly .10 in 1921. The inspectional method was continued by reading (from the original graph reproduced in Figure 22) the positive and negative deviations from the trend line.

Since they are necessarily inexact there would be no value

---

[13] As in the case of the lines shown in Figures 18 to 21, etc. The *method of semi-averages* would probably have been preferable here, or at least the determination of the average of the series as a fulcrum about which to rotate the line until the best "fit" seemed to have been obtained. (*Cf.* Chaddock, *op. cit.*, p. 320.) Neither of these devices, however, was employed.

in reproducing here the table of deviations from trend which Mr. MacDonald obtained. It was apparent, however, that the cycles which appeared might have some relationship to the business cycle. Employing for comparison the cycles of business indexes developed by Ogburn and Thomas (see page 290) the following coefficients of correlation were calculated:

1870–1920, without lead or lag, $r = -.11$
1870–1920, business cycle lagged two years, $r = -.34$
1870–1920,   "   "   "   three " $r = -.32$
1887–1920, without lead or lag, $r = -.33$
1887–1920, business cycle lagged one year, $r = -.445$
1887–1920,   "   "   "   two years, $r = -.47$
1887–1920,   "   "   "   three " $r = -.33$

All coefficients are seen to be negative, the highest $(-.47)$ appearing for the thirty-four year period, 1887–1920, with a lag of two years given to the Ogburn-Thomas cycle figures.

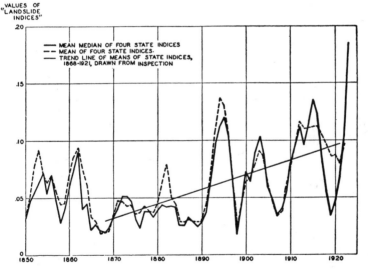

FIGURE 22 — TREND AND CYCLES OF "LANDSLIDE INDICES" DERIVED FROM POPULAR VOTES FOR GOVERNOR IN NEW YORK, NEW JERSEY, PENNSYLVANIA AND OHIO

It would be hazardous to contend that the data given above would warrant any particular inference. It does not run counter to the hypothesis, and it suggests a relationship between the business cycle and the size of subsequent political majorities. A number of questionable steps, however, intervene between the original data and the statements of the relationship. Perhaps the best evidence that the data mean something is to be found in the comparative regularity of the cycles of landslide indexes. The period of these seems to vary from eight or ten to twelve or fourteen years. The regularity disclosed could scarcely result from chance.

A POSTSCRIPT

As they have been assembled the papers of which this book is composed give an impression of incompletion. This is true also of some of them individually. It is more than a virtue ascribed to necessity when I contend that incompletion may be desirable. The entire book represents a *groping* toward a philosophy and a unity of method in social politics which will here and there permit a precise statement to be made concerning portions of the flux. Methods and results which are admittedly tentative may be of greater value in the present stage of development than a product which might mislead by its apparent completeness.

Disjointedness in the work may have resulted from two causes, of which the first is the way it has been constructed. While all of the studies fit into a general scheme of inquiry, or so it seems to me, they do not hinge on one another with the nicety that would be expected of a treatise written consecutively in an easy armchair. In the second place, the term "work" as applied to the present production may be used advisedly. Unless one has experienced the great amount of labor that is frequently involved in obtaining an inconspicuous statistical result, the amount of effort that has gone into the preceding pages may easily be underestimated. I hoped to bring a number of the earlier inquiries up to date by adding to them the appropriate data of current years. However, in most cases little would have been gained from the standpoint of method by this attempt. There was constantly, moreover, the contrary impulse to pursue new lines of inquiry that suggested themselves. This second alternative, as a choice for the utilization of a limited amount of time and energy, seemed the more profitable.

There are many untouched topics which I hoped to discuss here, but the investigations which might have given me something to say about them have not been undertaken or have not developed sufficiently. Among these has been a review of means of political *prediction*, including the value and validity of *straw votes* as indicators. Another inquiry looking in the same direction would have for its aim to discover whether *party enrollment* and the distribution of *primary registrations* by density (see page 98) in election districts whose past political behavior is known, could legitimately be made the basis of forecast of election results.[1] It was part of my original intention, also, to hazard a forecast concerning the development of method in politics. The difficulty and futility, not to mention the prematurity of such an effort have seemed increasingly apparent.

In conclusion, then, I can express little more than the hope, already indicated repeatedly in preceding pages, that this book will contribute to a genuine development of a science of politics by finding employment in the labor of other investigators. A working philosophy, a few hypotheses, a few evidences more or less successfully bearing upon verification, not a little "raw" and undigested statistical data, and some examples of technical devices which may suggest analogous procedure to others, are to be found in the foregoing pages. Whoever can put any of these ingre-

---

[1] "We made the statement at the outset that 400,000 Republican votes at the primary would mean the nomination of J. Hampton Moore. The registration of approximately half a million Republicans should guarantee more than 400,000 votes tomorrow." — Statement by William H. Emhardt, Chairman of the Moore campaign committee, as quoted in the *Philadelphia Bulletin*, September 19, 1927. Mr. Moore was not nominated but polled a surprisingly large "anti-machine" vote.

dients to use and in doing so discover the errors, short-comings, and unseen possibilities which are contained, is more than welcome. He will share in the creative enterprise to which the book aspires, the limited realization of which is to no one more apparent than the author.

INDEX

Abbott, Edith, 177

Adjacency of counties, criteria of, 139, 151 n.; relation to La Follette vote, 139 ff.

Aesthetics, domain of, 15, 17, 19

Age, calculation of congressional, 298; of Congressmen, 294-302; relationship to conservatism, 294

Agel, Max, 57 ff.

Agreement, between party opponents, 232-233; extent of, shown by votes, 231 ff.; overlooked, in attention to differences, 116; range of, in same party, 232; in deliberative bodies, 118

Alabama, Harding vote in, 1920, 175

Alignments, shifting political, 183-185

Allport, F. H., viii, 71 n., 81, 82, 83, 86, 91 n., 92, 176 n., 271

Almshouse pauper, unperceived change in definition of, 43

American Association for the Advancement of Science, 36

American Council of Learned Societies, viii, 36

American Historical Association, 36

American Political Science Association, 13, 191

Anderson, Nels, 110

Anthropologist, units of reality for, 40

Anthropology, as intermediate between history and science, 46-47

Anti-employment office bill in Washington, 158-162

Arkansas, Harding vote in, 1920, 175

Arneson, Ben A., 243

Ashurst, Senator Henry F., 217

"As if," scientific fictions, 44, 45

Assumptions, as objects of investigation, 189; impossible to avoid making, 189; in estimates of nonvoting, 246; of representativeness, 189-190, 194; philosophical, as a prerequisite to scientific inquiry, 9, 14

Atkinson, R. C., 70 n.

Attention, political, sources of data concerning, 241-250

Attitudes, as determinants of political events, 53; assumption of generalized political, 274 n.; atypical distributions of, 76 ff.; a valid subject of scientific inquiry, 92; certainty of, 87-89; classification of, 54; cleavages concerning in a graduate class, 207-208; culture areas of, 136-137; distribution of, 71 ff.; distribution of among students toward social change, 272-275; economic factors and diffusion of, 144 ff.; efforts at conversion of, 269, 270 ff.; factors affecting, 54; intensity of, 241; intensity of feeling of, 89; location in distribution of changes of, 86-89; meaning of, 51-52; occupational cleavages in, 125; political, 52; qualitative differences in, 75; social density of, 98-115, 138; social density of as a ratio, 101 n.; stability of distribution of, 156 ff.; toward communism, European affairs, late enemies in war, 242; toward evolution by students, 252 ff.; toward race by students, 252; variability of, 74 ff.

Attribute, concept of, 44

Averages, of La Follette vote by counties, 102-103

Ayers, Leonard P., 118

Barnhart, John D., 183

Bates, Non-Partisan Party candidate, 129-131

Beard, Charles A., 167

Behavior, as an index of attitudes, 92; of mental life, 29

Behavioristic political psychology, 9

Bi-modality, 113-114

Biographies, as source material for science, 69; of congressmen, 295,

School, fund equalization bill in Washington, 163–164; Medical Inspection Act of Washington, 158–164

Schwab, Charles M., 57 ff.

Science, and case method, 36, 37, 47; and history, 36, 37, 38, 46, 47; and statistics, 35; conceptual nature of 22–24; fictional nature of, 24; unity of, 21; natural, 14, 20, 29, 33; (see also *social science*)

Scientific Method, Committee on, Social Science Research Council, viii

Scientific spirit, 14

Seasonality, absent from political indexes, 281–282; ascertainable for political administration, 281; in economic time series, 281

Secular trends, in time series, 281; of Congressional age and experience, 299–301; of party turnover in New Jersey, 290–292

Sense organs, data of, 22, 23

Series, discrete, 72, 77

Service, length of, by congressmen, 294–302

Sex differences, data from street conversations, 242; in voting, 243–247; (see also *women's rights*)

Sheppard, Senator Morris, 217

Shibboleths, allied to stereotypes, 70

Shipstead, Henrik, 126, 168–170, 217

Shopping areas, 144 ff.

Shurz, Carl, 46

Simmel, Georg, 22 n.

Sixty-eighth Congress, blocs and parties in, 209–210, 216–218

Skewed distributions, 73–74

Skewness, of distribution of density of attitude, 107–198

Small, Albion W., 16

Smith, Adam, discussed by Albion W. Small, 16

Smith, Alfred E., 172, 173, 182

Social, distance, 71 n.; groups, existence of inferred from perceptual data, 23, 24; phenomena and natural phenomena, 27 ff.; philosophy distinguished from science, 16, 17; reform interest as bloc factor, 238

Social psychology, relation of present book to, vii

Social science, 13, 14; anomalous position of in the scientific world, 13; nature of differences from natural science discussed, 20 ff., 33; rapprochement with natural science, 14; scope of, 15 ff.; task of, 31; use of experimentation in, 29–31

Social Science Research Council, viii, 36

Social scientists, 15, 16, 33

Socialism, stereotypes of, 70

Socialists, in New York Assembly, 211 ff.

Sociologist, units of reality for, 40

Sociology, relation of to politics, vii, 7 n.; relation of present book to, vii; scope of, according to Albion W. Small, 16

Soil areas, a basis for political lines, 183

South, Republican vote in, 174–175

South Dakota, 99, 129, 134, 136, 137; Non-Partisan party in, 129–131

Space, material entity as occurrence in, 37

Speculation, essential for science, 14

Spencer, Herbert, 21

Sports, data concerning public attention to, 242

Spykman, Nicholas J., 22 n.

Stability, of distribution of attitudes, 156; of presidential preference, varied with conservatism, 278

Standpatter, more numerous among conservatives, 278

State, the, theory of, 191, 193

State bank of North Dakota, 126–129

State issues, in New York Assembly, 213–216

Statistics, and case method, 35; classification of units, 40, 41; errors in unit classification, 42, 43; and history, 36; and individual differences, 26 ff.; and science, 35; development of in politics, 7–8; in economics, 7; specialization within, 8

Stereotypes, allied to shibboleths and symbols, 69; as factors in attitude, 53–54; discovery of, 56 ff.; illustrated, 55–56; in face to face contact, 68–69; of doctrines or institutions, 69–70; of Germans, 56; political significance of, 67–68